*Imaginative Thinking and Human Existence*

# *Imaginative Thinking and Human Existence*

### by Edward L. Murray

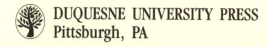
DUQUESNE UNIVERSITY PRESS
Pittsburgh, PA

Published in the United States of America
by Duquesne University Press
600 Forbes Avenue, Pittsburgh, PA 15282


First Edition

Library of Congress Cataloging-in-Publication Data

Murray, Edward L., 1920–
    Imaginative thinking and human existence.

    Bibliography: p.
    Includes indexes.
    1. Creative thinking.   2. Perception (Philosophy)
3. Self (Philosophy)   I. Title.
BF411.M87   1986       153.3′5       85–27368
ISBN   0–8207–0186–6
ISBN 0-8207-0213-7 pbk.
Second printing, May 1989

*To my*
*sisters and brothers*
*Margaret, Earl and Charles,*
*All now of happy memory,*
*and*
*Lillian and James,*
*With both of whom I still enjoy*
*Imaginizing life.*

# Contents

# Preface

This book was written primarily for professionals in the field: for psychologists, psychiatrists, counselors—all of whom are dealing constantly with persons in need of psychological help in the meeting of life problems. I would not expect that such persons will find it speaking a language that is totally new to them, although it may well present some considerations that could easily have escaped their serious attention in their previous study. Moreover I would anticipate that its contents will yield an understanding of the human personality that should enrich current appreciations of the human effort to integrate one's life. If so, it should prove valuable for those working in the field of human health services. To date, much written in the field has only tangentially addressed matters that we would raise herein. The time has come, however, to speak forthrightly to them; and a study originating in a phenomenological stance should do much to elucidate some very vital issues.

In addition, I would expect that graduate students in psychology, psychiatry, sociology, social work and education will find it speaking in terms that are theoretically meaningful and practically useful, once they have mastered some of the basic phenomenological and existential concepts that permeate these pages. This is not an incidental matter. With the changing social and economic scene in the world, and especially in the United States, there is a growing cry for more short-term therapy that is substantive, effective and not gimmicky. There are many people who stand in need of such help but simply cannot afford extended treatment sessions. In this regard, the understandings developed in these pages should render valuable aid to such practitioners of the future.

Finally I would expect that there are many professionals in life who are not engaged in formally psychological work, but who are still expected to deal with the area of human problems—people such as priests, ministers, rabbis, personnel directors and spiritual advisors. Such individuals will be able to find here ideas and insights that could prove valuable. There is so much that can be and must be gained from our study of the human personality, especially if we are going to bring about the transformations of society and life that the future of the human race will demand. And people such as the clergy are positioned to render this human effort extraordinary assistance—if they but understand. For them *Imaginative Thinking and Human Existence* should have much to offer, just as it should to many educated readers who simply want to understand more and more about the mysteries that attend our human existence.

Aware as I am that some of the book's readers may be non-professionals who are eager to learn but feel theoretically disadvantaged, I would venture a suggestion or two. Such readers, who are reluctant to throw themselves into highly theoretical discussion that appears, at least to them, of little practical value, would do well to skip chapters two and seven in their first reading of the text. The former builds around the work of Aron Gurwitsch on the field of consciousness while the latter wrestles with the issues of unity and temporality, both of which may appear highly abstract. Both chapters are important, but they could await one's second reading, and at that time will make far more sense to the reader. Likewise, it is not inconceivable that some might find it worthwhile to read the last chapter first—just to get a grasp of where the heart of the book might lead. For professionals, of course, such suggestions are empty; for others, however, they might prove helpful.

As to the content of the book, I would make two observations. In chapter one I speak of the growing interest manifested in the domain of philosophy for the subject of imaginative thinking. And I mention the work of several philosophers, one of whom is Paul Ricoeur. At that point the work of Ricoeur could easily have been expanded to book length, but I chose simply to mention his name. This was neither an oversight nor a slight. I have far too much respect for his contribution to human thought to treat him casually. The fact is, that I do mention his work quite often during subsequent pages, and shall be dealing with his contribution to the study of imaginative thought in another work that is scheduled for publication in the relatively near future. Hence the passing reference in chapter one was intended only as a simple and respectful acknowledgement of his work.

My second comment has to do with the final section of the book in which I treat briefly the significance of religion in the integration

of the human personality. To some readers this treatment may
appear irrelevant or maybe even inappropriate. I, of course, would
not agree. It will be noticed that in the first chapter I comment on
the growing interest in contemporary religious and theological
circles on the topic of imaginative thinking. In the final chapter, I
return to this matter to indicate its importance for personality
integration. This was done for two reasons. In the first place Freud
himself saw fit to devote an entire book to the question of religion's
relevance for human life, ultimately questioning its value for mankind's future. I speak of his work entitled *The future of an illusion.*
That illusion of religion, Freud felt, had served its purpose and
made whatever contribution it could to mankind, but was now of
dubious value. I would contend that time may well prove that
Freud's obituary was a bit premature. It behooves serious thinkers
to rethink the issue, and I for one have tried to show that it does
have a significant contribution to make to the rich living of our
human life. Secondly, it should be recalled that Hegel felt that
religion was attempting to do in the realm of symbols what philosophy was trying to accomplish in the realm of conceptions. If so,
then an appreciation of the importance of imaginative thinking in
both realms is even more imperative than we previously thought.
To those who share this conviction, I would refer them to my
article recently published in the *Journal of Dharma,* a periodical
dedicated to the study of world religions and published at Dharma-
ran College, Bangalore, India. It is an extended study of the same
subject that I treat only cursorily in the closing section of this book.

Finally I would express a note of gratitude to several people who
have contributed their time, talent and inspiration to the birth of
this work. To Ms. Linda Rendulic of the Department of Psychology, Duquesne University, who typed much of the manuscript, and
to Ms. Linda Rockey, a graduate assistant in the program, who
prepared the index, I am most grateful. In another way I am
indebted to my colleagues (and the students) in the Department.
They constitute a phenomenon all their own, and are gradually
receiving the national and international recognition that they deserve for the contribution they are making to contemporary psychology. Genuinely convinced of the value of phenomenological
and existential thought in their work, they have quietly and systematically pursued their study, distinguishing themselves on the
American scene in the classroom, books, journal articles and pro-

fessional conferences' presentations. When one stops to realize that Freud and Adler had parted company after only some half dozen years together, and that Freud and Jung did likewise, it is stunning to learn that the Duquesne faculty have worked together assiduously and brilliantly ever since the early 1960s. And there is every reason to think that their greatest work lies ahead, as the impact of their accomplishments is felt in many parts of the academic world. I feel honored to have been part of the work since 1964, and am indebted to their academic stimulation and intellectual contribution to my own life and growth during that time. To be sure, my colleagues may not quite recognize themselves in this book, but I can assure them that they are all there.

EDWARD L. MURRAY

# Acknowledgements

For permission to use the selections reprinted in this book, the author is grateful to the following publishers and copyright holders:

Argus Press. For excerpts from *The Dark Interval* by John Dominic Crossan. Copyright 1975 by Argus Communications, a division of DLM, Inc., Allen, TX 75002.

Sheed and Ward. For excerpts from *Image and Symbol* by M. Eliade. Copyright 1961 by Sheed and Ward. Reprinted by permission of the publishers.

W. W. Norton and Company. For excerpts from *Identity, Youth and Crisis* by Erik H. Erikson. Copyright 1968 by W. W. Norton and Company; "Oats" and "A Light Snow" from *My Voice Will Go With You: The Teaching Tales of Milton H. Erikson*, S. Rosen, ed. Copyright 1982 by W. W. Norton and Company. Reprinted by permission of the publisher.

Holt, Rinehart and Winston. For "Mending Wall," "Stopping by the Woods on a Snowy Evening" and "Hillwife" from *Complete Poems of Robert Frost*. Copyright 1949 by Holt, Rinehart and Winston.

Paulist Press. For "Nothing but a Loud-Mouthed Irish Priest" by A. Greeley from *Journey*, G. Baum, ed. Copyright 1975 by Paulist Press; "Historian as Believer" in *Journeys* by D. J. O'Brien. Copyright 1975 by Paulist Press. Used by permission of Paulist Press.

Duquesne University Press. For excerpts from *Field of Consciousness* by Aron Gurwitsch. Copyright 1964 by Duquesne University Press. Reprinted by permission of the publisher.

Harper & Row. For excerpts from *Being and Time* by Martin Heidegger. Copyright 1962 by SCM Press Ltd.; "The Thinker as Poet" from *Poetry, Language and Thought* by Martin Heidegger. Copyright 1971 by Martin Heidegger; "Words" from *On the Way to Language* by Martin Heidegger. Copyright 1971 by Harper & Row, Publishers, Inc.; *Basic Writings* by Martin Heidegger. Copyright 1977 by Harper & Row, Publishers, Inc.; and *Revisioning Psychology* by James Hillmen. Copyright 1975 by James Hillmen. Reprinted by permission of Harper & Row, Publishers, Inc.

St. Martin's Press. For excerpts from *The Critique of Pure Reason* by Immanuel Kant. Translated by Norman Kemp Smith. Copyright 1965 by St. Martin's Press, Inc. Reprinted with permission of the publisher.

Houghton, Mifflin Company. For "Endymion" and "When I have fears" from *The Complete Poetical Works of Keats* by John Keats. Copyright 1899 by Houghton, Mifflin Company.

Indiana University Press. For excerpts from *Kant and the Problems of Metaphysics* by

Martin Heidegger. Translated by J. S. Churchill. Copyright 1962 by Indiana University Press.

Viking Penguin, Inc. For "Climb down, O lordly mind" and "Song of a Man who has come through" from *The Collected Poems of D. H. Lawrence* by D. H. Lawrence. Copyright 1964 by Angelo Ravagli and C. M. Weekley, Executors of the Estate of Erieda Lawrence Ravagli. Reprinted by permision of Viking Penguin, Inc.

Random House, Inc. For excerpts from *The necessary angel* by Wallace Stevens. Copyright 1951 by Alfred A. Knopf, Inc.

Oxford University Press. For excerpts from "Mid summer's night dream" and Sonnet XXIX, "When in disgrace with fortune and men's eyes" by William Shakespeare. Copyright 1938 by Oxford University Press.

Cornell University Press. For excerpts from *The New Science of Giambattista Vico*, abridged and translated from the Third Edition by Thomas Goddard Bergin and Max Harold Fisch. Copyright 1970 by Cornell University. Copyright 1961 by Thomas Goddard Bergin and Max Harold Fisch. Copyright 1948 by Cornell University. Used by permission of the publisher.

Indiana University Press. For excerpts from *Metaphor and Reality* by P. Wheelwright. Copyright 1968 by Indiana University Press.

Doubleday & Co., Inc. For "Early Illusions" from *Bratsk station and other poems* by Yevgeny Yevtushenko. Translated by Tina Tupikina-Blaessner, Geoffrey Dutton and Igor Mezhakoff-Koriakin. Copyright 1966 by Sun Books Pty. Ltd. Reprinted by permission of Doubleday & Co., Inc.

# CHAPTER I

# The Centrality of Imaginative Thinking in Human Existence

My final point, then, is that the imagination is the power that enables us to perceive the normal in the abnormal, the opposite of chaos in chaos. It does this every day in arts and letters. . . . But when we speak of perceiving the normal we have in mind the instinctive integrations which are the reason for living. Of what value is anything to the solitary and those that live in misery and terror, except the imagination? (Stevens, 1942/1951, p. 153)

IN his discussion on the imagination Wallace Stevens has not hesitated to acclaim the imagination as the human access to the normal experience. In the work from which this passage is taken he suggested that human beings live in concepts of the imagination even before reason has had the opportunity to establish them. This is an intriguing statement, but one that seems to do violence to our own personal experience.

The imagination, as usually conceived, would seem to follow our normal perceptions, distorting them on occasion, embellishing them on others, but seldom preceding them. Nonetheless, Stevens pursues his point: when speaking of the normal, he is speaking of the instinctive integrations that are part and parcel of daily life and that constitute our reason for living. Finally, when speaking of those solitary folk who languish in suffering, Stevens sees no respite for them except that which their imagination provides. To deny them that, he feels, is to deny them the only thing that sustains them. In short, imagination in his view is in no way peripheral in human existence.

Shakespeare shared much of the same sentiment. Culling the

human experiences to which we are all heir, he spoke of imagination's influence.

> The lunatic, the lover, and the poet
> Are of imagination all compact.
> One sees more devils than vast hell can hold:
> That is the madman. The lover, all as frantic,
> Sees Helen's beauty in a brow of Egypt.
> The poet's eye, in a fine frenzy rolling,
> Doth glance from heaven to earth, from earth to heaven.
> And as imagination bodies forth
> The forms of things unknown, the poet's pen
> Turns them to shapes, and gives to airy nothing
> A local habitation and a name.
> *Midsummer Night's Dream*, Act V, sc. 1

This study is concerned with the question of personal integration: how human beings in the give-and-take of existence manage to put their lives together, some quite successfully, others less so. It cannot be disputed that such efforts were expended long before the advent of modern psychology and psychiatry. One need only scan the pages of the New Testament, for example, to learn how concerned the early Christians were with this matter; or, to cite another example, those of the Old Testament to see the famous Job painfully struggle toward realizations that enabled him to put his life together after a nightmare of suffering. Human suffering and failure have long been the focus of thought and study, but ultimately in the service of human wholeness, just as the study of physical disease has long been undertaken in medical circles in the interest of promoting human health.

In attending to the question of human integration, our study is primarily intent on the extraordinary role that imaginative thinking and language play in the individual's personal achievement. We shall center on the importance, indeed the centrality, of imaginative thinking. However much it may be disparaged or denied serious consideration in the human endeavor, the fact remains that people go on imagining all the time—and none more so than those who imagine that imagination has already made its contribution to their life and now imagine that it has no more to offer. The fact is, as one author has phrased it, that "imagining is so essential to human mental activity that its elimination would radically alter the character of man's mind." (Casey, 1974, p. 3) We would add to this that imagining is so essential to human activity that living is inconceivable without it.

To understand it, however, we must not abstract the issue of imagining from the living context in which it is to be found; namely, the context of human thinking. On the contrary, if its significance is to be properly understood, we must approach it precisely from our experience of it in the lived world, the *lebenswelt*, where it is to be seen as part of the semantic, thinking processes in which human beings are ever engaged.

## A. SIGNIFICANCE OF HUMAN THINKING IN HUMAN EXISTENCE

Ever since the early Greeks, the human person has been defined as a ζῶον λογον ἐχον, a living being endowed with the capacity of λογος, *logos*, languaging, discoursing. Unfortunately, the fullness and depth of the word λογος were lost in the translation of the Greek phrase into the Latin *animal rationale*, rational animal. The human person in this translation came to be seen as a person who was in effect an animal endowed with the capacity to reason. That the human person is this is readily granted, but the person is much more. Heidegger has phrased it this way:

> Man shows himself as the entity which talks. This does not signify that the possibility of vocal utterance is peculiar to him, but rather that he is the entity which is such as to discover the world and Dasein itself. The Greeks had no word for "language": they understood this phenomenon in the first instance as discourse. But because the λογος came into their philosophical ken primarily as assertion, this was the kind of logos which they took as their clue for working out the basic structures of the forms of discourse and its components. Grammar sought its foundations in the "logic" of this logos. (1927/1962, p. 208)

To identify discourse with reasoning is to err on the side of deficiency. The human being is remarkable for rational powers, but this does not exhaust the human genius. Human existence is characterized by both logical and imaginative thought, with the latter exercising a far greater significance in the person's life than has been hitherto appreciated. The failure to realize its proper role, however, has forced philosophy, science, and psychology in their efforts to understand existence to repair to countless hypothetical constructs, such as the unconscious, in an effort to formulate understandings of behavior that was sometimes rational and other times questionably so, while still remaining very human.

Such a comprehension of the human failed in its depiction of the person and embarked psychology in particular on a journey fraught with countless failures. Ultimately the acclaim heaped upon the rational dimensions of human thinking not only did an injustice to that imaginative thought of which the person was equally capable. It also led to the disparagement of the human rational achievements as well—soon to be dismissed as the tip of the iceberg, while the irrational and unconscious processes, primary and secondary, were extolled as the ultimate source of human genius. By this time the traditional pride of the human—his or her rational powers— was deemed imprisoned by the unconscious, instinctual ones.

This disservice to human thinking deserves to be pursued. The human's claim to fame is still that unique power to logos, to discourse, to name, to think—and it is for this reason that s/he stands forth as the head of creation, bringing it alive with our thinking genius. Human thinking, however, takes different forms, as we shall now seek to illustrate.

### 1. Common Sense Thinking

Neither common sense nor science can proceed without departing from the strict consideration of what is actual in experience. There is an inevitable distance required for human beings to commence the thinking that distinguishes them. If it is true that the human *Dasein* is at one with the world in which he exists, it is also true that the human being takes distance to commence reflection on the world of which he is a part. It is this distance that makes possible the thinking for which *Dasein* is acclaimed, and the entrance into what has been termed second- and third-order languaging: the languaging proper to common sense and to the logic that permeates sciences and philosophy. The pre-reflective experience of which phenomenology speaks ante-dates common sense and highly rational thought.

Common to all humans is that spirit of inquiry that constitutes ultimately the scientific attitude: the inquisitive, spontaneous Why?

And along with it, as Lonergan has pointed out, is the unsophisticated insight, or, better still, accumulations of insights with their proper interrogations, one following upon the other, at first spontaneously and later under some guiding influence (1957). Unlike the sciences, common sense is a special development of intelligence in a very earthy domain with little of the abstract and less of the theoretical. It is common; it is shared; it is generalized. Often it appears to argue from analogies or similaries, but they often escape logical formulations. It is verbal, but scarcely articulate, and makes no pretense at universally valid knowledge. It has little recourse to technical language or formal discourse. Its give and take between saying and meaning is often amorphous. At best it is experienced as if it were a homemade work of art with little theoretical pretension. Yet, like the sciences, common sense is the fruit of considerable collaboration with its homey share of tested results, imprecise though they be.

Heidegger has written on the impact of inauthentic existence in the life of *Dasein*: the shared content of commonsense thinking that is part and parcel of what Heidegger sees as the human They-self (*Das Man*) existence (p. 167). For the most part the human functions as a They-self that has been developed over time, by a people who have brought the individual into the world and have introduced him into an already imagined mode of existence in which he always already finds himself, and from which, as from within a circle, he must distantiate himself if he would move toward some measure of authenticity. In brief, we find ourselves living very much a They-existence in which our lives are dominated by the uncritical thought of everyman. Such thought, rooted as it is in the commonsense practice and unchallenged-unchallengeable axioms of centuries-old traditions, dominates our culture or a person until such time as it is called into question by new experiences and new ideas. It supplies for us the unseen skeletal structure with which we operate in life.

## 2. Rational, Logical Thinking

Commonsense thinking, then, is intrinsic to human existence, but its merits are quickly exhausted and its value circumscribed. It can never satisfy the aspirations of those who have come to see the great possibilities proffered humankind by a different style of rigorous thinking. The efforts of the early Greeks to establish a new mode of human inquiry beginning with the pre-Socratics and ending with the post-Aristotelians are well known and need not be recounted. During the Christian Era such thinking was developed further and gave rise to richer understandings of existence, now explicated within the Hebraic-Christian tradition. These efforts were permeated with the logical dimensions of thought and reason working together with faith. *Fides quaerens intellectum*; *Intellectus quaerens fidem* (Faith in the pursuit of knowledge; Knowledge in the pursuit of Faith) provided the moving inspiration. Such efforts sought to formulate for human living the solutions called for by the exigencies of life as lived in the Christian milieu impacted by historical developments such as wars, persecutions, plagues, diseases, poverty, the emergence of new mathematics, new world discoveries, and so on. In all this, thinking advanced far beyond common sense, and rational thought reached new heights through the genius of such persons as Augustine and Aquinas, to mention two of many. In the fields of engineering, architecture, navigation, art, and music tremendous strides were made. Some there were who began the scientific method, such as Roger Bacon (d.1202) and Albertus Magnus (d.1280). Then, during the late medieval and Renaissance periods, astronomy sustained breakthroughs principally because of men like Copernicus (d.1543), Brahe (d.1601), Kepler (d.1630), and Galileo (d.1642). Of these Galileo's work was most extraordinary, meriting him the honor of being one of the greatest discoverers of all time. As Husserl has stated, the work and thought of Galileo provided the impetus for the modern scientific thrust.

> One can truly say that the idea of nature as a really self-enclosed world of bodies first emerges with Galileo. A consequence of this, along with mathematization, which was too quickly taken for granted, is the idea of self-enclosed natural causality in which every occurrence is determined unequivocally and in advance. Clearly the way is thus prepared for dualism, which appears immediately afterward in Descartes. (1954/1970, p. 60).

It was indeed not until the advent of René Descartes (d.1650), a brilliant Frenchman of profound faith and intellect, absorbed in the philosophical and mathematical excitement of the growing rational thought, that a style of thinking was developed that gave logical thought its pronounced scientific quality. His conception of philosophy and the world came to dominate. Although Galileo had established the initial founding of the new natural scientific method, it was Descartes, himself the founder of analytical geometry, who conceived and set in systematic motion the new idea of universal philosophy: a mathematical, physicalistic rationalism. Its effect was immediate and powerful.

It is remarkable to note that the Descartes to whom modern science is so much indebted is the same Descartes to whom Kant, Husserl, Heidegger, Wittgenstein, and others, critical of the contemporary preoccupation with logical, rational, scientific thought, also gave acclaim. This paradox is striking, and it serves to illustrate the magnitude of his bequest. Descartes's understanding of the person as essentially a *cogito* served as a springboard for contemporary thought and, for example, provided phenomenological study (which would repudiate his subject-object dichotomy as disastrous for a full understanding of human nature), with a profound grasp of the role of human consciousness and subjectivity in human endeavor. There is no mistaking the vital presence of his ideas. In the words of Husserl:

> But it was not merely in the inauguration of this idea (i.e., philosophy as "universal mathematics") that Descartes was the founding father of the modern period. It is highly remarkable at the same time that it was he, in his *Meditations*—and precisely in order to provide a radical foundation for the new rationalism and then *eo ipso* for dualism—who accomplished the primal establishment of ideas which were destined, through their own historical effects (as if following a hidden teleology of history), to explode this very rationalism by uncovering its hidden absurdity. Precisely those ideas which were supposed to ground this rationalism as *aeterna veritas* bear within themselves a *deeply hidden sense*, which, once brought to the surface, completely uproots it. (p. 74).

Such was the setting for the meshing of logical discourse and current scientific discourse. The development of any science is a gradual occurrence. Some, such as astronomy and mathematics, have their origins lost in antiquity. Others—few in number—spring from the combination of fields already well established, such as biochemistry. For the vast majority, however, the growth is cumulative, tending over a period of time to crystallize in some coherent form. Thus mechanics and motion originated in the medieval period; physical optics sprang out of the efforts of the seventeenth century; electrical research came into being in the first half of the eighteenth century. Each field has its prehistory and then its formal history. When, as Kuhn points out, a field witnesses the integration of its data in a formulation that is unprecedented and significantly impressive so that it appeals to a number of scientific practitioners who find the formulation helpful and sufficiently provocative to elicit further ideas and research, a paradigm can be said to have been established. At this point, historically, the gestation period ends and a science would seem to be born.

In all such endeavors the presence of logical, rational thought is obvious. Various methods are used, depending on the science in question and the stage of scientific development in the given area. It is rare indeed that there is not some recourse to models of diverse kinds: systematically developed metaphors, to use the phrase of Max Black (1962), highlighting similarities in concepts that have yet to be fully conceptualized. Such models are sometimes termed heuristic fictions, useful fictions that seemingly are to be taken seriously but not literally, all with the intent of ordering the experiment and the study despite the wide assembly of detail. Whatever the model, the respective methods, however varied, are employed in accordance with the dictates of the rationalism from which they originally sprang (Barbour, 1974).

There remains a final and crucial aspect of the logical, rational thought that has been instrinsic to the modern scientific pursuit: the issue of approach. It is seldom specified in the scientific enterprise, but along with method and content, it forms a scientific triumvirate, critical for the pursuit of scientific research. Giorgi has put it this way:

> By establishing the category of *approach* we mean to take into account the researcher himself in the enterprise of science. By approach is meant the fundamental viewpoint towards man and the work that the scientist brings, or adopts, with respect to his work as a scientist, whether this viewpoint is made explicit or remains implicit. We also recognize that in a very real sense this task is inexhaustible. That is, no person could ever make completely explicit all of the characteristics of his approach. However, we would also maintain that it is worthwhile to make explicit whatever one can. We would argue against the position that would say that since one cannot make fully

explicit his presuppositions, or his approach, there is no sense in trying at all. The very nature of science, or any human effort for that matter, is such that there is this note of incompleteness in its very core. Yet in spite of this incompleteness, we must strive for a knowledge that transcends the particular and the momentary. This is where the social aspect of science comes in. From his limited viewpoint each scientist states the truth as he sees it or understands it, and then he lets the rest of his colleagues criticize or modify it until what is true stand and what is false is shed away. Thus far, it has been the practise to do this with both method and content; we are merely stating that the same thing should be done with respect to approach. (1970, p. 126)

With the domination of rational and logical thought in the modern scientific scene and its almost exclusive emphasis on mathematical and objectivistic method for serious study, the question of approach has been simply ignored. It is as though the researcher with his strongly logical thought were inconsequential in the study, and that the faithful observance of all canons of objectivity need not involve the researcher and his presuppositions. The truth is, however, as Giorgi has stated, such objectivism does not remove the presence of the researcher at all; it simply makes him present in another way.

## 3. Imaginative Thinking

It has been shown thus far that human thought can take the form of commonsense thinking or of logical, rational thinking. To stop here, however, would be to sell human nature short. There remains much more to the human being than this, and it is to this domain of imaginative thinking that we now give our attention.

During the medieval period the curriculum of the universities allowed for the trivium and the quadrivium. The former included the lower division of the seven liberal arts: grammar, rhetoric, and logic. The latter included the upper division: the mathematical sciences of arithmetic, geometry, and astronomy, along with music. In substance the trivium handled matters of language while the quadrivium treated science and mathematics. Of the areas in the trivium grammar was rated least significant and logic by far the most significant. In between was rhetoric, more important than grammar but less prestigious than logic. This was no happenstance, for rhetoric had declined from its glorious days in pre-Aristotle Greece when it flourished as the art of persuasion and gained prominence as the favored form of higher education. In the hands of the sophists it had indeed become a powerful tool that gave distinction to its masters. Aristotle for one saw it as critical for political life, legal proceedings, and festive celebrations. Subsequent centuries, however, under both the Greeks and the Romans, saw the entire nature of rhetoric change, its influence in effect becoming less valued and more ornamental. By the early centuries under the Roman emperors, many of whom sought to encourage rhetorical training in their schools, it had become highly imitative and declamatory. By the eleventh and twelfth centuries it was a study of lesser consequence. Periodic revivals of interest usually proved short-lived. Even the Renaissance was unable to bring about the significant rebirth of permanent worth, although the humanists of the Renaissance were the first to see the literature of a people in its totality as a cultural achievement. As Bolgar has put it,

> They were not content merely to write classical Latin. Desiring to equal the cultural triumphs of antiquity, they attempted every classical genre, thus giving imitation a range it had not had before. And this was also the age when the national literatures of Europe were attaining their maturity, so that imitation was no longer limited to Latin. It was practised in the vernaculars, and with striking success. (1972, 19, p. 259)

The eighteenth century saw revivals of interest in the topic, but the nineteenth century, which had become convinced of the value of logical thought and especially scientific experimentation, dismissed traditional techniques of style and formal rhetorical study. It was this appraisal of the topic that prevailed until the second quarter of the twentieth century, when a new appreciation of language and its use emerged in Western civilization. Even here, it should be noted, the new realizations about language came about in the area of logic—at least at first. Logical positivism and its emphasis on meaning gave logic an impetus that it really did not need, for any emphasis on language by the very nature of things was destined to concentrate on logic. Since that time, to be sure, many new developments have come about.

It should be pointed out that while the philosophy of language, at least in Western thought, has always been based primarily on logic, there have been those who questioned its priority, or at least its strong emphasis. Among the most outstanding was Giambattista Vico (d.1744), the Italian philosopher, whose genius is becoming more apparent every decade. It is to Vico that our own age has turned to understand a whole new dimension of what it means to be human.

> Vico interpreted the Greek maxim "Know Thyself" as signifying the possibility of a science of mankind as revealed in the ethnohistory of man. Man, he maintained, acquired an objective knowledge of himself, not through critical reflection and analysis of his individual ideas as Socrates and Plato attempted to do, but rather through reflection on the historical evidence of the mental and cultural development of man in society. Thus the study of myth became for Vico an integral part of his science and philosophy of history—a thesis which has since been developed by the ethnologists E. B. Tylor, in *Primitive Culture*, and Max Muller, in *Science of Thought*, and by Ernst Cassirer, in his classic *Philosophy of Symbolic Forms*. (Bidney, 1969, p. 259)

Today the position of logical eminence in language is undergoing a serious challenge. The new position sees in rhetoric much more originary power and significance than has hitherto been acknowledged. It would appear, according to this growing school of thought, that much of the vitality and ingenuity of language derives from its so-called rhetorical constituents, and that the genius of a language is to be found in those areas that have not been treated as part of the logical sphere. This analysis is relevant for our purpose, for it is part of the tardy appreciation of imaginative thinking: the rhetorical, aesthetical, creative, originary dimension of language. This thrust toward rhetoric and the originary power that it entails, and the focus on the imaginative dimensions of human thinking would appear to be part of the same realization. Owen Barfield has observed that we have had, to the full, language as it is grasped by the logical mind. What is needed now, he insists, is language as it is grasped by the poetic mind—something that we have seen sketched only in bits and pieces to date (1964, p. 62).

Obviously language and linguistics, linguistics and logic, logic and language are all interrelated, but the powerful mediation of imaginative thinking throughout this trinity is just beginning to surface. In essence, imaginative thinking has been making its contribution to human thought and study, and even to the human sciences and to natural science. For the most part its presence has been felt in the domain of rhetoric rather than that of logic. It is beginning to appear at this stage of our understanding of matters, however, that the foundations of rhetoric may well be offering more support to the logical superstructure than we have been wont to admit.

## B.   THE GROWING RESPECT FOR IMAGINATIVE THINKING

The struggle for primacy between logic and rhetoric has begun to take shape, but it must be said in all candor that the confrontation was sooner or later inevitable. The Greek concept of λογοσ, as we have seen, included more in its fullness than the notion of rationality that was developed in Western civilization. With the latter now reduced, two millennia later, to a powerful but highly circumscribed area of mathematics and science as the paragons of rationality and objectivity, it was only a question of time until the question was raised: whether human thinking does not encompass more in its purview than the contemporary notion of rationality would allow. The ironic truth is that imaginative thinking has contributed mightily to human accomplishment. While not lost totally in the shuffle, it was certainly relegated to the periphery of solid thought; or, when taken seriously, it was allowed its artistic and delightful moment in the sun, and usually an aesthetic one. Needless to say, this underestimation has wreaked havoc with the human effort to understand the fullness of being human, or the individual person's attempt to realize his or her personal integration.

### 1. Imaginative Thinking and Aesthetic Experience

We have been mentioning the deepening appreciation of the value of imaginative thought in the human enterprise of existing. Its role in the aesthetic experience was always recognized. However, Heidegger has pointed out in his poem "The Thinker as Poet" that it is not enough to see the thinker in the poet; we must see the poet in the thinker:

> Singing and thinking are the stems
> neighbor to poetry.
> They grow out of Being and reach into
> its truth.                              (1971, p. 13)

That thinking should be akin to singing and poeticizing appears unusual, but not if we see thinking as imaginative, creative thought, with a lilt of its own. Indeed in such a context the relationship is most appropriate. Singing, thinking, poetizing are all modalities of Being, and each contributes its disclosure of Being, its unveiling of Truth while remaining in some respects part of each other. The novel, the play, the oratorio—all allow one to enter in unique, tender ways the lives of characters. The same can be said of the musician, the sculptor, the architect—artists all, who invite others to enter their domain and taste of their offerings. Their appeal is to the imaginative thinking of their guests, and their hope is a genuine sharing of the wealth of their rich experience of life, now captured in its art form. Poetry, with its own profound thought, would have us sing of life's wonders and mysteries. Singing, with its creative uplift, would have us ponder anew and revel in its profundity, much in the spirit of St. Augustine's famous dictum: *Quis cantat, bis orat*, He who sings prays doubly. In a truly remarkable way singing does heighten the poetic disclosure and enrich profoundly the meditative act. Thinking, with its immense spread of our horizons and unearthing of life's depths, graces us with the creative vision of the poet and the power to enthrall as befits the singer.

Few poems have succeeded in capturing so exquisitely the power wielded by our imagination in the aesthetic experience as has Keats's opening lines to "Endymion". It constitutes a glowing tribute to the force and significance of the imagination in its vital aesthetic draw upon the hearts of poets and thinkers alike.

> A thing of beauty is a joy for ever:
> Its loveliness increases; it will never
> Pass into nothingness; but still will keep
> A bower quiet for us, and a sleep
> Full of sweet dreams, and health, and quiet
> breathing.
> Therefore, on every morrow, are we wreathing
> A flowery band to bind us to the earth,
> Spite of despondence, of the inhuman dearth
> Of noble natures, of the gloomy days,
> Of all the unhealthy and o'er darken'd ways
> Made for our searching: yes, in spite of all,
> Some shape of beauty moves away the pall
> From our dark spirits. Such the sun, the moon,

Trees old and young, sprouting a shady boon
For simple sheep; and such are daffodils
With the green world they live in; and clear rills
That for themselves a cooling covert make
'Gainst the hot season; the mid-forest brake
Rich with a sprinkling of fair musk-rose blooms:
And such too is the grandeur of the dooms
We have imagined for the mighty dead;
All lovely tales that we have heard or read:
An endless fountain of immortal drink,
Pouring into us from the heaven's brink.

Nor do we merely feel these essences
For one short hour; no, even as the trees
That whisper round a temple become soon
Dear as the temple's self, so does the moon,
the passion poesy, glories infinite,
Haunt us till they become a cheering light
Unto our souls, and bound to us so fast,
That, whether there be shine, or gloom o'er cast,
They always must be with us, or we die.

John Keats, "Endymion"

"The grandeur of the dooms that we have imagined for the mighty dead." Keats could have spoken just as truly of the magnificent symphonies composed in tribute to loved ones, or the Pietas of Michelangelo, or the Taj Mahal. The list is endless. The appeal of the drama, the concert, the novel, the poem attests to the power of such artistic accomplishments to stir the heart of the human being. And the more successful the artist may be in touching the imagination, the more powerful the work in question. Poetic imagination, creative imagination it is that allows the trees about the temple to become soon dear as the temple's self. Artistic imagination it is that allows the flower show to soothe the soul as does the symphony; that introduces the person to a Hamlet, a Tess, a Beatrice in whose company the reader is granted precious glimpses into the human heart and profound understandings of the human soul. Creative imagination it is that enables the thinker to contemplate the *mysterium fascinans et terribile* and metaphorize it anew in the face of the impossible. Such is its genius. Indeed, Santayana felt that the role played by the imagination in human life was truly noble: "Without it his thought would be not only far too narrow to represent, although it were symbolically, the greatness of the universe, but far too narrow even to render the scope of his own life and the conditions of his practical welfare." (1900, p. 8)

## 2. Imaginative Thinking and Science

In his work, *Personal Knowledge*, Michael Polanyi addresses the question of mathematics and draws an analogy between it and novel writing (1958, p. 186). In the course of writing a novel, the novel grows. In the course of developing a system, a theory, a hypothesis, it too grows. The growth that a science undergoes is dependent to a significant extent on the rational decisions, imaginative thinking, personal risks, empirical findings and systematic verifications that emerge in the course of years, or a particular lifetime. Much depends too on the serendipitous, unexpected discoveries that take place, as well as the personal acumen of the individual scientists who have undertaken their respective quests. And, even though it may appear incidental, if not irrelevant, much depends on the personal biases, experiences, prejudices, and beliefs of the scientist at work, just as much depends on the reactions, personal and professional, of the scientific community to the individual's findings: its evaluation of the uncoverings. In all its forms science is a human achievement, and as such it is subject to human limits as is any other study. In some ways this would appear to be a laboring of the obvious, were it not a fact that the rise of logical and rational thinking, and their domination by the scientific endeavor, would or could lead one to overlook this truth. We could be led to identify scientific objectivity with extranormal attributes, just as scientific thinking itself has often been depicted as pure rationality. In science we are dealing with a very human enterprise, from the beginning to the end. Whether we focus on the remarkable emotional outburst that Kepler indulges in his *Harmonices Mundi*, during which he gives vent to what he terms his "sacred fury," or study the intensity that characterized the academic and scientific wars over the years, we see in action the explosiveness that can and has surrounded many a scientific debate. The competition between paradigms is not the sort of confrontation that is resolved by quiet and cool reflection on proffered proofs. As Thomas Kuhn has pointed out, proponents for competing paradigms may well battle

over the definition of science and the demands of standards—
indeed the incommensurability of standards. Thus Copernicanism
made few converts for almost a century after Copernicus's death.
So too Sir Isaac Newton's work had to wait a half century before it
gained acceptance on the continent, once the *Principia* appeared.
Joseph Priestly never would accept the oxygen theory, nor Lord
Kelvin the electromagnetic theory, and so on. In one dramatic
passage Kuhn describes something of the intensity that is felt in
various quarters:

> The difficulties of conversion have often been noted by scientists
> themselves. Darwin, in a particularly perceptive passage at the end
> of his *Origin of Species*, wrote: "Although I am fully convinced of the
> truth of the views given in this volume . . . I by no means expect to
> convince experienced naturalists whose minds are stocked with a
> multitude of facts all viewed, during a long course of years, from a
> point of view directly opposite to mine. . . . But I look with con-
> fidence to the future,—to young and rising naturalists, who will be
> able to view both sides of the question with impartiality." And Max
> Planck, surveying his own career in his *Scientific Autobiography*, sadly
> remarked that "a new scientific truth does not triumph by convinc-
> ing its opponents and making them see the light, but rather because
> its opponents eventually die, and a new generation grows up that is
> familiar with it!" (1970, p. 151)

Lest it appear that we are now suggesting that scientific decisions are made for or against paradigms solely on grounds that are
imaginative, emotional and unscientific, let us point out that such
is not our intent. Even when one is not dealing with the question of
a paradigm shift, it remains a fact that there are independent
criteria of assessment to which scientists can, and do, have recourse
in moving toward their preference. Kuhn concedes this in his
reiteration that the development of science witnesses paradigmatic
changes, less through a dramatic group conversion of scientists
toward a new theory than a gradual but increasing shift in professional allegiances. Such shifts, and such failure to shift, are fully
understood, however, in terms of thinking that is at once highly
logical, as is to be expected, but also quite personal, imaginative,
and even aesthetic.

At this point a second consideration would be advanced. It was
stated above in the discussion on scientific, logical thinking that
science employs many models of various sorts to explore its under-

standing of nature. Black has termed such models systematically developed metaphors, designed to enable the scientist to treat of one system in terms of a second system, in a different medium so to speak, whose structure may be currently better understood or more easily manipulable. Whatever the basis for the selection, the models themselves provide for the elucidation of a given scientific position or for the extension of a theoretical formulation. One familiar example is the billiard-ball model which serves as an analogue for the kinetic theory of gases; another is the planetary model which served as analogue for the Bohr theory of electrons.

The critical point at issue is the fact that such models are an imagined mechanism or process which is selected by analogy with familiar mechanisms or processes. Such models, particularly theoretical ones, are obviously intended to further the understanding process, but they are also used to make possible predictions. As is evident, this process calls for considerable creative imagination on the part of the scientist himself. Model theory, to be sure, is a field unto itself, but the function of the models in question is apparent enough. Some theorists, such as Mary Hess, term the theoretical explorations in sciences metaphorical redescriptions. Such models, of whatever type, are never intended to exhaust the subject at hand. They serve merely to bring certain aspects of the world into prominence, while admittedly ignoring other aspects of the world at hand. Such a model, for example, is the double-helix model of the DNA molecule. As a model it comes close to being identical with the molecular structure of DNA. Nonetheless it represents only the spatial relationships among the DNA components, not the character of the bonds between them. The issue of debate among scientists in regard to models is the question of whether there is any essential and objective dependence between an explanatory theory and its model that goes beyond a dispensable and possibly subjective method of discovery. Whatever the merits of arguing that models should be taken literally—and few would push this far—there is general agreement that models, when used, should certainly be taken seriously.

In summary, we have seen that the world of science, with all its emphases on the priority of logical, rigorous method along with rational, objectivistic thinking, finds the recourse to imaginative thinking inevitable and indispensable on various levels. Thanks to this, it can move into the unknown on the basis of previous experiences or study that it can now metaphorize. It can conjure up hypotheses, theories, and systems that await its verification. It can uncover information of such a diverse nature that its synthesis would appear to be inconceivable. Yet, by imagining things otherwise, it can eventually originate or formulate or even guess paradigms that in time can render its discoveries intelligible. And, when the data permit it and scientists are scientifically and emotionally able to confront it, it can move to the formulation of a new paradigm for a better understanding of its own discoveries.

Without imaginative thinking the scientific enterprise would have long ago died aborning. Without continued imaginative thinking the scientific enterprise would soon grind to a halt.

### 3. Imaginative Thinking and Philosophy

It is no secret that Plato had his misgiving about poets. And it should come as no surprise, then, that he had misgivings also about the imagination. This he considered a lesser form of knowledge, analogous but inferior to perception. The image, being an imitation of an imitation, was held in suspicion. Aristotle, on the other hand, saw in imagination a faculty situated somewhere between perception and intellect, and bearing a unique relationship to memory, itself an outgrowth of perception also. In his *De Anima* he clarified his thinking on the subject and proposed a view that held sway clear into the medieval period. Aquinas, for example, makes many references to the image, the sensorium, the fantasy, the dream, and allows considerable respect for all aspects of the question in his works in philosophy and theology. Basically he espoused the Aristotelian position, as did most of his contemporaries. All this, of course, was prior to the logical and scientific preemption of the modern period. In Descartes, himself a product of the scholastic tradition, considerable reference is made to the imagination along with the inevitable confusion that so often attends the word. Many such references are to be found, for instance, in his *Meditations* (1972, v. 1, p. 186).

Subsequent to the time of Descartes the imagination was relegated to a lesser role, devoid of genuine cognitive value. During the Romantic period in Germany and England it did assume authority as a constituent of art and metaphysics with claims, however, that in time became self-defeating. Immanuel Kant, in his *Critique of*

*Pure Reason* and *Critique of Judgment,* made serious contributions toward the better understanding of the imagination's role in human existence. The latter work is considered a decisive event in the history of modern aesthetics (Kerrane, 1971) while the former, particularly in its early edition of 1781, had a profound effect on the development of Heidegger's own thought. Also influenced by Kant, Samuel Taylor Coleridge extolled the virtues of what he termed the primary imagination. Others like George Santayana, Friedrich Schiller, and Ernst Cassirer also acclaimed its virtue, but the emphasis with the majority of thinkers concentrated on the subject of aesthetic criticism. In time the term became much overused and was associated with the exotic and vague. A turning point was reached, however, with the rise of phenomenological thought: Brentano's *Psychology from the Empirical Standpoint* (1874) and Husserl's *Ideas: General Introduction to Pure Phenomenology* (1913). Both these works are considered basic documents for modern aesthetic study, but they are also critical for the philosophical interest in imaginative thought. At the core of that renewed interest, not surprisingly, were the three critiques of Kant, particularly the *Critique of Pure Reason.*

Mention must be made here of the work of Martin Heidegger, a philosopher whose early work was profoundly influenced by Kant and whose later work, still in the Kantian tradition, gave eloquent testimony to his genuine appreciation of the significance of poetry and art. His magnum opus, *Being and Time,* was published in 1927; his *Kant and the Problem of Metaphysics* was published in 1929. In the former, speaking of the matter of temporality and its relation to the Kantian doctrine on schematism, which is at the heart of Kant's teaching on imagination, he expresses deep regret that Kant saw fit to recoil from a position of affirmation of the imagination that Kant had enunciated in the first edition of the *Critique of Pure Reason* in 1781. In his *Kant and the Problem of Metaphysics* Heidegger returned to this theme, and again expressed regret at Kant's decision:

> By his radical interrogation, Kant brought the "possibility" of metaphysics before this abyss. He saw the unknown; he had to draw back. Not only did the imagination fill him with alarm, but in the meantime (between the first and second editions) he had also come more and more under the influence of pure reason as such. (1929/1962, p. 173)

This mention of Heidegger's works provides some insight into his appreciation of the importance of the imagination in *Dasein's* understanding of existence. His decision to critique Kant for recoiling represents a strong feeling indeed. Ironically, Heidegger himself also subsequently seemed to recoil from the challenge—at least from a direct confrontation. Whatever his reason for sidestepping it, Heidegger did return in full force to take it up indirectly—through recourse to language, poetry, and art.

It should be mentioned here that the name of Husserl is relevant in two different contexts: first, in any discussion on the developments in the area of logical thinking that took place early in the twentieth century, and second in any discussion on the renewed interest in imaginative thinking that has occurred during this century. This calls for some comment. The development of Husserl's thought shows that his appreciation, like that of Heidegger, was for both kinds of thinking. His volumes in the *Logical Investigations* speak for themselves regarding his efforts expended in the clarification of logical thought. His respect for the imagination, however, was equally genuine, although his work deals sparsely with the topic as such. Nonetheless, the role of the imagination is central to the entire Husserlian project. The epoche, the phenomenological reduction, the eidetic reduction, the imaginative variations, and the role of adumbrations in perception—all bear witness to the depth of that respect. Casey has phrased it accurately:

> No other philosophical method, with the possible exception of Descartes' method in the *Meditations*, makes so explicit or so extensive a use of imagining. And this is the case in spite of Husserl's abiding logocentrism, which prevented him from according to imagination a central place in his official philosophy of mind—where it is held to be a mere modification of memory. (1974, p. 7)

A final and significant instance of contemporary interest in imaginative thought is Jean-Paul Sartre. Two of his works were focused on the topic: *Imagination* (*L'Imagination*, 1936) and *The Psychology of Imagination* (*L'Imaginaire*, 1940). The first work depicts Sartre's critique of the classical concept of imagination, while the second seeks to explicate in a more phenomenological presentation the essentials of the imaginative experience. In so doing Sartre proposed that the art object as image is necessarily unreal and that imagination is to be conceived as a preoccupation with the absence of a present object or the presence of an absent object. Subsequent to these works, however, Sartre wrote his *What Is Literature?* (*Qu'est-ce que la litterature?*, 1948). A noticeable development had taken place during this time in his thinking about imagination. In this work he developed a theory of the novel, a theory in which the imagination has a central place in the human engagement with reality. While never completely renouncing his position as stated in the *Psychology of Imagination*, Sartre did come to see the imagination as part of the aesthetic imperative having a moral imperative of its own. As he puts it,

> When the writer thinks that he has pathways to the eternal, he is beyond comparison. He has the benefit of an illumination which he can not communicate to the vulgar throng which crawls beneath him. But if it has occurred to him to think that one does not escape his class by fine sentiments, that there is no privileged consciousness anywhere, that *belles-lettres* are not *lettres de noblesse*, that the best way to be bowled over by one's age is to turn one's back on it or to pretend to be above it, and that one does not transcend it by running away from it but by taking hold of it in order to change it, that is, by going beyond it toward the immediate future, then he is writing for everybody and with everybody because the problem which he is trying to solve by means of his own talents is everybody's problem. Besides, those among us who collaborated in the underground newspapers addressed themselves in their articles to the whole community. We were not prepared for this kind of thing and we turned out to be not very clever; the literature of resistance did not produce anything to be excited about. But this experience made us feel what a literature of the concrete universal might be. (1948/1965, p. 224)

In brief, the activity of the imagination changed and moved from a philosophical freedom that enabled it to produce unreal images to a situated freedom that required that it function as an ethical instrument in personal communication. In other words, while the earlier Sartre may have seen the imagination as a focus on the unreal, the Sartre of the postresistance period saw it as intently engaged in the real world of activity. Unfortunately he never formulated an extended theoretical presentation of the latter position as he had once done for the former. Had he ever done so, there is certainly reason to think that he would have allowed considerably more theoretical room for its rhetorical dimensions and living engagement with the *lebenswelt* than the earlier Sartre ever had.

It is thus evident from the preceding treatment that imaginative thinking has concerned philosophy from the very beginning, but at no time has it become as central as it is becoming today. A striking instance of the current thinking is Paul Ricoeur, as well as Derrida, whose *White Mythology* is an invitation to philosophy to examine itself anew and discover itself as an imaginative enterprise that has forgotten its own metaphorical origins (1974). The white mythology of which he speaks is Western thought which has covered over its rhetorical base and allowed itself to be mesmerized by its own logocentrism. Derrida is convinced, as are others, that a return to its ground—its metaphorical, imaginative, rhetorical ground— could conceivably give philosophical study today new life.

## 4. Imaginative Thinking and Psychology

The study of imagery through introspection was one of the earliest endeavors in the field of psychology. Under Wilhelm Wundt in Leipzig and E. B. Titchener at Cornell classical introspection, focusing on sensations and feelings, came into prominence, only to be modified significantly by Oswald Kulpe and the Wurzburg school in the early 1900s. Their emphasis, however, was on higher mental processes, such as thought and will. The inherent defects and serious limitations of the methods, along with the almost inevitable unreliability surrounding the controversy on imageless thought, eventually brought the introspection movement to a halt. In contemporary psychology it is still used as a complementary method as in subject's reports on sensory experience in psychophysical experiments, or in psychopharmacological studies on drug effects on humans. For the most part, however, no prolonged serious efforts in the study of imagination or imagery were conducted after the first decade of the twentieth century. Some fifty years or so later, the studied neglect gave way to a new interest in mental imagery in various areas of psychology. Although there are still those who remain unconvinced of its significance or reliability, it has returned as a matter worthy of its own investigation in some instances, or as an explanatory construct in cognitive psychology in others.

These developments in no way exhaust the contribution that psychology has made to the question of imaginative thinking. If one turns at this point from the area of experimental psychology to that of clinical psychology, one soon realizes that its emphasis on imaginative thinking has been simply tremendous. And this is true in the areas of theory and praxis. It would be no exaggeration to say that clinical psychology, more than any other professional field, has exploited the field of imaginative thought in its attempts to deal with the serious problems of practical life. The most prominent example is Sigmund Freud himself. In his *Interpretation of Dreams* he speaks of the adoption of an attitude of mind that is an abandonment of the critical function; as a result the person may enter a state of imaginative associations, free of evaluation and full of meaningful implications. And this he sees as a distinct bonus, particularly in therapy. Freud quotes with approval a letter from Friedrich Schiller, the German poet and philosopher, who reprimands a friend for allowing a constraint to be imposed by his reason upon his imagination, thus reducing his productivity. For creative work, he feels, the reason must step aside, so to speak, relax its vigilance and let ideas rush in pell-mell, for such momentary and transient extravagances allow the genius in the artist to flourish. And Freud sees something akin to this in the therapeutic experience (1900/1953, p. 102).

This passage is one of the rare formal references that Freud makes to the imagination as such. The constraint of reason to which he and Schiller speak is directed against the imagination; and when reason does relax and open the gates to free association, they state, it is allowing the advent of the imagination. Schiller's point is clear, as is Freud's: the realm of the imaginative is in many ways the key to understanding the human.

It can be stated in another way. Freud's heroic efforts to uncover the illusions of life, to cut through the subtleties of painful psychopathological experiences, and to liberate the human being from the grip of his or her own neurotic fabrications, were directed ultimately to a skillful exploitation, in the best sense of the word, of the imaginative potential of the person. His appeal was made to the imaginative resources of the individual to release the person from the imaginative restraints by which the person was hindered. To bring this about, Freud, over time, built his theory of the human personality engaging the problem of false consciousness (to use a phrase of Ricoeur) via dreams and neurotic symptoms and working toward an economics of instincts. Nor was this all. His entire theory represents an imaginative effort to depict a psychic structure of the human and to plot the vicissitudes of its abnormal functioning.

It is clear to any thinking person that the theoretical construct of Freud, to say nothing of his diagrammatic depiction (1932/1964, p. 77) is a metaphorization of human existence. This, of course, is not to be faulted, but simply acknowledged. Indeed it represents an ingenious effort to render human existence intelligible and to provide some comprehension of psychological difficulties with which individuals may be afflicted. But for all that it remains a metaphorization, nonetheless, not unlike the scientific models mentioned previously, and as such it constitutes a highly imaginative creation. To be sure, Freud was not the first to construct such a model. The mystics had done the same long before him, as he readily conceded (1932/1964, p. 80). And many other theorists have done likewise since his time.

What has been stated about the theoretical description of human nature depicted by Freud may also be said of the various constructs that he developed in the course of his therapeutic practice: the defence mechanisms, those imaginative means used by the ego to ward off danger, anxiety, and displeasure. As Freud himself said, it was from the study of one of those defence mechanisms, repression, that the study of neurotic processes took its start. These mechanisms were imagined by the person, says Freud's theory, to protect the individual in question, but at a certain phase of their development they themselves became the danger, thus allowing the person to become fixated in his infantilisms.

The Freudian analysis of human nature, in short, and the therapeutic built around that analysis are a highly imaginative account of the operation and development of the person, along with a proposed analysis of the genesis of psychological and psychosomatic illnesses to which it is prey. To pretend that the theoretical picture totally covers the entire study of human development is grandiose. To propose that it answers every question that can be raised is absurd. To see it, however, as a metaphorization of human existence and a heuristic for the understanding of the genesis, development, and possible healing of human problems is quite intelligible indeed. Many obviously have, while many others see in it some plausibility but are keenly aware of its shortcomings. In either case Freud's psychoanalysis remains a theoretical stance that has had powerful impact on human lives and human thought, and it is a stance that offers a highly imaginative understanding of life and its foibles, along with a profound appreciation of human creativity, art, and civilizaton. The irony, of course, is that while it is such a powerful metaphorization of life that owes so much to its imaginative depictions, its creator himself seldom took stock of the fact that it was just that and nothing more: a significant metaphorization.

Another example of the same principle is the theoretical stance of Carl Jung, one of Freud's early followers who opted to break with Freud and present a theoretical picture of his own. Unlike Freud, however, Jung made no apology for his recourse to the imagination, and his theoretizations give overwhelming evidence of his own respect for thinking of this kind. Despite his many writings Jung himself never reduced his theory to a diagram as had Freud, but one of his colleagues, Jolande Jacobi, did so with Jung's expressed approval (1962, p. 125).

Our point should be evident. Jung's theory, diagrammed or otherwise, is another attempt to capture the constituents of the human personality, all in the hope of promoting an understanding of human growth and providing a resource for the understanding and alleviation of human ills. Like Freud's, Jung's theory is itself a metaphorization of the human person, in some respects analogous to that of Freud and in other respects quite different.

More to the point, however, is Jung's own expressed discussion of the imagination, and there are many. The *Two Essays on Analytical Psychology* provide strong statements on his own advanced thought on the matter. To cite only one:

> It is in the creation of fantasies that we find the unitive function we are seeking. All the elements engaged by the active tendencies flow into the imagination. The imagination has, it is true, a poor reputation among psychologists, and up to the present psychoanalytic theories have treated it accordingly. For Freud as for Adler it is only a so-called "symbolic" view disguising the tendencies of the primitive desires presupposed by those two investigators. But one can set against this opinion—not upon theoretical principle, but essentially for practical reasons—the fact that, though it is possible to explain and to depreciate imagination in respect of its causality, imagination is nevertheless the creative source of all that has made progress possible to human life. Imagination holds in itself an irreducible value, for it is the psychic function whose roots ramify at the same time in the contents of the conscious mind and of the unconscious, in the collective as in the individual. But whence has the imagination acquired its bad reputation? Above all, from the circumstance that

its manifestations cannot be taken at their face value. If one takes them concretely they are of no value; if, like Freud, one attributes semantic significance to them, they are interesting from the scientific point of view; but if we regard them, according to the hermeneutic conception, as authentic symbols, then they provide the directive signs we need in order to carry on our lives in harmony with ourselves. (1956/1965, p. 298)

It is clear that Jung's comprehension of humankind and its history calls for clear and forthright recognition of imaginative thinking as being at the center of individuation, the process of personal becoming. Imaginative realization is the human quest, as Jung sees it, and such a realization is unintelligible unless full recognition is given to the imaginative thinking of everyone. Casey, a student of Jungian thought, would suggest that three types of imaginative experience be allowed within the confines of such theory: conscious imagining, to be explored through phenomenological inquiry; active imagination, to be pursued by depth psychology; and archetypal imagination, analyzable through the study of archetypal topography. Such a conception of imaginative thinking, as Casey sees it, would

land us in a world which is neither perceptual nor conceptual in nature—nor, for that matter, merely imaginary in the derogatory sense of unreal. This intermediate world is an imaginal world, teeming with transmuted substances, subtlized sensuous forms, and legions of figures each with a proper place within the endlessly variegated topography of the *mundus imaginalis*. It is a world no longer human—or, at least not exclusively or primarily human. It is *another* world, with *another* kind of reality, to which we have access through active imagination but which we explore by the exercise of an archetypal imagination. It is with reference to this world that Rimbaud said that "one must be, must make himself, a seer," for we come to know it only through the enactment of an authentically visionary imagination. (1974B, p. 27)

Whatever the merits of this suggestion, it certainly corroborates the contention that Jungian thought not only allowed for imaginative thinking, but saw it as the critical component in human growth and individuation.

Countless other examples of such metaphorizations can be found in the study of various personality theories. One recent publication takes up the subject of personality theorizing and terms it a form of human mapping (Von Eckartsberg, 1981). Still another current movement, that of hypnotherapy as developed by the late Milton H. Erikson, gives the issue a powerful praxis orientation, centering around the effective, skillful, and respectful use of imaginative thinking on the part of the therapist and the client. As seen by members of the Eriksonian school, the royal road to success is to be found, not in dreams à la Freud, but in imaginative thinking in all its forms.

In short, psychology indeed has always taken imaginative thought seriously, even though it often failed to advert to the fact theoretically.

We have concentrated on the growing appreciation that is slowly but surely being bestowed on the imagination and imaginative thinking; in the study of aesthetics, in science, in philosophy, and in psychology. With the exception of aesthetics one would not have expected to witness this transformation of evaluation, but witness it we do. These areas, however, do not exhaust the fields in which the awakening to the significance of the imagination is taking place. The past two decades have seen the phenomenon occurring in the fields of theology and law, to cite two more areas where the effects of the awakening are so pronounced. In theology the importance of imaginative thought for the individual believer who is living out his faith as well as for the professional theologian who is seeking to conceptualize his grasp of religious mystery is growing steadily. (Tracy, 1981). In law it is being suggested that the lawyer's life in many respects is an activity of the imagination, that the task consists in the making of metaphors, and that the judge is an artist whose opinion issues forth as a poem. As one author puts it,

> What can be learned from the study of poetry and its criticism that will help us understand, engage in, and criticize the arts of lawyer and judge? To put these two forms of expression side by side will not lead to a system of exposition and analysis, of classification and categorization, but it may give us a way of asking new questions and expressing new hopes. To suggest that the judge is like the poet—or the historian or the mathematician—seems more promising than to say he is like a man using a pair of scales or a tape measure of an inclined plane. (White, 1973, p. 16)

It remains now to reflect more explicitly on the meaning of that imaginative thinking about which we have been writing thus far.


C.  TOWARDS A BETTER UNDERSTANDING OF IMAGINATIVE
    THINKING

No attempt will be made here to present an elaborated theory on imagination or imaginative thinking. That is a topic that calls for a book of its own. Suffice to say that a decade ago Ricoeur made the statement in an address at the Veterans Administration Hospital in Lexington, Kentucky, that a theory of the imagination is badly needed (1973), and six years later he stated that the theory of imagination is in its infancy (1979). At present both the phenomenological and cognitive psychologists are moving toward a clarification of the subject, but the engagement has only just begun. It is evident that the issue of imagination, imagery, imagining, fantasy, reverie is considerably befuddled. The words are used indiscriminately, and overlap is inevitable. Some authors speak of images as that sensory reverberation that accompanies every experience, presumably even a highly abstract experience. Some would term it the picture of a loved one before the eyes. Some would term it the experience of the impossible, such as a red, white, and blue crow. Some would restrict imaging to these experiences and reserve the word imagination for practical projects that await future implementation. And so on. A real problem arises when we attempt to delineate precisely what it does mean, and authorities themselves cannot agree. The disagreement preceded Plato; it engaged the medievalists; it haunts contemporary thinkers.

In the light of this history one might do well to speak first to what is not meant here by the imaginative thinking that is so relevant to the question of personality integration. To begin with, it does not mean that which one does when conjuring up one's mother, now long dead, standing in the kitchen and happily embracing an infant grandchild. Popular parlance refers to this at times as imagining, but it is better described as remembering: calling back a sensory impression. Nor would imaginative thinking be that experience which we would have if we should experience ourselves getting off the chair, walking outdoors, soaring far and wide over the city, and gliding gently back down to earth. That would indeed be an imaginative experience—quite different from the experience of one's mother—but it would not constitute the imaginative *thinking* about which we are occupied. One might term it a revery or fantasy, but the latter usually takes on the form of a narrative. At any rate this is not the imaginative thinking that is our concern, however worthwhile it might be, as Bachelard has well said:

> Thus a whole universe comes to contribute to our happiness when reverie comes to accentuate our repose. You must tell the man who wants to dream well to begin by being happy. Then reverie plays out its veritable destiny; it becomes poetic reverie and by it, in it, everything becomes beautiful. (1969, p. 12)

To come to the point. Imaginative thinking is just that: it is thinking, intellectual effort designed to move us toward an end. Like all thinking, imaginative thinking is a task, a work demand made upon the individual who indulges in it. But it has a character all its own, and to appreciate that character, we shall focus attention on the question of thinking as an enterprise and then on imaginative thinking as a form that a person can elect to undertake.

In the process of thinking one is confronted with a problem, the terms of which must be known and the solution of which is sought. With the complexity of the issue, one must begin to sift through the mass of detail confronting him and attempt to make as clear as possible just what the critical matter is with which he must cope. This is not an easy task, since obscurity abounds on all sides, and the project can take on a semblance of a fog or storm, in whose spaces appear elements of darkness, twilight, and occasional shafts of light. These can seem almost as beams or streaks of lightning that appear sharply, throwing momentary light but increasing thereby the darkness at their inevitable disappearance. One moves into it all, circumspectly locating himself and tentatively trying to gain some glimpse of the whole. Only gradually are certain features highlighted and ideas formed that tend to bring some intelligibility into the scene. One gains a foothold by formulating ideas, most of which are tentative and doubtful, but some of which truly allow one to grasp the situation with a modicum of hope. It is the problem that gradually becomes lightened up—not the answer—but even that enlightenment proves valuable, for the destination toward which one is struggling becomes less obscure, if not less hopeless.

Only when the person has grasped some degree of intelligibility in the chaos does he begin to intuit here and there (and by intuition we mean an immediate grasp that leaps up before us) some solid ideas of the dimensions with which he is faced. The problem becomes clearer and some of the irrelevancies become apparent as just that: irrelevancies that can be set aside. Amid all this, critical notions about the problem, now increasingly evident, are slowly formulated. Our ideas grow, if not in depth at least in breadth, and the tools with which we will operate are gradually placed in hand. At this point the reasoning process has reached its first plateau, so to speak. At this point, when all is said and done, one has simply assembled his material, his ideas, such as they are; has provided a context of sorts in which to view matters; and has clarified to some extent the problem, still unsolved but far less amorphous. Why reasoning should be called discursive and not intuitive is now apparent enough: one is ever running to and fro, moving from idea to idea in an attempt to gain his foothold, almost like a person in a burning room trying to detect a creditable opening to safety. Intuition—the only recourse one had at the outset—is still at a premium, and vagueness must constantly be engaged.

At this stage one is only beginning; and before one leaves the plateau to begin his further ascent, he must dwell with his thoughts, his concepts, ideas until they begin to yield their secrets. This stage is critical in logical thinking, for the task to be undertaken at the second ascent will presuppose some solid grasp of the critical issues involved and the tools (concepts) with which one labors. In other words the thinker must dwell with his material, study it at length, and begin to understand just what the meaning and potential of the concepts relevant for the task might be. Even then, he labors in considerable obscurity, for the fuller meaning of concepts and concept potential comes to light only in the deliberate effort to compare and contrast them with others at hand.

This presupposes that one has a strong or stronger grasp of the other concepts germane to the present endeavor. Thus mush testing must go on at this stage, the first plateau, of thinking. Ideas are to be explored and weighed vis-à-vis other ideas—all in the anticipation of forthcoming judgments which one is not as yet prepared to make. Unfortunately, many thinkers, in their anxiety to move, settle for less at this stage and hasten for hurried formulation. Such a decision is, of course, illogical in the sense that it is not the decision that logic would dictate. Logic does not gamble; it is not impulsive; it is cautious and careful. If it errs, it does so on the side of caution. Logic demands that one knows what he is dealing with and knows it well. Furthermore, as one comes to grasp better the contents of his ideas and judgments for the problem at hand, he looks to the derivations or implications of what he is saying. For having moved now into the making of judgments, one should learn just what he or she has really said or established. Logic asks of us whether, in having stated and shown that all carbon is a chemical, we have also established by that finding that all chemicals are carbon. In other words, can we convert the statement and have the proof of the second stand in virtue of the proof of the first? If not, if in the second statement we find ourselves saying more than we have stated in the first judgment, how does one convert a judgment properly? We must know what we have established and not established. To say more in the second statement than in the established first statement is to exceed one's proof, one's evidence, and thus endanger the entire thinking process. Too much blood, so to speak, has been spilled in our attempt to establish certitude to warrant gratuitous leaps. Logic demands that we face up to the fact that, if we have established that all carbon is chemical, we have merely established that some chemicals are carbon. Thus it is that, in geometry, the reciprocal of a proposition (which appears to be saying the same thing but is actually saying much more than the original) must be given its own proof. This, of course, is the danger in any conversion of propositions. One may think that in proving that skyscrapers are tall structures, one has also proved that all tall structures are skyscrapers. The truth is that he has not done so.

Thus the thinking process has begun to tighten up. We are well into our second ascent and engaged in a higher order of thought than at the outset: the trial by error, the purely intuitive, the experiential givenness of findings. Again and again one is forced to examine what it is that he has come to see, what degree of certitude marks the knowledge at this state, and what degree of vulnerability attends his statements. The ascent is steeper, the danger of slips greater. Obviously truth is our goal, but consistency is the sine qua non of our path. We cannot proceed to further understandings if our implications are unwarranted or our premises doubtful. If we exceed them, we shall find ourselves building on quicksand in no time.

Returning to the pursuit of the purely logical thinking that is undergoing its second ascent, it is apparent that logical thinking is intent on its certitude, its validity, its consistency—all of which are tied with the truth of its respective judgments, those predications made by the logical thinker once he feels that he has grasped with sufficient clarity the concepts that are vital for sound judgments. At this stage the thinker finds himself well in command of sufficient knowledge, so that he can make the necessary distinctions and clarifications that will enable him not only to rest at a second plateau, but also to venture forth to further heights by inferences that follow from the careful study of concepts and the profound grasp of judgments, which contain within themselves the wherewithall to mount profound deductions for the thinker who has mastered the intricacies of third-term mediation. It is at this point that logical thinking truly blossoms and enables the thinker to see in seemingly disparate truths the *tertium quid* that allows him in effect to build truth upon truth. Whether it be within a mathematical system that allows for astounding deductions, or a philosophical system that opens up glorious horizons of understanding, it is accomplished through careful, precise, and respectful syllogisms that show, within the respective judgments that he has made, a common element, carefully circumscribed, that propels him to a deeper or a higher level of understanding nature and reality. If cautiously monitored, the power of the syllogism will enable the thinker to move to the heart of his problem and bring forth the full dimensions of the issue that has haunted him. He has at his command the rational instruments of logical thought to see, within the limits of the specific and technical language that he has employed (be it that of philosophy, chemistry, physics, mathematics, and so on), no more or no less than the truth for which he has labored. Assuming his fundamental assumptions, basic ideas, judgments, and reasonings to have been carefully established, his conclusions will stand forth in all their verity—at the same time commanding the assent of other thinkers who have followed the path of thinking with him.

Such in brief is the triumph of rational thinking—the ratiocination that distinguishes the human being and is the basis of all his wondrous scientific, philosophical, aesthetic, and engineering accomplishments. There is no denying its fruit. Human history over the ages attests to it.

There is, however, another kind of thinking that characterizes human living: the imaginative thinking, the base of that meditative thinking of which Heidegger wrote, a thinking that certainly graces the intellect of the geniuses of humanity but which is also to be found in the most common of people (1955, 1966).

Imaginative thinking, as has been stated above, is just that: it is a cognitive task that proceeds in a way all its own, thinking that is distinguished by unique features that bring with them a potency that is not to be found in purely logical thought. In proceeding in such a manner, the thinker is every bit as intent on arriving at a solution of a problem as is the logical thinker. However, his method allows him to love with a suspended judgment as to the facts of the case. Concepts are brought into the picture and their intrinsic veridicality at the moment is not allowed to create any obstacle in the procedure. Such a thinker is no less interested in the outcome than is anyone else. He is interested, however, in allowing to come to the surface as quickly as is feasible any and every consideration that holds promise. To put it another way, the imaginative thinker is free from the outset to move in many directions, even though his movements may temporarily endanger or challenge the sacred cows of his industry or field. It is not a form of iconoclasm that he espouses; it is a new metaphorization of thought. The traditional logical thinker is intent on cautious plodding, testing, building with critical acumen brought to bear on the process of sifting, of dividing, of distinguishing, of negating. Such a procedure guarantees the logical thinker that he or she is on solid ground, and the need to retrace steps will be minimized. The imaginative thinker, however, will proceed in a more lateral fashion, going a long way around with leaps, small or gigantic, that enable him to cover much ground quickly and cursorily, until he is brought to a position or stance that holds up to him the promise for which he was seeking. To her or him everything in sight holds up some possibility, and the choice, if choice one makes, is between possibilities. The logical thinker carefully establishes his or her ground, finding building blocks and testing the progress at each stage. The imaginative thinker sees building blocks everywhere, so to speak, and selects for the time being any and all, knowing full well that he or she ultimately will settle for certain ones at the appropriate moment. Unlike the logical thinker, the imaginative one will suspend decision after decision. All such may indeed enter the picture in due time but only in due time and then only to the extent that they are truly required.

To cite a simple example, facing bankruptcy, the imaginative thinker will not panic in despair. He will not settle for the tried and true methods that have now seemingly failed him. A situation that others might term a dung heap, he will describe as a compost pile teeming with vitality and energy. True, he must be prepared for the collapse of the long-treasured dream to which he has given his life—and he is. Failure is not beyond him, any more than it is beyond the next person. But failure is not to be identified with the end, and failure in a given venture does not mean that his resources are now exhausted. It means that they must be addressed in a different manner, with different concepts, different rules, and different expectations. To him it is not inconceivable that the collapse of the enterprise may well be the birth of a new one—at least he is willing to entertain that notion. And should the collapse prove to be the eventual outcome, he is willing to look for the possibilities that lie in the impossible situation that is now his. To call such thinking polyannish is to miss its power. A Polyanna just will not admit the possibility of failure or wrongdoing; such cannot be imagined. The person of whom we are speaking admits it all the time and lives with it. And he moves toward a restructuring that brings with it a vitality all its own.

To contrast briefly the two styles of thinking, let us say that imaginative thinking is strongly intent on the realization of its goal. In this respect it is no different from logical thinking, but it is convinced that the roads to the goal are many. The fact that others have not found them is no proof that they do not exist. Second, it employs a bracketing procedure, termed epoche, allowing for a suspension of judgment in several respects. Above all, one's goals must remain wide open for considerable time. And one's means— concepts and judgments—must remain tentative or hypothetical as long as possible. Options are kept open to allow for the onset of new possibilities on every side. As is apparent, this kind of thinking is quite far from the logical thinker's method. Third, it not only does not ask for clear and distinct ideas at the outset, it actually welcomes conceptual ambiguity as the seed of possibility. Even though it may move rapidly and laterally, imaginative thinking would maximize the complexity of situations in the hope of bringing them to life. Exploiting the nebulous and the vacuous is itself a liberating and strengthening experience. Fourth, it allows for the non sequiturs that creep into the human picture of thought, considering them a small price to pay for the compensation they can render to one who is patient and tolerant. For such a person there rests in the experience of illogicalities the makings of significant metaphorizations that can alter the course of our lives. Fifth, imaginative thinking is willing to entertain even the unimaginable as long as one can, not ruling out its generative potential, such as occurred when negative numbers or imaginary numbers were introduced into mathematics, and such as occurred when Euclidean axioms were reversed, despite their productivity, and non-Euclidean postulates were entertained for what they were worth—and their worth, as history later showed, was invaluable.

Obviously, if one were intent solely on the logic of the issue, such an entertainment would be suicidal. That is not the case, however, if one is focusing on the creativity of it all. Hence, the imaginative thinker notes resemblances and uses them for stretching the mind, but the imaginative thinker would go far beyond the real or imagined resemblance. He would even favor, if only for a while, the contradictory thought, if only to see the quality and kind of yield it might have. Hence, the imaginative thinker will deal in analogies, in contrasts, in antinomies, but his indulgence in such dialectic often proves in time to be immeasurably fruitful. He is forever seeking ways to render the familiar unfamiliar, which is a way of making it new and exciting. He is also seeking ways to make the unfamiliar familiar, for this brings into his ken worlds that would otherwise elude his grasp. This is not to be construed as magic brought about by the waving of a wand. It is a feat accomplished by the sound application of hard word, serious preparation, and patient scrutiny. In brief, imaginative accomplishment is the hope of imaginative thinking, but it proves to be a realizaton only if and when it is seriously and humbly pursued. It is in no way an alternative to logical thinking; for without the structure that logical thinking provides, imaginative thinking could degenerate into intellectual chaos. Provocation, discontinuity, delayed and suspended judgment are ingenious and creative procedures, methods, employed in the process of imaginative thought, but they gain their respect and prove efficacious only within the confines of the structure that is provided by sound, rational, logical thinking. Neither is successful without the other; both are creative and fruitful when together.

DeBuono has written of lateral and vertical thought, an analysis that is akin in some respects to our discussion on imaginative and logical thinking:

> Lateral and vertical thinking are both required. Lateral thinking is concerned principally but not solely with the earlier stages of thinking, the stages of patterning, perceptual choice, and approach to the problem. Vertical thinking is concerned with the middle and later stages, processing and working out. Lateral thinking is concerned with choosing concepts, vertical thinking with using them. Lateral thinking required vertical thinking to select and develop the ideas that are generated. Vertical thinking required lateral thinking to establish an effective starting point. Skill in lateral thinking magnifies the effectiveness of skill in vertical thinking. And the other way around. Although both types of thinking are distinct, they are not substitutes; they are complementary. (1971, p. 22)

It is in the richness of imaginative thought that we find bases and the resources for pursuing the meditative thinking of which Heidegger speaks in the *Discourse on Thinking: Gelassenheit.* In this meditative experience we pause to contemplate the meaning inherent in things, to dwell on the interrelatedness of Being in all its forms, to behold the unity that the manifold of Being presents to the caring seer. At such moments calculations are set aside, logical thought bares its wealth, imaginative thought allows for the possibilities of Being, and the beholder stands in wonder before the "is" of everything. And it is this capacity to imaginize that transports a person to the meditative realm and experience.

The relevancy of these considerations should become apparent in subsequent chapters. Suffice to say for the present that a person's integration is a lifetime pursuit that continually calls for the best in the person. However one brings it about, and however productive that integration, it makes demands. One thing is certain: it will be neither a purely logical achievement nor a purely imaginative one. It must be a blending of both. Phenomenological research has established the importance of consciousness in human living. That consciousness, however, is not to be identified with human rational dimensions any more than the imaginative is to be identified with the unconscious. Human consciousness embraces both the logical and the imaginative. It is a proper human accomplishment to live both logically and imaginatively, and it may well be that the greatest human achievement of all lies in the experiential realization of genuine poetic living, thus optimizing the strong presence of both kinds of thinking in human existence.

# CHAPTER II

# Perception: Its Primacy, Limits and Possibilities

## A. SOME BASIC PHENOMENOLOGICAL CONSIDERATIONS

IT has been pointed out by Maurice Merleau-Ponty, the French phenomenologist, that there are several ways for the body to be a body and there are various ways for consciousness to be consciousness. This chapter will focus on consciousness as it is disclosed in the act of perception, since human perception is so basic for the human project of existence. A better understanding of the phenomenon of perception will enable us to grasp the marvels of human integration better, since the task of integration is designed to bring some unity in the complexities of life, the knowledge of which originates in the perception act itself.

### 1. Perception and the World

The study of perception is critical for our project. It begins in mystery, however, and ends in more of the same. For the astounding thing about it is, as Merleau-Ponty has pointed out, that we must back up from perception to try to understand it, much as a movie projector runs backwards, pulling the diver back out of the water so that we might then restudy the forward dive into it. We never find ourselves unperceiving and then set ourselves to the task of perceiving. We find ourselves always already perceiving and have to make the effort to distance ourselves from that world of which we are already perceptually a part. That being the case, we would expect that the integration of our personality would be tied to the world of our perception. How we put ourselves and our perceptual world together would appear to go hand in hand.

Indeed it remains a question whether or not we can even separate the two issues; they may end up to be two sides of the one coin of our existence. Perception, like consciousness, makes one conscious of everything but itself. One is not conscious of consciousness; one is not perceptive of perception; one is conscious, perceptive of the world in some respect. Thus, objects are enabled to appear and display themselves in the lived life of the human being.

This is another way of remarking that perception and reality have a unique affinity of mutual implication. Were there no human perception, and thus no human awareness, of what reality could one speak? To put it another way: of what is one conscious when there is no consciousness to be conscious of it? And conversely, of what is one conscious when there is no reality of which one can be conscious? When he deals with this question, Heidegger points out that the human being is a being (a *Sein*) who is by his very nature already in the world: a *Da-Sein*, a There-Being. By this he means to emphasize that the person is not one who finds himself and then decides to step into a world. On the contrary, a person is one who always finds himself already there. Thus to speak of the human is to speak of a being who is already there in the world, a being already engaged; and, by the same token, to speak of the world is to speak of an entity already engaged, an entity already at one with the person. Heidegger has spoken regretfully of the futile effort that has been expended in an attempt to bring the world and the human together, whereas the real dilemma, as he sees it, is the very opposite. It is the task of separating them, determining, if one can, where one truly ends and the other truly begins. This is not an easy assignment.

Merleau-Ponty, speaking of the attempt to institute a break or suspension, a thinning out, or a phenomenological reduction between the subject and the process of transcendence toward the world that we are, observes,

> In order to see the world and grasp it as paradoxical, we must break with our familiar acceptance of it and, also, from the fact that from this break we can learn nothing but the unmotivated upsurge of the world. The most important lesson which the reduction teaches us is the impossibility of a complete reduction. (1946/1962, p. XIV)

Thus we can attempt to suspend the transcendence we are, but we do so only with great effort and then only with partial success, much as we would have were we to try to walk backwards down an ascending escalator. For purposes of study we may simulate a break, but only for purposes of study, not for those of living. It is an artificial and highly imaginative art. Thus perception brings us upon the birth of beings, in virtue of which distinct entities are seen in and on the earth. To be sure, that birth is marked by finitude and ambiguity, and calls for considerable sophisticated care to ensure the ongoing development of those beings brought to light. But it has all taken place in the light of the perceptional consciousness that is the human person.

It should be noted, by implication, that the object of perception has its own reality and Being, but nothing can be said for or against it without human intervention. There is no such thing as meaning or significance unless it is meaning for someone. That someone is the person perceiving. Furthermore, the subject is not to be conceived as a passive, helpless recipient who is completely overwhelmed by an in-dependent object. Far from it. The person brings with him an activity all his own, a spontaneity, a creativity, a meaning-filled, meaning-bestowing illumination, a Midas touch, so to speak, that is awaited by some object, and in virtue of which that object springs to life, called as it were from darkness into light. Gurwitsch has spoken to this in a slightly different way:

> From the phenomenological point of view, consciousness cannot be regarded as one mundane realm among others. To whatever mundane realm an object belongs, it necessarily involves, implicates and in this sense, presupposes consciousness, namely, those acts through which the object in question appears and displays itself as that which it presents in our life. Consciousness thus reveals itself as the universal domain or medium of presentation of all objects, a domain to which every mundane realm necessarily refers. Herein consists the privilege and the priority of consciousness to every mundane realm. (1964, p. 159)

Thus, for Being to come to light, for the event of Being to transpire in whatever form, the human must be present to perceive it. If such is not the case, then nothing whatsoever can be said—so critical is the presence of *Dasein*, humankind. In a truly remarkable way, then, the person and the world are part and parcel of each other. But this is only the beginning. To further our understanding of this event of Being, this primacy of perception, we must say more.

## 2. Perception as Meaning-Bestowing

It was observed above that the person, even in perception, is meaning-bestowing. To grasp this is essential, for it is at the heart of the integrating process in the person. By virtue of our being endowed with intentional consciousness, and thus open to reality such as it is, the person is both significative and signifying. We elevate everything toward which we are intending and to which we are attending to a meaning. Human consciousness has the capacity to bring together in a whole or totality all that to which it is present, even though that totality may be nebulous, chaotic, and not fully delineated. Human consciousness can bestow on it an orientation to all other beings, if it deals with an individual object, or can treat each being as a sign referring to other realities. Through this unique power to contextualize and relate being to being, human consciousness is said to constitute meanings for things. This could occur through an elaborate thought process, or it could occur in the relatively simple intuitive act of perception, making the object in question a moment somewhere in the field of consciousness. Thus no truly human act—no act characterized by human intentionality—is empty or meaningless.

Having said that our perceptions are meaning-bestowing, we are not suggesting thereby that those efforts at meaning-bestowing are purely arbitrary. Perception is a light-giving act of the person, it is true, but in all its virtuosity it operates under constraints. It cannot give meaning arbitrarily, independently, completely, or even adequately. The illumination of the moment that perception gives is illumination of an object that possesses a structure, richness, a wealth far surpassing the lighting-up of the perceptual moment or moments. Husserl was aware of this fact and stated so quite clearly:

> Intentional analysis is guided by the fundamental cognition that, as a consciousness, every cogito is indeed (in the broadest sense) a meaning of its meant, but that, at any moment, this something meant is more—something meant with something more—than what is meant at that moment "explicitly," In our example, each phase of perception was a mere side of "the" object, of what was perceptually meant. This *intending-beyond-itself*, which is implicit in any consciousness, must be considered as an essential moment of it. That, on the other hand, this intending is, and must be, a "meaning more" of the Same becomes shown only by the evidence of a possible

making distinct and, ultimately, of an intuitive uncovering, in the form of actual and possible continued perceiving or of possible recollecting, as something to be done on my initiative. (1970, p. 46)

Thus perception partakes of a dual character: it gives meaning but it does so in the light of what it perceives. With the perception there is a percipiend, as with the multiplier there is a multiplicand. And what is perceived is but a portion of what is perceivable. Nonetheless, perception has put the person in touch with the world—indeed, since perception is a certain openness to the world, one could rightfully say that when the person perceives, it is not the ego, or even the ego engaged as a *cogito* in cogitating, but rather the cogitatum that reveals the first specification of the perceptive act. In other words, the first closure of the openness that is the human person is the cogitatum of the world. It is this that determines that and how one experience differs from another. In brief, consciousness is an openness that is specified or closed by that to which it is open in the perceptive act.

### 3. Perception as Historical

There is still more to perception. As we have seen, it is constrained by the cogitatum or, if you will, by the world perceived. It is also constrained by history. Perception, in other words, is historical, having a decided, pronounced relationship with one's history. This means, in effect, that one's perception is signifying in the way and to the extent that one is historically prepared for the perception. Traditional psychology would like to refer to this as one's conditioning, but this phraseology is misleading. It is not what has happened to a person—his so-called conditioning—that is most critical in one's history: it is what has been picked up and used by the person that is critical. In other words classical conditioning would explain our history in terms of the associations that formed or the reinforcement that we received, making us the victims of the entire experience. We are suggesting here that it is the associations that *we* formed and the meaning *we* gave to the so-called reinforcing experiences that matter in our history. It is not a question of tweedle dee or tweedle dum with both views being equally important. It is a question of realizing that the subject takes from his so-called conditioning experience the significant events and meanings that *he* or *she* decides upon and that the sum of all this constitutes one's history that is brought to bear on a given perceptual experience. To repeat what we said above, our perception is signifying in the way and to the extent that we are historically prepared for the perception and that means in the way and to the extent that we have put it together for ourselves.

## 4. Perception as Perspectival

There is one other significant limitation with which perception is beset. It is perspectival—and therein lies a whole story. To use a phrase of Paul Ricoeur, it has to do with the narrowness that characterizes the human's perceptual openness. We have seen before that the openness of perception is brought to relative closure by the cogitatum, that specification of the world that was related to the kind of perception that was ensuing: seeing by the object seen, hearing by the object heard. However, we are here drawing attention to something else: the narrowness of the openness itself. It is much as though we were to narrow the focus of our flashlight as it rests its light on its target. The target would be analogous to the cogitatum, while the greater or less narrowness of the light beam would be analogous to the more or less narrowness of perspective.

In speaking of this, phenomenologists employ the words "noetic" and "noematic." These terms, technical in nature and coined by Husserl himself, speak to the finitude of the human being. A person, after all, does not create beings out of nothing, as though one were God. But our presence is necessary so that beings themselves may have a presence and meaning, that they may be contextualized, de-contextualized, and recontextualized, acquiring thereby more and more meaning. This is the bequeathal of human consciousness, thanks to which we are able to categorize the various presences named, reflect upon them, analyze them, synthesize them, and ultimately study them in many different disciplines and sciences. On the other hand, there would seem to be no limit to the variety of ways in which entities can be studied. Ultimately this means that there is seemingly no limit to the multitude of ways in which entities can be perceived. This is true whether one elects to study an object in one discipline or in two disciplines, as carbon in chemistry and biology. It is true too even if one elects to study the naive experience of everyday life, such as a child opening a Christmas gift or a person receiving a disheartening phone call. Whatever the study, the object in question far exceeds in its wholeness the perceptive capability of a single perception. Thus we are forced to return to the object time and time again for restudy or further perceptions.

Since, then, knowledge never really comes to an end on anything, it would appear that we are moving toward some variation of sheer relativism, if not skepticism. That, however, is not the case. What our analysis does breed is caution, especially about precipitous judgments, early closure on a study, easy answers. At the same time it indicates the need for knowing and weighing the assumptions upon which a study is made, a judgment is based; the methods used in arriving at conclusions voiced; the history of an era that generated certain now-taken-for-granted views that seemingly are unchallengeable. It breeds a recognition of the need for intersubjective cooperation and, hopefully, agreement. It extols an appreciation of significant contributions to thought (new noemata hitherto unseen, unexpressed), a respect for disclosures already captured in various traditions, an openness for new models or paradigms. In short, the perspectivalness of human perception and knowledge points to man's limits. It points to the parameters of his knowledge, the shortcomings of his understandings, the impossibility of exhausting the knowability of nature, much less human nature. Thus, paradoxical as it is, the finitude of human knowledge generates a seeming infinity of possibilities. Learning never really ends. In no way should this realization lead one to deny established truths. On the contrary, it points up the fact that one's appreciation of truth can ever grow deeper and more profound. In a remarkable way the finitude or perspectivalness of human knowledge is at once the human's agony and ecstasy.

## B.   THE STRUCTURE OF CONSCIOUSNESS

### 1. Perception's Object a Unity

In speaking thus far of perception, attention has been concentrated on an object that comes into view: a table, house, vase, field, person. And the concentration focused on the fact that the perception of the object was meaningful, historical, and perspectival. Such considerations, however important, were actually quite limited, and did not begin to take account of other dimensions that feature in the perceptive act. Nothing was said, for example, about the other sides of the object, about the back, or the left or the right. It was recognized that the perception was limited, that it allowed for a perspective from which to grasp the totality, but it did not speak of other perspectives that are not immediately apparent in the special perspective that has been grasped in the act to this point. What, if anything, can be said of this matter?

First of all, let it be reiterated that in perception one grasps the object, the totality, although admittedly from a given perspective. Yet it must be said that one feels the football, listens to the violin, sees the man in the hall, touches the statue, and so on. One is perceiving, in short, an object through the perceptive act, which may include one or several sensory modalities. Yet it does remain a fact that one does not see the back of the person, does not feel the entire football, does not even see the wood of the violin, and so on. Such dimensions do not fall under the direct purview of a given perception, and yet they belong to the totality of the object that has been perceived. The truth of the matter is that one does not perceive them as he perceived the original modality, and yet he does. It is not that one has an abstract idea of a man that he then applies to this individual perspectivally perceived. In Merleau-Ponty's words, a practical synthesis is achieved in perception wherein the object, the totality, is grasped in the whole setting, in the "*L'entourage*" of the perception. No football player, for example, fondles every inch of the ball as he throws it or catches it. The player running down the field to make his catch sees a slight portion of the ball, and yet he never experiences himself dealing only with a profile. He reaches for, catches, and pulls toward himself that thrown ball. Having made his touchdown, he holds the ball aloft amid the cheers of the spectators, all of whom have seen the ball as well as he but none of whom has seen it totally. Everyone has experienced the object in its totality, though only from one of several perspectives.

What is one to make of this? Does it give lie to what has been said thus far? By no means. The point is, that in the direct perception by the given individual there are contained in the entire perceptual complex many other tangential perceptions that go to comprise the totality of the experience. This could conceivably occur in the sports instances cited above or in an impersonal setting, where no one else was present except the perceiver alone.

In the first instance, the sports scene, the perceiver experiences the ball watched by many other perceivers as well. That is to say, that the other percipients provide the seer with their perspectives as well, and one experiences in the *l'entourage* of the perception much more than his own limited vision. As Husserl terms it, a passive synthesis has taken place, the benefit of which has been reaped by the perceiver in question. In the second instance, where one is found in an impersonal setting and perceives an object, that object in its *l'entourage* is surrounded by many other objects whose presence redounds to the fullness of individual perceptual experience. These objects, in short, tend to swell the perceptual experience and allow one to perceive the object in a many-sided manner even though he himself has only a very limited perspective. It is as though one were to behold the object that is backed by several mirrors, all of which converge to disclose to the viewer other perspectives of the object in question than that upon which he directly gazes. In Husserl's words, one finds that the unseen side is given to him as "visible from another standpoint." Merleau-Ponty refers to this as a practical synthesis, while Husserl terms it a horizontal synthesis, or synthesis of transition. The principal point here, of course, lies in the fact that one does perceive in his perception the object from a perspective but at the same time he experiences in a remarkable way the many other perspectives that the *l'entourage* provides for his understanding. In other words, strange as it may sound, in perception one perceives much more than he perceives. And this is done, not by way of grand deduction or a purely intellectual act. It is part and parcel of the perception that one has experience, albeit from his own limited point of view. It is almost as though others, without him even realizing the fact, have entered into his perception. What he sees he sees—thanks to himself and them.

## 2. Consciousness an Organizational Field

The totality or wholeness that surrounds perception has been carefully described in the phenomenological study of consciousness by Aaron Gurwitsch. His book, the *Field of Consciousness*, points up the autochthonous nature of perception, meaning that the act of perception is not a scattered, disarrayed act. On the contrary, it is highly organized with a pattern all its own, even though the perception itself may admit to unclear, vague, or highly ambiguous content. His thinking on the subject is worthy of further study, for it will make possible a better understanding of the integrational achievement(s) of the personality about which our present study is primarily centered, and can serve as a base for the material to be discussed in subsequent chapters.

Says Gurwitsch:

> we venture to assert the existence of a universal, formal pattern of organization, realized in every field of consciousness regardless of content. Every field of consciousness comprises three domains or, so to speak, extends in three dimensions. First, the *theme*: that with which the subject is dealing, which at the given moment occupies the "focus" of his attention, engrosses his mind, and upon which his mental activity concentrates. Secondly, the *thematic field* which we define as the totality of facts, co-present with the theme, which are experienced as having material relevancy or pertinence to the theme. In the third place, the *margin* comprises facts which are merely co-present with the theme, but have no material relevancy to it. We shall endeavor to bring out the type of organization which prevails in each of these domains and determines both the relationship between the data that belong to that domain and its relationship to the two others, particularly to the theme. By dimensional differences between organizational forms we mean differences between types of organization which pertain to, and are characteristic of the three dimensions in which every field of consciousness extends. Each of the above types of organization has a *specific formal structure* of its own, independent of the organized content and the particular forms of organization, which depend upon the content to some extent. It is the formal structure of these types of organization which will primarily interest us here. *With the pattern theme-thematic field-margin, we intend to present a formal invariant of all fields of consciousness.* (1953/1964, p. 55)

Reflecting on this passage, one can glean much that is relevant to the present attempt to understand the full picture of perception. As Gurwitsch sees it, in a given perception one can distinguish the noema or presented profile of the object in question. This is what arrests the attention of the perceiver, and it can be captured, if need be, in description. Its apprehension, to be sure, leaves much to be desired unless the perception is augmented by subsequent perceptions of other dimensions of the object. Even so, there is a certain inner horizon that pertains to the noema or profile that enables one to grasp more of the object than a perception itself would seem to allow, even without subsequent perspectives being added. This inner horizon gives, so to speak, a certain shading to the noema that in turn gives it a glimmer or glow that augments the presumably stripped noema. This is not to say that other qualities or attributes are directly perceived in the act, but it is to say that some possibilities, or at least apparent possibilities, begin to present themselves for consideration, provided they are compatible with the object perceived. This means in effect that certain anticipatory references may conceivably be interwoven with the constituents of the perceptual meaning, thanks to the cultural or personal history of the individual involved, without as yet entailing any additional perspectives. The perception, in essence, is the perception of an historical person who brings much to the meaning-giving experience even at this incipient stage.

The thematic field mentioned by Gurwitsch in his triumvirate is something else. He likens it to William James's fringes, psychic overtones, which James looked upon as conscious counterparts of faint brain processes 1953/1964, 309ff. It will be recalled that Rubin made famous the significance of the figure and ground in his analysis of paintings. Merleau-Ponty, on the other hand, emphasized the figure and ground dimensions of perception: how every perception takes place within a field from which the figure emerges (1962, p. 13ff). Gurwitsch here applies the significance of this consideration as a further development of Merleau-Ponty's ideas. The thematic field is the background, as it were, from which the noema emerges for consideration, as well as the background from which the impact of the *l'entourage* cited above is felt. It is the penumbra of items to which a theme points and refers to in some manner, and which forms the context within which the theme presents itself. As seen by Gurwitsch, it would comprise those aspects of a perception that are not intrinsic to the noema of the perception, but which do bear some relevancy to the theme, such that they are a natural for the purposes of contextualization.

The third dimension of the organizational structure of consciousness for Gurwitsch is the margin, those conjunctions of the perception that are not intrinsic for the theme or noema, nor immediately relevant for the constitution of the perceptual context, but are nonetheless cotemporal with the perceptive act. To speak of such dimensions as irrelevant would be inaccurate, for their copresence would belie that. Their contribution to the perceptual act, however, is highly minimal, and hence marginal. They do constitute some portion of the experience, but not an essential ingredient. Nonetheless they are there, and certainly constitute an element of the experience.

### 3. Indeterminacies in the Field of Consciousness

There is one very significant aspect of Gurwitsch's telling analysis of the organizational structure of consciousness that must be highlighted. It lies in his insistence on the anticipatory possibilities that lie in all dimensions of the perceptual experience. In regard to the theme of the perception, he speaks of the inner horizon: those anticipatory references that are conceivably interwoven with the constituents of the perceptual meaning, the noema. Speaking, then, to the thematic field, Gurwitsch also gives attention to the indeterminacies that characterize its relevancies. And such indetermination, needless to say, is subject to further determination by the perceiving subject.

Finally, when addressing himself to the margin, the third aspect of his structure of consciousness, Gurwitsch again accedes to the indeterminacy—hence the determinableness of this dimension of perception. It will be remembered that the margin, as Gurwitsch described it, comprised those elements in perception that were copresent with the theme and thematic field but which were not intrinsically relevant to the theme itself. At best they might be termed as being of minimal extrinsic relevancy. Nonetheless they were embedded in the perceptual experience and cannot be considered totally meaningless; their presence in the experience, as we indicated before, would belie that claim. They too belong to the perceptual experience, however incidentally. Gurwitsch, in speaking of the marginal aspects of consciousness, allows for its possibilities as he did for those of the thematic field, but granted that they were of far less consequence. To phrase it in his words:

> In analyzing the thematic field and also the margin from the noetic point of view, we are confronted with potentialities of consciousness. We have already encountered potentialities of consciousness in our earlier discussion of the perceptual inner horizon or perceptual implications under the noetic aspect. Here as before are anticipations of further acts, references to future experiences through which

what at the present moment appears in a certain mode of presentation will be given in a different mode. There is the consciousness "I
can if I choose," that is, the awareness of the actualization of the
experienced potentialities as depending only on the free choice of the
experiencing subject. In both cases, the potentialities involved are of
elucidation, explicitation, and actual exploration. Indeterminate-
ness thus acquires the sense of determinability. Finally, in both
cases, there may be a solicitation to actualize the experienced
potentialities and a corresponding tendency towards yielding to
such solicitation. Descriptively speaking, the potentialities involved
in the experience of both the thematic field and the margin seem so
similar to the potentialities related to the experience of the perceptual inner horizon that we may refer to the characterization given
above. On account of the difference in organizational structure
between the perceptual theme and the thematic field, the potentialities involved in either case, however, have a different sense. For the
sake of convenience, we refer to potentialities concerning the noetic
aspect of the phenomenon of perceptual implication as *intrathematic
potentialities*, whereas we reserve the term *field-potentialities* for those
connected with the thematic field.(1953/1964, p. 370)

By way of summary it is apparent that Gurwitsch, in his descriptive analysis of the structure of conscious experience, sees within
the theme itself and its inner horizon, within the thematic field and
its relevancies, and within the marginal area of perception with its
copresent but incidental references a hugh area of indeterminacy—
hence determinableness—that awaits further elucidation. There is
no suggestion here that indeterminacy has overshadowed the
noema of perception, that the individual perceiver is unable to
distinguish that upon which he is focusing because of them. By no
means. Likewise we recognize the contextualization that surrounds
the perception and from which the figure, the noema, emerges for
the perceiver. Nor is there any suggestion that the marginal features of the experience are meaningless. Far from it, for they
provide the rich matting and frame that surround the perception
and make it somehow palatable or nonoverwhelming for the subject in question. The issue is something quite different. It is a
matter of the indeterminacy that accompanies in one way or other
all areas of the conscious experience, the unmentioned possibilities
with which the perceiver is faced as he gazes upon his object. And
in his brilliant description of this totality Gurwitsch finds himself
confronted with that indeterminacy at all levels—and admits that
the indeterminacy cries out for some semblance of articulation.

It would appear that in the analyses of both Gurwitsch and Husserl that the fringe elements (indeterminacies à la Gurwitsch and adumbrations à la Husserl) that permeate the entire organizational field in one way or other are significant dimensions of the perceptual experience; and that each noema or adumbration of the perception makes its contribution to the full experience and suggests a ground for further explicitation. It must, for the person has grasped it all as a flowing stream. Says Husserl:

> We must note the following distinction also: Even an experience is not, and never is, perceived in its completeness, it cannot be grasped adequately in its full unity. It is essentially something that flows, and starting from the present moment we can swim after it, our gaze reflectively turned towards it, whilst the stretches we leave in our wake are lost to our perception. Only in the form of retention or in the form of retrospective remembrance have we any consciousness of what has immediately flowed past us. And in the last resort the whole stream of my experience is a unity of experience, of which it is in principle impossible "swimming with it" to obtain a complete perceptual grasp.(1913/1931, p. 127)

A perception in other words, being an act of consciousness, is a transient synthesis in which a noema stands out. One grasps much of it but never in its full unity. Following Gurwitsch's description of the field of consciousness, we would seemingly grasp the noema with its theme and indeterminacies, the thematic field with its greater indeterminacies and the margin with its even greater indeterminacies. It is apparent, then, that our perceptive intuition is remarkable especially for the fact that it is so pregnant with form. It would appear capable of giving birth to so much, if it be but attended. And that further attention is indeed necessary. With all its illumination, along with its countless indeterminacies, we still must be wary of judgments and decisions made solely upon it. A perception, in brief, calls for further perspectives, not only because the indeterminacies it has are so vague and tentative, but especially because the illumination it provides yields highly circumscribed knowledge.

## C. Perceptual Field Indeterminacies and the Integrating Effort

At this stage of the current study it is too soon to undertake an investigation of the integrational process that is ongoing in the life

of every human. Such an investigation will require a deeper appreciation of the significance of language and its power in human life.
That topic will be dealt with in the following chapter. For the
present, however, we should rethink some of the considerations
that we have advanced thus far, particularly as they might relate to
the integration achievement.

It would appear that the effecting of a personal integration calls
for an imaginative synthesis of our life, but a synthesis that effects
some kind of a restructuration of the components of life. In other
words it is at once a synthesis of our life constituents and their
emotional components. In a very real sense we are all undergoing
such a process at every moment, but at some times more dramatically than at others. A man who has broken his leg will somehow
have to integrate that facticity into his life, but with all his discom-
fort it would appear inconsequential compared to the ordeal of
integrating the death of one's child. How successfully one inte-
grates both experiences is another issue, but both must be fit into
the picture of life in some manner or other. And both will be—even
if one should opt for self-destruction.

The previous articulations of perception and its autochthonous
nature give one reason to pause. It will become evident in due time
that metaphorizations, symbolizations, and mythicizations, all of
which figure so prominently in the integrational process, are closely
allied to one's perceptual life. And yet they seem to involve so much
more than a simple perception. The truth is that they do. Nonetheless, they are not mindless achievements, aperceptual accomplishments. On the contrary, they are related to the process of
perception in a very special way.

It is interesting that Husserl considered the perception to be a
profile that shadowed forth the reality, the object, *an abschattung*, an
adumbration. This intriguing description captures the enticing
features of a perception: the fact that the perception emerges from
the darkness into the light bringing with it enough of the darkness
that serves only to make the light more attractive, thus luring the
percipient on, making him want to learn more. It is, as it were, a
bait set up by the reality in virtue of which the person, curiosity
now aroused and interest generated, wants to move forward toward
the noema dangling, as it were, before the eyes. The perceiver is in
effect captured by the object. It is even a bit ironical. The perceiver
brings his or her luminescence into the scene and endows the object

with a radiance. Once having done so, the perceiver finds himself or herself now captivated and fascinated to learn all she can about the being to which she has given a place in existence. Such, if you will, is the love affair between the person and the world.

There is another consideration that we would deal with, even though inadequately, at this time: that having to do with the indeterminacies that beset the organizational field of perception, and hence, of the world perceived. This consideration may appear somewhat subtle, but no less significant for all that.

It was seen above that Gurwitsch's analysis of consciousness took cognizance of three dimensions in the field of consciousness: the theme, the thematic field, and the margin. Gurwitsch identified the noema as the center of the theme. In so doing he was allowing for the synthetic aspects that are entailed with the temporal dimensions of which we have spoken: the retentions and the protentions. Even in the theme, however, he found it necessary to recognize some element of indeterminacy, qualities that were certainly germane to the theme but nonetheless inadequately determined, features that were obvious enough in the perceptional noema but which left something unsaid or ununderstood. Thus their meaning, however clear the noema, was, if not problematic, at least vague. They belonged. When he addressed himself to the indeterminacies of the thematic field and the margin, Gurwitsch conceded their need for further specification far exceeded that of the indeterminacies of the theme. The indeterminacies of the margin in turn were scarcely discussed, but their presence was readily granted. It is to these aspects of the perceptual act that we would now speak.

Much of Gurwitsch's basic thought took inspiration from Husserl and from William James, a psychologist whose work in many ways predated that of the phenomenological school. James had addressed himself to the stream of consciousness and the efforts made by human consciousness to grasp adequately the world with which humans must cope. Gurwitsch has credited James for his treatment of the indeterminacies that characterize human thought. In the words of James they constitute the "fringes" of consciousness and are to be found most notably in that domain of consciousness that Gurwitsch himself would characterize as the thematic field, and these fringes are said to convey a sense of affinity, one of the most interesting features of the subjective stream. In Gurwitsch's words, "Fringes, 'psychic overtones,' 'suffusions' are defined by James as conscious counter-parts of faint brain-processes. Such counterparts are experienced in the form of some awareness of 'relations and objects but dimly perceived' " (1964, p. 309).

Gurwitsch made these references to James concerning the theme itself. Affinities were acknowledged to be present even at this most central area of the field of consciousness, right at the heart of the noema: affinities the experience of which gave rise to some subtle neurological responses. When, however, Gurwitsch speaks to the indeterminacies of the thematic *field*, he is far more explicit:

> We have repeatedly stated the relationship of the pointing reference between the theme and the thematic field need not necessarily be completely articulate and distinct. It may be dim and penumbral with little or no differentiation of structure. Relations between the theme and items of the thematic field may be more or less indiscriminate and somehow nebulous and obscure. If such is the case, the theme-thematic-field-structure presents a rather compact, concrete, and confused aspect. Not all items of the thematic field appear in clear distinction from one another. In some way, they fuse and coalesce with, blend and melt into, one another. Items emerging from the otherwise hardly articulated field may still be rather vague and indistinct, present no precise contours, and exhibit little, if any, inner differentiation. Admitting of degrees, such vagueness, indistinctness, indetermination may be almost complete, so complete that the pointing reference is to a kind of total diffuse field rather than to definite and determinate items. (p. 336)

At this point, lest the presence of fringes and indeterminacies be misunderstood as pure negativities, Gurwitsch hastens to point out their positive value and contribution to the conscious experience. Such transitive states, characterized by James as vague, penumbral, indefinite, and inarticulate, would scarcely lend themselves to introspective analysis. Yet James saw the recognition of the vague and indeterminate as truly contributing to our mental life. Vagueness, he argued, does not merely mean the absence of determination. The feeling of an absence is not to be construed as the absence of a feeling, for a word not remembered is experienced as a gap.

A final reference, one of Gurwitsch quoting and referring to James, is in order. It constitutes a recognition of the deep implications that may be contained in the respective indeterminacies. Says Gurwitsch:

> For our interpretation of fringes, we may refer to James own formu-
> lations. James speaks of "affinity," of relevancy, of appropriateness,
> of the "relation . . . to our topic or interest . . . particularly the
> relation of harmony and discord, of furtherance or hindrance of the
> topic." All these terms obviously apply to mental states with regard
> to their contents, that given in and through each mental state, rather
> than their sequence in phenomenal time. Because of the fringe, a
> thought or representation occurring to the subject's mind is wel-
> comed or rejected, according as to whether that thought is experi-
> enced as being of concern to the theme. (p. 353)

Gurwitsch felt, as did James, that the most important feature of
the fringes was their feeling of harmony or discord, of a right or
wrong direction in the thought. This reference of James and Gurwitsch to the feeling of harmony or discord as the most important
element of the fringes introduces into the picture, along with the
cognitive elements that we have studied to date, the affective
dimension of the perceptual experience. As James saw it, the
indeterminacies and fringes that attend perception not only give
rise to suggestions of vague, cognitive possibilities, but also have
emotional or affective nuances that enable one to experience conceivable harmonious feelings or rumblings of discord. No doubt it
was this aspect of the fringe concept that led Gurwitsch to sub-
scribe to James's notion that fringes were psychic overtones that
were experienced as conscious counterparts of faint brain processes. Thanks to the fringes, one has the feeling of affinity, of harmony, of moving in thought in the right direction. Seemingly, then,
the perceptual noema is not alone in setting off affective experiences
for the subject. The fringes and indeterminacies, though obscurely
or indirectly perceived, would appear in the thought of James and
Gurwitsch to do likewise.

It is evident, then, that the indeterminacies of perception are not
incidental. They have much to do with the direction that one's
thoughts may choose to take. In other words, our perceptions open
up meanings, bring the world to light, set the person in readiness
for future movements toward additional perceptions, and awaken
emotional responses, thanks to the clear disclosures and the many
vagaries that characterize them. We generate affective responses
through both the clearer cognitive dimensions that they possess
and the more nebulous and emotionally laden dimensions of their
indeterminacies. Such a realization is never inconsequential, but

particularly in regard to the matter of personal integration. The latter is a highly cognitive process, to be sure, but by no means exclusively so. In our wordings, metaphors, symbols, and myths there are powerful affective overtones and undertones, and, to boot, they are heavily weighted with perceptual indeterminacies despite the guidance and clarity that they undoubtedly afford people.

What has begun to emerge from this discussion on perception is an intimation that more may be involved in the perceptual act than has been presupposed. That there is cognition has never been doubted. That there is considerable affect bound up with the act, not only in its principal thematic dimension but also in its many indeterminacies and fringes, is something else. But that there is great provocation for imaginative thinking throughout the entire perceptual experience simply because of the inviting and fascinating dimensions of the vagaries of both the adumbrated noema and the field indeterminacies is an entirely new appreciation of the fullness of the perceptual act. It is provocative that both James and Gurwitsch were prone to concede an affective component to the fringes of the conscious experience; that they were prone to relate it to the neural and cerebral—and presumably endocrine—systems of the human body; and that they both granted the personal significance and need for the many indeterminacies to be brought to some measure of further determination. This, of course, is precisely what the task of imaginative thinking would perform. The theme and the principal thrust of the thematic field derive their determination from further perspectives, gained as the subject pursues the many retentional or protentional dimensions to which the perception gives rise. This is not the case, however, with the indeterminacies, since they are too vague, amorphous, uncertain, and subtle for the subject to address himself to them expressly in the way in which he could seek out further perceptions. They are not too inaccessible, however, for imaginative speculation, wonderment, excitement, historical leaps, surmises, and so on for the individual who has begun to experience a certain delight for reasons that are not totally clear, even though they are not irrational, or for the person who has begun to experience a revulsion of sorts for reasons that are not inane but certainly too obscure at the moment to allow for any sorting. Far from being too inaccessible, they are precisely what one might expect from a subject who does not *have* but who *is* his or her own lived body.

In phenomenological thought the body is seen not as a thing to which other things relate, any more than the person is seen as a thing to which other things relate. The body is seen as part and parcel of the subjectivity that is the person. The lived body, when it is experienced or phenomenologically studied, is not the body of bones, muscles, joints, and so on; it is the integrated synaesthetic synthesis that I am and is essential to the experiences that I am. Thus, this would be given to me along with parts of my body in a living connection identical with that existing between the parts of my body itself. With such an appreciation of the body, a person's perception would be understood in its perspectivity as moving a living human body, in virtue of the adumbrated profiles, toward further complementary perceptions, while our imagination, in virtue of the many cognitive intimations and emotional stirrings of the indeterminacies within the perception, is moved toward many imaginative speculations and/or possibilities. This indeed is precisely what the interrogation of one's experiences does reveal. We look at a beautiful flower in our hand, and, after having gazed admiringly upon it for some time, gently turn it so that we might gaze all the more, experiencing within ourselves delicate but unmistakable feelings that are aroused by the seemingly intangible and almost inexpressible attendants of the experience. Already we have been imaginatively transported. In this experience our consciousness, our fingers, our nerves, our muscles, our eyes, our history, our dreams, our memories, our imagination have all played their part—and seemingly all we had was a few glimpses of a beautiful, black red rose. Or so it seems. Actually those few seconds saw us imaginatively caught up and touched over and over again. True there were only a few perceptions, but only one would have been needed to send us on this poetic excursion. Consciousness, the body, imaginative thought—all were copresent.

Experiences such as this are at the heart of the integrational achievement of every person. To understand them we must appreciate the significant role played by human perception. But it is not the only factor in the process. What we imaginatively think, both during the perceptions and later when we imaginatively transform them, is equally important. But that belongs to the rest of our story.

# CHAPTER III

# *Imaginizing, Saying, and Presencing the Real*

THE preceding reflections on the phenomenon of perception
have introduced into our discussion that aspect of existence
that is so basic for human living. For one to exist and to live
that existence, one must perceive: one must meaningfully experience the existence that we are. Obviously that perception is limited,
has its ambiguity, requires further elaboration and fulfilling ad-
denda; but in no way does this suggest that the perception is
expendable. For the human being perception has a primacy and, as
such, provides a cognitive base for all subsequent thought, reflection, and abstraction. For us whose life is at issue, perception is our
*terminus a quo*, our place from which we begin, and our *terminus ad
quem*, our place to which we repair to gain our moorings, to gather
our poise, to assemble our data, to ground our lives. Our personal
integration takes place in the light of our perceptions, however
clear, however obscure. And yet perception has a context that must
needs be disclosed.

To speak of perception is to speak of the imagination. To speak
of perception is to speak of language and words. To speak of
perception is to speak of the real, the realities of life with which we
are beset and with which we must cope. In brief, perception is not
an isolate. It is very much an experience that involves the entire
human being and is intimately related to the imaginative pursuits
of the person as well as the language that the person has embodied.
We say embodied advisedly, for the language pervades our entire
makeup. And in a real sense the language has us as much as we
have the language. That which we perceive, the realities that take
form before our eyes spring up, as it were, not out of nowhere and
not nearly as arbitrarily as one might think. The realities of life are

those which humankind and human individuals have brought into being. They obviously are what they are, and they might have been otherwise. They are not otherwise, however, and it is the human lot—and privilege—to deal with these presences such as they are.

## A. IMAGINATIVE PROJECTIONS: THE HORIZON

The perceptions that lie at the heart of a person's integration of life are not made in darkness. They have their limits and their obscurity. But they are also integral to the openness and the illumination that the human person brings into the scene. There is a clearing of sorts that takes place that enables the perceived entity to be experienced by the percipient, in some way or other. The figure is in some fashion brought forth from the background in which it was buried, and it is the perceiver who does the figuring of the entity. Be it the duck or the rabbit that appears before us in the picture, or the vase or face that rises up from the page, the percipient has entered the birth of the object. A certain luminosity has been bequeathed, a certain light has been shed upon the scene, and an entity comes forth, as did David from the marble of Michelangelo. To put it in another way, the perception is not made in darkness; it is made in the light of the human light we throw upon the scene.

Medieval philosophy spoke of a *lumen naturale*, a natural light, which the person brought into experience and in virtue of which entities were lighted up for the person. Heidegger affirms such a concept, preferring, however, to speak of the disclosedness that is man, *Dasein*. To quote his own words:

> When we talk in an ontically figurative way of the *lumen naturale* in man, we have in mind nothing other than the existential-ontological structure of this entity, that it *is* in such a way as to be its "there." To say that it is "illuminated" means that *as* Being-in-the-world it is cleared in itself, not through any other entity, but in such a way that it *is* itself the clearing. Only for an entity which is existentially cleared in this way does that which is present-at-hand become accessible in the light or hidden in the dark. By its very nature, Dasein brings its "there" along with it. If it lacks its "there," it is not factically the entity which is essentially Dasein; indeed, it is not this entity at all. *Dasein is its disclosedness.* (1927/1962, p. 133)

Heidegger, in essence, is pointing up the fact that the person, being a being that is of its very nature intentional, thrown out into the world of its perception, is always found "there," casting its light. Thus the human being is a There-being, a *Dasein*. His being ever "there" entails a constant disclosure. Whatever else may emerge on the scene owes its emergence to the light of human consciousness, whatever form that light may have taken in a given instance. Thus we move into life, bringing with us our own luminosity and setting for ourselves the relevant contexts or horizons in which the illuminations or perceptions take place. To put it in another way, we are ever moving forth into our existence by casting ahead of ourselves a horizon in the midst of which and in whose parameters the tone of our existence is set. Such a horizon is much more than a mere logical projection, for no individual has at his or her command an adequate enough comprehension that would enable one to grasp the niceties of our world in all their clarity. Indeed, we move into life having embodied the traditions, the values, the perspectives, the preferences, the prejudices, the limitations of our heritage. This factor is critical. In fact that heritage in which we have been conceived, in which we were nurtured, of whose milk, so to speak, we have drunk, which we have experienced, that we have come to know, is the where-with-all with which we now move ahead. It is only by degrees, and with much trial and error that we come to appreciate what its meaning might really be. Ambiguity surrounds us on all sides.

This is not to suggest that we are unaware, nor is it to say that we are not knowing. It is to say that we do not really and fully understand that of which were are aware and do not fully understand that which we find ourselves already knowing. In a certain sense it could be said that we find ourselves laboring within the ambiguity of chaos, but this would be an exaggeration. Even amid all the uncertainties of our life, our being there, we put it together in some fashion. Sense is made out of it all, and we find ourselves coming to grips with whatever it is that is emerging. This achievement is a remarkable feat—one that is permeated with much of the imaginative and a little of the logical and reasonable, less certainly than we are prone to assume. Already we project forth our light, and that light is a highly imaginative light.

Kant and especially Heidegger, among others, have spoken to this. They see the person moving forward in life guided, so to speak, by the light of his or her imaginative projections. Such projections, setting the horizons in which our perceptions are born, are the accomplishment of our productive imaginative thinking. As one might expect, their (Kant and Heidegger) understanding of imaginative thinking is quite different from that which others have espoused, but it is extremely valuable for grasping what the human experience really is. Those there are who consider imaginative thinking as a focus on an object, the reality of which is a matter of indifference. Such, for example, is the thought of Croce and Collingwood, both of whom are of the mind that the object of imagination is essentially independent of the question of reality and unreality. That which one imagines is that which one imagines, and the reality of the object is not germane. The distinction between reality and unreality, they contend, simply does not enter the picture. Sartre, on the other hand, concentrated on the contention that the object of the imaginative effort is imaginative simply because it is a negation of the real or the present. As Hofstadter has phrased it, Sartre

> describes the imagination as the great function by which consciousness creates a world of unrealities. He is concerned with consciousness of the image, which he interprets as the act by which an object is supposed to be presented as absent or as nonexistent, hence in some way as a nothingness. The presentation occurs by means of a physical or mental content, like a portrait, or spots on the wall, or hypnagogic images, or the mental materials of a mental image. This content serves as an analogical representation of the imaginary object and thereby delivers the object to us in its absence or nonexistence. (1967, p. 47)

Thus, for Sartre, the imagination is a mode of consciousness that enables one to relate to the world of unreality. In the imagination one can hold something as unreal, nonreal, nonexistent, and by so doing can gain distance, as it were, from the real world, at least for a while, and establish some basis for one's freedom. Hence, Sartre would see imagination as identified with the world of consciousness in the process of realizing its own freedom.

The Heideggerian notion of imaginative thinking, as has been said, is quite different. He would not deny the fact that we can imaginatively think of an object as indifferent to the question of reality, nor that we can imaginatively think of it as absent or unreal. These two views of imaginative thought, however, do not begin to exhaust the imaginative achievement, nor do they in fact come even close to depicting the singular contribution that imaginative thought is constantly making to our existence. In this view that contribution of the imagination is what it bequeathes our experience of being and of reality. Hofstadter, for example, terms the imagination our "organ of actuality." Seen from this perspective the imagination moves from the periphery of existence to the center of actuality. It is human thought now setting the stage for the creation of actuality, for the birth of being, for the realization of possibilities, for the construction of life and transformation of one's existence. As he phrases it,

> Imagination becomes the central function in the production of experience, hence of the meaningful form of our encounter with reality, rather than being restricted solely to secondary functions like the aesthetic, artistic, fantastic, imaginary, magical, incantatory or nihilative. (1967, p. 49)

This reference to Heidegger's appreciation of imagination is important for understanding the full impact of his thought in the articulation of man, *Dasein*. In his book *Kant and the Problem of Metaphysics* Heidegger first spelled out his respect for this dimension of the human being. He never took up the issue again thematically, although the path of his later thinking was carved out in the light of this understanding. The appreciation of language, the recourse to poetry, both of which dominate from the outset but especially in his later years, are testimony to his realization of the power that the imagination wielded in human life. It was seen as the *Einbildungskraft*, the unity-building power within the person; and Heidegger saw the significance of time in the constitution and comprehension of being as due to the fact that time, as the distinguishing feature of *Dasein*'s existence, was essentially identical with that imaginative thought of which *Dasein* was capable.

Heidegger sees the transcendental imagination as dealing with more than the unreal or the absent. It is not to be understood as dealing with the "merely imaginary," as the term is often used. Far from it. He sees the imagination much as a farmer sowing seeds in the field, sketching a horizon in which objectivity is to be encountered. Things will come into being. Thus it is that the comprehension of Being takes place, for the comprehension of Being as the comprehension of anything must take place within a horizon, and imagination provides that horizon. And it is within that horizon, then, that the experience of any essent takes place. A kind of envisioning thinking occurs that enables beings to rise up before us, as it were. That thinking is both forming and projective thinking. In Heidegger's words,

> If what Kant terms "our thought" is this pure self-orienting reference-to, . . . , the "thinking" of such a thought is not an act of judgment, but is thinking in the sense of the free, but not arbitrary, "envisioning" of something, an envisioning which is at once a forming and a projecting. This primordial act of "thinking" is an act of pure imagination. (1929/19, p. 158)

In this passage Heidegger is concerned with the famous Kantian schemata in which the imaginative ground is laid for the encounter with essents of various kinds. Heidegger was quick to point out, however, that such "thinking" is not intellectual judgments but the freer, though not arbitrary, envisioning that enables beings to emerge for and in *Dasein*'s perceptions. It is indeed thinking, but not as traditionally understood; it is in essence imaginative thinking, without which no ultimate ground or context for the perception of emergent essents is provided.

Hofstadter, in his depiction of the imagination as the organ of actuality, elucidates the role of imaginative thought in human living, basing his articulation of course, on Heidegger's understanding of Kant:

> Take any concept you please. Let it be one of a quality or a quantity, a thing, a phenomenon, a whole of parts, an outward manifestation of an inner impulse, a causal action, a feeling, a thought, a moral action, a work of art, a philosophical system. Its very invention is the work of imagination as the latter branches out from the common root into the region of understanding. And what is of greater interest is its development in relation to the matter of existential, perceptual reality, so that the latter becomes progressively structured, deepened, shaded, colored among these conceptual lines as it condenses into the world. Imagination operates at the forefront of this process of distinguishing and connecting perceptual existence with conceptual essence so as to articulate the being in the world. (1967, p. 49)

In his own work, *Being and Time*, Heidegger addressed himself to the question of human understanding (*verstehen*), a topic closely related to the present discussion. He indicated that understanding must of necessity take place with a world or horizon that the person has projected before himself. It is of the nature of *Dasein* that it is both thrown into the world (*geworfen*) to face up to the facticities that surround it, and it is in a constant state of projecting itself to run ahead of itself, so to speak, toward its possibilities (*entwurf*). This latter observation does not mean that one perceives the nitty-gritty of specific agendas; it means rather that man sees himself as a being who is his possibilities that await their awakening. Projecting, of course, has nothing to do with comporting oneself toward a plan that has been thought out and in accordance with which *Dasein* arranges its Being. The character of understanding as projection, to which Heidegger makes reference, is such that the understanding does not grasp thematically that upon which it projects—that is to say, possibilities. Grasping it in such a manner would take away from the projected character as a possibility and would reduce it to the given contents which we have in mind. Projection, in Heidegger's view, is throwing before self the possibility as possibility, and letting it *be* as such. As projecting, understanding is the kind of Being of *Dasein* in which it *is* its possibilities as possibilities (1927/1962, p. 145).

This point is not incidental to our discussion. Man is a being who ever finds himself in the world and never finds himself otherwise. At the same time, as experience attests, man is being who, being in the world, is ever ahead of himself, caught up in bringing things alive with his projection, and providing all the while the horizon in which beings of whatever kind can be brought to light. Thus we can say that the human person is ever writing large for himself the broad outlines of a living projection and at the same time throwing the light of that projection on the entities with which he is confronted. Whatever comes to light owes its presence to the fact that man has provided the overall imaginative sunlight for viewing, and as well the individual calls with which to flood existence with beings.

These considerations are helpful for grasping the manner in which the person is at work in life. The imaginative horizon projected by the human sets the stage, as it were, for what it will effect, and such a stage is always being set, for man is ever at work in some manner. Even the highly depressed person—contrary to common opinion—who seemingly has written life off and is caught in paralyzing depths is one who has effected a tremendous imaginative achievement, which unfortunately has darkened him to the other dimensions of the life that surround him. Just consider for a moment: to imagine that everything is meaningless, that nothing good is to be found anywhere, that no purpose resides in anything, that every person in one's life has walked away and left one abandoned, that even the seeming good of life is really a sham— this is a huge imaginative accomplishment. With one gigantic stroke such a person wipes away everything, and no amount of reasoning can convince him otherwise. Knowledge, logic, truth, facts, figures are now devoid of meaning—not because they cannot be meaningful, to be sure, but simply because the person has imagined them so. Without doubt this represents a gigantic imaginative feat, but unfortunately it is one that suffers, despite its imaginative dimensions, from the fact that it is not imaginative enough. The depressed person is like the person who tries to imagine a railroad stretching out into the desert before him; the more he throws himself into the imagining, the more the tracks converge in the distance without, however, ever coming to meet. Investing one's life in a depression is indeed an imaginative accomplishment—futile, exhausting, unproductive, but imaginative nonetheless. But not imaginative enough. Such a person is crippled, not principally because he is imaginative, but because he has come to imagine that there is no other way to imagine his life. He ends, caught on his own petard.

Let us return to the question of one's traditions, one's culture, one's people. Traditions among a people, cultures on a continent are a people's way of imagining their lives, bringing imaginative thinking to bear upon their lives. Much experience, much thought, much suffering, many disappointments, great successes and failures go into the making of a culture, a tradition. It grows bit by bit and is formulated in customs, ways of doing, of looking at life, of entering into situations, of putting things together. At times some may wonder about the values and appreciations of their people and call them into question. Still others may question possible injustices that seem to befall certain segments of their people, and urge adaptations, regulations, procedures to be effected. Laws may even be enacted to correct abuses or to guarantee a modicum of justice on all sides. Such developments occur in every culture, and each group forms its own ways of dealing with the contingencies of life that befall the inhabitants.

To think, however, that the mores, values, laws, and so on of a people cover every aspect of a given culture is to overlook the endless subtleties that permeate a people's relations together and the innumerable nuances that characterize life among a people. The culture is filled with dimensions that are never articulated and in all probability will never be articulated. The people just live them and the common mentality is simply formed and embodied. Unless somewhere someone rises up to question it, as did Socrates in ancient Greece, the vast majority of people just assume that theirs is a way meant by nature, that theirs is a style beyond challenge, that any significant alternative is unthinkable. In brief, a culture is a people's imaginative creation, which here and there may be rethought for needful reasons, but which for the most part constitutes the "way it is done." Handed down from generation to generation, the authority of tradition is brought to bear and render it all even more unchallengeable. By this time the people's way of imagining life is conceived as the only way to do so.

Speaking of the question of authentic living, Heidegger addressed the same issue. He speaks of the "they existence" (the *Das Man* existence) that everyone for the most part lives. One imagines his life as it has been imagined for him by his elders, forefathers, founding fathers, and so on. To move from such a style to a critical owning of it is to move toward a more authentic mode of life; but such a movement is not common, and even in a truly authentic person is not constant every minute. He says,

> This Being-with-one-another dissolves one's own Dasein completely into the kind of Being of "the Others", in such a way, indeed, that the Others, as distinguishable and explicit, vanish more and more. In the inconspicuousness and unascertainability, the real dictatorship of the "they" is unfolded. We take pleasure and enjoy ourselves as *they* take pleasure; we read, see and judge about literature and art as *they* see and judge; likewise we shrink back from the "great mass" as *they* shrink back; we find "shocking" what *they* find shocking. The "they", which is nothing definite, and which all are, though not as the sum, prescribes the kind of Being of everydayness. . . .
>
> The Self of everyday Dasein is the *they-self*, which we distinguish from the *authentic Self*—that is, from the Self which has been taken hold of in its own way. (1927/1962, p. 127ff)

Subsequently, Heidegger expresses the same thought in this manner:

*Authentic Being-one's-Self* does not rest upon an exceptional condition of the subject, a condition that has been detached from the "they"; *it is rather an existentiell modification of the "they"—of the "they" as an essential existentiale.* (p. 130)

These passages were intended to illustrate that, in Heidegger's eyes, the individual *Dasein* is caught up—and necessarily so, since pure authenticity every moment of every day is both impossible and indeed needless—in a way of life that has been imagined for him by his or her people, the "they" of one's ancestral culture. And this culture has extended into every phase of life, although few could tell one how. On occasion and in specified areas, to be sure, one comes to honestly face her or his culture and own it in honorable ways, thus moving toward a more authentic style; but even these moments and efforts rest on an underlying view that we have taken unto ourselves of necessity. Without such an embodiment of life and life values bequeathed us, we could never even commence our life.

Having seen thus far that we go about our living imaginatively projecting a horizon in which we constantly function, that we bring into existence the entities with which we are ever confronted, that our imaginative projection is very much a they-projection, it is now important to note several features of this movement that have been merely alluded to and only tangentially treated.

Mention was made above that human beings bring into the picture of existence the realm of possibilities. This is obviously not intended to suggest that we do not have to cope with realities or hardships, the fait accompli of life, with that which has already been imagined and even already actualized. Nor does it suggest that that we can shut our eyes to the pain and suffering that surround us. It is to say rather that the presence of humans on the scene means that the scene becomes engulfed in possibilities, with so very much that *can* be, no matter what actually is. Again, it is not the individual agenda that one has lined up, or the strategy that one has worked out, or the steps that one has planned to take that occupies us here. The significance of understanding, of dealing with the possibilities of existence lies in none of this. What it does mean is that the presence of the human on the scene renders possibilities possible. To say that the human brings possibilities is to say that the human brings into the scene the possibility of possibilities.

Behold! her or his presence has rendered all anew, not by the creation of any individual object or entity, not by laying out a plan of attack, not by actualizing any particular potentiality or talent that the individual may seem to have—important as all these might be—but rather by the fact that a being whose nature it is to make possibilities possible has now appeared on the scene.

We are now dealing with the realm of the unexpected, and who can say what the unexpected might mean? It may very well mean in some instances unexpected tragedy of some kind, but it does certainly mean that there is one now present whose being enables it to deal, even with the unexpected tragedy, in unexpected, marvelous ways. The situation, however unexpectedly tragic, itself provides us with unexpected possibilities for creative, courageous, and ennobling, even inspirational response. It is this giftedness that lifts the human above, enabling him or her to transcend the apparent impossibilities and to provide further ineluctable proof that hope is the truly human lot, grounded in the giftedness that is *Dasein*—a giftedness that is most called into action when the situation is apparently most hopeless. Such is the power of imaginative thought—the basis of human possiblity—that it welcomes the unexpected and glories in the hope that it extends to the hopeless.

A further consideration, buried in the previous treatise, should be advanced. Our discussion on the nature of culture and tradition could conceivably be misunderstood. To say that a culture is a people's way of imagining life, and that one, in living his culture, is imagining life in a way that has already been imagined for him, was not intended to be facetious or demeaning. On the contrary, it points happily to the intrinsic sociality of the human being, and the fact that no human being could ever move toward greater authenticity in one's life without the grounding bequeathed to him or her by others, by the "they" of the culture, of the family, of one's friends. Thus to find oneself living the life that "they" have imagined for him is to show living respect for the value of the Other in human life. And that Other is paramount for one's own becoming. Some no doubt would conceive of the Other as one from whom one distances the self; but, as Heidegger has so beautifully expressed it, the truth is quite otherwise. He says:

> To avoid this misunderstanding we must notice in what sense we are talking about "the Others." By "Others" we do not mean everyone

else but me—those over against whom the "I" stands out. They are rather those from whom, for the most part, one does *not* distinguish oneself—those among whom one is too. (p. 154)

The Other, then, is not foreign or alien to the person; the Other is those of whom one is a part and who conversely are part of the person. Thus to suggest that the Other who is one with the person should in any way be repudiated is to misunderstand. One does indeed become what the Other has imagined him to be, and vice versa. Were one to reject the Other and the Other's proposed imagined mode of existence, one would guarantee one's own demise. However, having embodied the culture and traditions of our people, we can imaginatively distance ourselves from such and in due time move toward an authentic owning or even repudiation of the customs, values, or mores. But such is not possible at the outset. Thus there arises the remarkable fact that to repudiate whatever from the Other's bequeathment is to presuppose that one is using that which has been uncritically accepted to do so. As Heidegger has shown, the accepted, inauthentic mode of life is that upon which one builds and with which one functions. Obviously the more mature the culture, the more mature the persons embodying it may presumably be, and the more readily may they move toward their own authenticity. But this simply means in effect that the Other has bequeathed to the person, its people, a richer foundation with which to move forward into life. And with it one moves forward toward one's own richer integrations, such as they are.

What the above observations are indicating, of course, is the fact that learning is intrinsic to the entire process of integrating our life. If a person is the possibility of possibilities, he is nonetheless one who comes to learn that which has been imagined for him, and he learns it in a manner that has been modeled for him. In due time with sufficient given experience, however, he moves to a questioning of the cultural values and mores—or at least may move—but does so always within the understanding and parameters of that which he has learned. This is another way of pointing up the famous heremeneutical circle of which phenomenologists speak, wherein one employs what one has been given to critique what one has been given. We grow toward authenticity by using and even transcending what has been given to us so that we may from within it rethink what has been given to us and perhaps even better it.

This is not ingratitude; it is the grateful and proper use of the Other's graciousness.

All this bespeaks the remarkable plasticity that becomes the person. While not denying the person's finitude in any respect, it remains a fact that our capacity for thought, logical and imaginative thought, allows us almost unlimited growth possibility, thanks indeed to our own imaginative possibilities and to the endeavors that Others have considerately made on our behalf, the opportunities they have opened up, the learning that they have shared to promote our own learning launch. However it occurs in the individual's life, the person retains and perfects the capacity to envision his life, to plenish it with fulfillments of divers kinds, to learn anew and to reflect on those learnings, such as they are. Learning examined, like the life examined, is an enrichment of the learning or life unexamined. Taking imaginative distance in our thinking about our experience, our learning and our life make possible a genuine appropriation of that which has been found worthy and the eventual replacement of that which has been found wanting. Obviously the person's full endowment would be called into use in such an enterprise, his thought capacity in every respect challenged, his own integrity confronted; but such is not beyond the limits of a human being. Needless to say, to make this achievement come to pass, imaginative thinking would be the order of the day.

Even if one should fall short of this, however, it still remains a fact that his life will witness an imaginative flooding, as event after event, object after object, project after project are found permeated with the imaginative accoutrements that one bequeathes the respective settings. It is the human way to imaginize life: to flood it with imaginative dimensions in every sphere. To be sure, there is more to the human life than this, but it can never be properly understood if this realization is not given its due.

Giambattista Vico, whose sensitivity to this issue is well known, spoke of early man and his poetic wisdom:

> Hence poetic wisdom, the first wisdom of the gentile world, must have begun with a metaphysics not rational and abstract like that of learned men now, but felt and imagined as that of these first men must have been, who, without power of rationination, were all robust sense and vigorous imagination. This metaphysics was their poetry, a faculty born with them (for they were furnished by nature with these senses and imagination). (1970, p. 74)

The observations that Vico has made about early humans are provocative. They enable one to see how the human person could conceivably have once put his life together as a poetic achievement in a highly imaginative way. Withal, however, his comments remain relevant even today. Much, indeed most, of the integration effected by human beings is of a highly imaginative variety. It is only with this insight that considerable sense can be made of the human preoccupation with the irrational and paralogical dimensions of life, and the extreme ways in which so many see fit to effect some semblance of personal meaning and transpersonal understanding. But even in the lives of those whose integration manifests considerable thought and rationality, the imaginative horizons in whose light they labored are not to be overlooked. Imaginizing—flooding one's life with imaginative thought—remains an ongoing human acitivity, even when one is engaged professionally in the most rational of occupations.

## B.   LANGUAGING, WORDING, SAYING

The preceding discussion on the role and power of imaginative thinking is incomplete. To be fully understood, it must undergo further development and be seen in relation to language. The two topics are not by any means unrelated. As will shortly be seen, a language—any language—is truly an imaginative creation, to say the least. This truth will become increasingly clear in subsequent chapters as the topics of metaphors, symbols, and myths are brought into view. In each of them the imagination is a dimension that must always be reckoned with, but it is likewise a dimension in an area, the mere act of wording or saying, where it seemingly does not belong. It would appear that wording is a relatively minor responsibility and, except for unusual circumstances, uncomplicated. Such, however, is hardly the case, and even at this level one finds the imaginative dimension significant.

On the other hand any endeavor of imaginative thinking is a languaged endeavor. This twist may be surprising, but it merits some thought. In his own working notes in his book *Visible and the Invisible* Merleau-Ponty reflects on his own work over the years. He refers back to his famous opus, *The Phenomenology of Perception*, and he speaks of it in this way:

> The Cogito of Descartes (reflection) is an operation on significa-
> tions, a statement of relations between them (and the significations
> themselves sedimented in acts of expression). It therefore presup-
> poses a prereflective contact of self with self (the non-thetic con-
> sciousness of self-Sartre) or a tacit cogito (being close by one-
> self)—this is how I reason in the *Phenomenology of Perception.*

Then he goes on to ask himself:

> Is this correct? What I call the tacit cogito is impossible. To have the
> idea of "thinking" (in the sense of the "thought of seeing and of
> feeling"), to make the "reduction," to return to immanence and to
> the consciousness of . . . it is necessary to have words. It is by the
> combination of words (with their charge of sedimented signfications,
> which are in principle capable of entering into other relations, than
> the relations that have served to form them) that I *form* the transcen-
> dental attitude, that I *constitute* the constitutive consciousness. (1968,
> p. 170)

In other words, it was not until years later that Merleau-Ponty,
who had dealt with the topic of speech and language frequently in
his earlier works, came to realize the full import of words in
thought, including imaginative thought. As he states, he came to
see the necessity of words even in constituting the constitutive
consciousness. We have seen in the previous chapter that consciousness plays a constitutive role in the bringing of reality into
being. Here Merleau-Ponty is saying that it is words that enable
one to constitute that constitutive consciousness. In effect this
means that without one's language and words one's imaginative
thinking would be unworded, speechless, nonsignificative, unproductive, impotent. Heidegger came to see the same truth, and
phrased it quite succinctly:

> In order to be who we are, we human beings remain committed to
> and within the being of language, and can never step out of it and
> look at it from somewhere else. Thus we always see the nature of
> language only to the extent to which language itself has us in view,
> has appropriated us to itself. (1971, p. 134)

In a very real sense, then both Heidegger and Merleau-Ponty
are pointing to the unique significance of words and language in the
makeup of the human person. Heidegger would say even more. He
saw language as fulfilling a special role in the entire gamut of
Being. His comment was as follows:

> According to this essence language is the house of Being which comes to pass from Being and is pervaded by Being. And so it is proper to think the essence of language from its correspondence to Being and indeed as this correspondence, that is, as the home of man's essence. But man is not only a living creature who possesses language along with other capacities. Rather, language is the house of Being in which man ek-sists by dwelling, in that he belongs to the truth of Being, guarding it. (1977, p. 213)

In describing language as the House of Being, Heidegger has indicated that it is in language that Being is born, in language that Being dwells, in language that Being comes of age, in language that Being finds the care, the succor, the protection, the solicitude that would nurture Being. On another occasion Heidegger spoke of man, *Dasein*, as the Shepherd of Being, the one who is entrusted to Being and in whose watchful care Being is attended and respected. In the above passage he is indicating that it is in language that the Shepherd (*Dasein*) and his sheep (Being) both dwell. Thus the significance of language in the event of Being cannot be overestimated, nor can its unique position in the existence of *Dasein* be exaggerated.

In a very real sense one may speak of language as that communicative art that the speaking person uses to bring forth meaning from the realm of the unspoken. In another sense one can speak of a culture as a people's language written large. In this sense one's language and thus one's thinking can be found mirrored, captured in a people's ways, mores, customs, roads, buildings, architecture, art, dance, technology, modus vivendi. All such are the embodiment of their thinking, their language. In this sense too the sciences are to be seen as highly specialized languages, as is mathematics, logic, metaphysics, philosophy, and music. In all and similar instances the specialist must master his language and then use it toward his respective ends. Now it is evident that language has taken on larger and greater meaning than was suspected when words were heard coming from the mouth of a speaker. And yet there is an affinity among the senses indicated.

To appreciate the relevance of these remarks to the topic of a person attempting to integrate or better integrate his or her life, it is important to grasp just what it means to word, whether it be on an individual level of a speaker or on a grand scale as a culture, a science, a philosophy. The question might be posed by asking what it is that happens when one words, one says, one languages in discourse, whatever the nature of that discourse. In understanding this, one moves toward understanding how the *logos*, the word, the saying plays such a vital part in the event of Being and in the integration of a person's or a people's life.

To word is often identified with the same meaning as to name, and to name is often made to appear a purely arbitrary exercise. It is everywhere acknowledged that a rose by any other name would smell just as sweet. In this sense, then, the wording of anything is quite inconsequential, if not whimsical. Aristotle seemed to favor this notion when he described the word as a *vox significativa ad placitum* (a sound endowed with an arbitrary meaning). However, when one considers such words as automobile or television, it would appear that there is more to wording than appears at first sight. An automobile is a self (*autos*) moving (*mobilis*) vehicle, which is precisely what the word indicates. A television is a piece of equipment designed to issue forth at its end (*telos*) the picture (*visio*) of an event transpiring elsewhere in the distance. Again the word indicates that idea. In these instances, then, the word is seen to have much more in it than the mere whim of the namer.

Vico, in his work *Scienza Nuova*, makes the point that words are far from arbitrary creations, and indeed have a unique relationship to people. In his words:

> It is noteworthy that in all language the greater part of the expressions relating to inanimate things are formed by metaphor from the human body and its parts and from the human sense and passions. Thus, head for top or beginning; the brow and shoulder of a hill; the eyes of needles and of potatoes; mouth for any opening; the lip of a cup or pitcher; the teeth of a rake, a saw, a comb; the beard of wheat; the tongue of a show; the gorge of a river; a neck of land; an arm of the sea; the hands of a clock; heart for center (the Latins used umbilicus, navel, in this sense); the belly of a sail; foot for end or bottom; the flesh of fruits; a vein of rock or mineral; the blood of grapes for wine; the bowels of the earth. Heaven or the sea smiles; the wind whistles; the waves murmur; a body groans under a great weight. The farmers of Latium used to say the fields were thirsty, bore fruit, were swollen with grain; and our rustics speak of plans making love, vines going mad, resinous trees weeping. Innumerable other examples could be collected from all languages. (p. 88)

To Vico, then, a word is given with pause and care, for it

bestows significant meaning on an entity, and it often bears a distinct relationship to the human body. Thus the issue grows more complex than it first appeared. Certainly a word does not have the sheer arbitrariness that some would claim, nor would it be proper to speak of the name as being the only substance that an entity can be said to possess. This nominalist understanding would reduce a substance simply to its verbal understanding—a position just as extreme as that which would see the word as purely arbitrary. Thus a word is not everything for an entity, but neither is it nothing. To word is to say something about a being, to bestow identity on it with some measure of rationale, and, in the spirit of Vico, with some reference, at least in many instances, to the human person or body.

Thus to word is to say and to say is to reveal something to another about an entity. This is captured in the Greek word, λεγειν or, to used the verb, λογοσ which means to speak, to say, to lay out in the open, to disclose. Consider what it is that happens when one words. Thanks to the words employed, one reaches over and picks up, so to speak, the object of his attention and sets it before himself and his listener. If he would speak of a hill or a mountain, he reaches over and lifts the mountain from its setting to bring it into the room in which he is engaged in discourse. If he speaks of a river, he reaches out and lifts it up, bringing it before them both so that he might attend to it in the exchange. On the other hand, he may elect to pick up, not the mountain, but the valley; not the river, but its bank. In these instances he gathers up the lowlands at the foot of the mountain, the land that runs astride the river. In a certain sense it could be said that the valley belongs to the mountain and vice versa, or the bank belongs to the river and vice versa. The demarcation, to be sure, is not clean, for there would be no mountain without some valley nor valley without some hill, no river without some bank, and no bank without some river. Thus the gathering up that takes place in the transaction of wording has its share of leavings. It is as though one, in wording, were to gather up a being or beings, much as one would gather up leaves that have been swept together in a pile. As he reaches down with his arms and lifts a large pile of leaves, carrying them to the bin for deposit, the bulk of the leaves is contained in his arms but there are many that drop off from his arms as he moves from the pile to the bin. A falling of sorts occurs, while it is still true that the majority of the leaves are carried over. In much this way, the word gathers up the entity and carries it into the conversation, but the transition is not entirely clean, and there are leavings along the way. Things are not so clearly demarcated, nor are the words that gather them up. The things melt into each other in many ways in nature or culture or existence, as one cares to phrase it. To say father, for example, is also to point to mother; to say grandchild is to say grandfather; to say mountain is to say valley, terrain, foliage, depth, height. To say car is to say driver, engine, tires, gasoline, oil. To say bed is to say mattress, springs, pillows, sheets, slats, headboards. Things have a way of running into each other as existents, or essents, and the words used to say them do the same.

This is not to suggest that everything means everything else. It is to suggest, however, that the limits of realities are not always, if ever, clean, and that the words one employs to say them depict that same kind of limit. Nonetheless words try to present the objects of their saying and to make their disclosure, laying before us that of which we are speaking. The demarcations leave something to be desired, just as the objects themselves leave traces of themselves in each other. One could imagine the mountain, for example, far beneath the surface of the ground becoming part of the foundation of the nearby mountain. At that level they would both be of each other's foundational depths. Yet the person wording cuts the one mountain off from the other at some specified point, and they are seen as distinct. The exercise is not futile, to be sure, and must be done in the discourse, but the overlap remains and the words, like the entities, run into each other if one but looks to see how.

From this point of view, then, the comments of Vico take on added meaning. The brow of the hill and the shoulder of the road speak of relationships that obtain, and they overlap just as the muscles of the forehead, cheeks, shoulder, and the neck do on the person. The teeth of the rake, the saw, and the comb speak of a relationship that obtains, as it does in the mouth of a person where the anatomical parts concerned spread over into each other. The belly of the sail, the flesh of the fruit, the vein of coal do likewise. Without laboring the issue, it becomes clear that wording of the objects or the parts is neat, but not too neat, clean but not too clean, distinct but not too distinct—and whatever else, it is laden with its share of the imaginative. In short, to word is to lay out in the open the entity in question after having gathered it up in nature. The whole process was not idle, not purely fanciful, not completely arbitrary, not perfectly clean—certainly not as clean as one would like to pretend. But this is the human achievement of wording, such as it is. And it makes all kinds of things now possible.

It is easy to understand from this account the dissatisfaction that scientists feel with this process, and their great need to establish clean and precise definitions. One can understand, too, the great emphasis that the social sciences placed on operational definitions, despairing, as it were, ever to describe the entities that abound cleanly but setting down instead the operations upon which they were to concentrate and by which they would evaluate the outcomes of their study. Paul Ricoeur speaks to the stresses of ambiguity with which scientific endeavor can be plagued and the various steps taken by the sciences to cope with this problem. As a first step, scientific language uses a procedure rooted in ordinary language, that of definition. This it does by extending the definatory procedure by refining it with the help of classificatory and taxonomic measures. Its second step, as he indicates, would introduce technical terms into our vocabulary to satisfy a specific rule, that of denoting only quantitative entities, to the exclusion of the qualitative aspect of our experience. At a third stage of abstraction, words are replaced by mathematical symbols, that is to say by signs which can be read, but not vocally uttered. At this stage, then, the link with natural language is broken. Scientific language henceforth is beyond the boundary line which divides artificial language from natural language. Finally, at a fourth stage, an advanced degree of formalization, the meaning of all the formulas and all the laws of a formal system are governed by a set of axioms, which assign each elementary meaning its place in the theory and prescribe the rules for reading the whole symbolism. At this stage new rules of translating are employed to exclude all ambiguities. Reflecting on these procedures, Ricoeur mentions the dream of a *langue bien faite* that some entertain in the hope of eliminating all ambiguity in human discourse, but despairs of it because of the countless new problems that it would generate (1973).

It should be noted that Ricoeur speaks of the scientific effort as a strategy of discourse that has been deliberately designed. Even it, as he illustrates, has its shortcomings and imperfections, precise though it tries to be. Moreover, as was indicated in the opening chapter, the scientific enterprise has had to have recourse to countless metaphors for the mere naming of its field and its respective elements and forces, to say nothing of its recourse to imaginative creations in the effort to construct models, theories, hypotheses, and ingenious resolutions. Thus even in a highly sophisticated language deliberately designed to minimize, if not eliminate, ambiguity and imprecision, the effort has always been clouded by the inevitable process of imaginative embellishments and extensions. And the effort to maintain purity of expression even in a very limited sphere requires constant monitoring.

This being the case, the hope to eliminate such in the field of ordinary discourse where most people, including the scientists themselves, are always living will never end or succeed. Having left their laboratory and returned to their homes and families, the super-precise scientists find themselves indulging in all the familiar wordings of the everyday lives where they themselves, their spouses, and their children carry on in the attempt to put their own lives together with all the languaged creations that are ever in a process of change or extended applications: the world of polysemy. In this endeavor the imaginative is ever holding forth. But by the same token imaginative thought is helpless without the words.

Pursuing this last thought, let us now examine a poem that Heidegger frequently quotes from the German poet, Stefan George. Among other places Heidegger quotes and comments upon it in his work, *On the Way to Language*: (p. 140)

"WORDS"

Wonder or dream from distant land
I carried to my country's strand

And waited till the twilit norn
Had found the name within her bourn—

Then I could grasp it close and strong
It blooms and shines now the front along . . .

Once I returned from happy said,
I had a prize so rich and frail,

She sought for long and tiding told:
"No like of this these depths enfold."

And straight it vanished from my hand,
The treasure never graced my land . . .

So I renounced and sadly see:
Where word breaks off no thing may be.

Stefan George

This poem depicts a world traveler who, in all his wanderings about in distant lands, would gather up wonders of many sorts to bring home to his own land; but before sharing them with his people, would submit them to the wisdom of the twilit norn, the goddess or Scandanavian fate, who from the depths of her well, would seek to extract the word that would most gracefully and properly befit it. Once found, that word would render the prize known and precious to the traveler, who then would proclaim it for what it was to his fellow countrymen. "It blooms and shines now the front along" treasured dearly by all.

At this point, however, the traveler relates a different story. Returning home once with a finding that was beautiful and delicate, his prize won the admiration of all. The norn herself stood in silent awe before the wonder and turned to her bourn to extract the precious word that would give name to the treasure. She was unable to find such, and long she sought until, realizing that there was no word with which she could presence it, she turned and confessed sorrowingly, "No like of this these depths enfold."

At this announcement the traveler felt it slip from his hand, vanishing forever. Sadly he was to learn that it would never again appear in their midst. Says he, "The treasure never graced my land."

Then it was that the supreme realization struck him: the truth that he had never come to realize over the many years of travel and discovery. It was a truth, however, that he came to appreciate as never before: "Where word breaks off, no thing may be."

He died to the wonder, the dream, the prize, and his death of abandonment awakened him to this new appreciation, something he had never ever considered: Where word breaks off, no thing may be.

It was with this realization that he came to understand how other gifts and treasurers could bloom and shine the front along. It was not to his own discoveries that they owed their presence in his land. It was to the word that gave them identity and presence and preservation. Without the word he and his people were left empty-handed, bereft, deprived, saddened, impoverished. And they could only imagine what might have been, had the word for it been found. But found it was not, and it vanished. A thing of beauty, John Keats has said, is indeed a joy forever. Its loveliness does increase; it will never pass into nothingness, but will still keep a bower quiet for us and a sleep full of sweet dreams, and health, and quiet breathing. Keats was so very right—provided the thing of beauty has been worded by someone, and preferably by one of life's twilit norns.

## C. Presencing and Reality

Thanks to the wonders of imaginative thought and to the efficacy of words, reality takes on substance in human life. Usually, however, the significance of both in the event of reality is simply overlooked. Seemingly the real or reality is that which is before one, and it stands over against the person as verily as a building confronts the onlooker. Nothing could be more obvious. To suggest, then, that the matter should be thought through, or given second considerations, is presumably to ask one to labor that obvious. Or so it certainly seems.

The preceding reflections of this chapter, however, should give one reason to rethink the issue. If perception is the human sine qua non for integrating life in whatever form that integration may take; if perception does take place within an imaginative horizon projected before human consciousness; if objects and things and happenings do emerge from within that horizon and are brought into being under the light of that projective endeavor; if words do gather up and set something before the speaker and the listener; and if, when words break off, no thing may be; then one has to ask oneself just what it is that occurs when all this does take place. And one has to ask also just what it means to speak of reality. Is it in fact an *en soi*, existing solely in its own right, standing off from consciousness and compelling our surrender to the ineluctable facts with which we are confronted? Or is reality something else, something that shows forth given certain conditions? These two questions remain to be asked.

Let us speak to the second question first, and then, in its light, look at the first. If the conditions cited in the previous description of perception and its concomitants do aptly depict the perceptual encounter with whatever is engaged in the imaginative horizon, then, we ask, what is it that is effected when the word words, the saying says?

When one says something, lays it out in the open, gathers it up for the speaker and listener, a presence is effected. It might be the presence of a person, a thing, a relationship, a concept. To word the gathered entity as a hill or river is to bring the gathered entity into the forefront of the discussion as a hill or river. Focus now settles on it and the emotional resonances are those that attend the experience of a hill or a river, not the word "hill" or the word "river." To be sure, the word presences the entity perspectivally, just as the perception itself grasped the entity perspectivally; but the object as a profiled whole takes on presence for all parties concerned. And the give and take that ensue center about the object presenced, not the word used. We may, of course, focus on the word and make it the object, but now one would speak of a verbal presence, since that is the object engaged. Whatever the object, once it is said, layed out in the open, it now enjoys its own presence in the discussion, has its own meaning, its perspectivalness, its possibilities, and its unfolding history. Had the word broken off and never been said, it would remain unknown, unpresenced and lost, much as a wave that has returned to the ocean, its constituency unmarked. Because, however, it has been gathered up in its name, it is not lost or forgotten. It is certainly possible that it may be set aside for a while, allowing other worded entities to occupy the center of the stage, but it can and will be resurrected and reengaged in due time. Meanwhile, it can bloom and shine the front along.

This phenomenon is witnessed in ordinary life as well as in the selected areas of science or the arts. Over the centuries countless realizations were on the verge of their advent onto the human scene; but words having failed us, these realizations slipped back into oblivion—there to await the formulation that would someday give them birth. When that day arrived, if ever it did, their presence on the human scene was that depicted by their saying. That saying, then, has its historical dimension: it is said at the moment of history as best it can be said at that moment. In time, of course, it may grow, taking on structure, stature; it may undergo metaphorizations of various kinds. All this is its history. The electron of the nineteenth-century physicist was what it was as it was brought forth in its presence. The electron of today enjoys a different and much richer presence in the language of contemporary science. But whatever presence each was heir to was effected through its gathered exposure. Without that, the electronic presence would ever have remain unsaid, unknown, unheralded. In Heidegger's phrasing:

> Saying is showing. In everything that speaks to us, in everything that touches us by being spoken and spoken about, in everything that gives itself to us in speaking, or waits for us unspoken, but also in the speaking that we do *ourselves*, there prevails Showing which causes to appear what is present, and to fade from appearance what is absent. Saying is in no way the linguistic expression added to the phenomena after they have appeared—rather, all radiant appearance and all fading away is grounded in the showing Saying. Saying sets all present beings free into their given presence, and brings what is absent into their absence. Saying pervades and structures the openness of that clearing which every appearance must seek out and every disappearance must leave behind, and in which every present or absent being must show, say, announce itself.
>
> Saying is the gathering that joins all appearance of the in itself manifold showing which everywhere lets all that is shown abide within itself. (1971, p. 126ff)

In thus depicting language as that which marks the birth of beings, that which effects the presence of beings, that which makes truly possible the presence of presences, language, wording, saying is seen to be singular and unique. It is evident now why language is regarded as the house of Being, the dwelling for Being, for it allows for Being and being, as a home allows for its inhabitants. We can see too why language and the word are so precious for the human being in particular. We cannot fulfill our human function without language and wording, for they are the wherewithall that *Dasein* employs to give presence to the beings over whose birth *Dasein* presides.

Having stated this, we now turn to the remaining question we raised. If language, wording makes a presence present, as we have shown, we would ask the legitimate question: what might reality then be? Is it an in-itself, an *en-soi*, standing opposite consciousness, now languaged, and compelling the latter to surrender to its undeniable verity? Or is it to be understood otherwise?

In his book *The Politics of Experience* R. D. Laing raises this question in his own unique way. To quote him:

The theoretical and descriptive idiom of much research in social science adopts a stance of apparent "objective" neutrality. But we have seen how deceptive this can be. The choice of syntax and vocabulary is a political act that defines and circumscribes the manner in which "facts" are to be experienced. Indeed, in a sense it goes further and even creates the facts that are studied.

The "data" (given) of research are not so much given as *taken* out of a constantly elusive matrix of happenings. We should speak of *capta* rather than *data*. The quantitatively interchangeable grist that goes into the mills of reliability studies and rating scales is the expression of a processing that we do *on* reality, not the expression of the processes *of* reality. (1967, p. 62)

Laing, in essence, is pointing out that the so-called objective data of human science is not that which is objective, independent of people, given uncontaminated to the researcher. It is that which is seized upon, taken up, by the researcher in a highly constructed research language. There are no data, hard or soft, that has not been somehow worded in the respective sciences. That being the case, what is taken up (the capta, captum) is taken up in the sophisticated language. Thus the datum or data should be more appropriately described as the *captum* or the *capta*; the given is actually the taken or captured.

This point is akin to the preceding discussion. Without words, no thing may be; with words, much may be. And research, despite its claim to objectivity and seeming independence from the researcher, remains very much a human enterprise, highly languaged and necessarily so. The language is needed for the constituting of the data and for the study of the constituted data. It will be remembered that language operates within the horizon sketched out or drawn by the human imagination. Thanks to that language, whether it be in the sciences, the arts, or the commonplaces of the *lebenswelt*, we set presences before us, disclose them to other humans, make presences of all kinds present. These are the realities with which humankind must deal, but that reality is not what it is independent of the human and his consciousness. Their being what they are emerges from the confluence of human imaginative projections, the human's imaginative and informed sayings, and the presences that we have brought about. This does not imply that the person has created them from nothing, as though we were God.

Nor does it imply that they are what they are without human languaging. It does imply quite emphatically, however, that the finite human being needs the presences, the presences need the language and sayings, and that the language/sayings need the human consciousness with its imaginative horizons.

Once one understands the significance of these dimensions, the understanding of the meaning of reality and the questions raised about reality take on depth. Thus, to ask if reality is something independent is to ask if it is independent of consciousness. That is why it is asked. But the very asking of the question is presupposing consciousness to begin with; otherwise the discussion is meaningless, and the question cannot even be raised. People are what they are, thanks in part to the world of which they are part and parcel. Reality, on the other hand, is what it is, thanks in part to the human consciousness and genius that have given it presence through its imaginative wordings and sayings.

In his *Being and Time* Heidegger has a magnificent passage in which this very issue is addressed briefly, thoroughly, and honestly:

> Of course only as long as Dasein is (that is, only as long as an understanding of Being is ontically possible), "is there" Being. When Dasein does not exist, "independence" "is" not either, nor "is" the "in-itself". In such a case this sort of thing can be neither understood nor not understood. In such a case even entities within-the-world can neither be discovered nor lie hidden. In such a case it cannot be said that entities are, nor can it be said that they are not. But now, as long as there is an understanding of Being and therefore an understanding of presence-at-hand, it can indeed be said that in this case entities will still continue to be. (p. 255)

To ask, on the assumption that the human is nonexistent, questions that are intelligible only on the assumption that the human is existent, is to ask meaningless questions. Such questions cannot be raised for they are raised only by human consciousness. To raise them anyhow is to guarantee that no answer will be rationally given by way of affirmation or denial, since there is no human consciousness to answer. However, if we proceed on the assumption that the human is existent, such questions do have meaning, but they now presuppose the presence of that consciousness whose wording has lighted up the entities in a very imaginative and rational way, making such questions meaningful indeed and their answers very vital.

Hopefully it is now apparent that the project of integrating one's personality, putting of one's life together, entails not only the perceptions that a person makes in life, but also the realities of life with which one must deal. Such realities have much to do with our efforts, decisions, and plans as we move forward into our life challenges and encounters. We achieve our measure of integration amid the world in which we exist. We are not first integrated and then step into the contingencies of our life. The engagement with reality and putting life together are one and the same process. It should be clear at this point, however, that those realities are not what they are independent of human consciousness and the person. Far from it. Much imaginizing, reasoning, languaging, and say-ing—and many people as well—have entered into the construction of reality with which we deal. As Berger has convincingly shown, the construction of reality is very much a societal creation (1967). The They enters, not only the traditions, cultures, and mores of life, but also the countless realities that everyone must face. Hence the person and the They of one's life actually pool their resources to bring about a social reality that must be effectively faced. To be sure, many of a person's realities in life are principally of his or her own making, but the vast majority of those realities are social constructions in whose building he or she plays some small but not insignificant part.

Be all this as it may, the individual person, living amid the They of our life and pulling upon the interpersonal strengths provided by the significant and even less significant others in our life, must move into his or her realities and seek to put them together for him or herself. Every person does it, some more effectively than others; and in this process everyone has recourse to language and words. Without them, there is nothing. With them, there is reality with all its promise.

CHAPTER IV

# The Metaphor: The Midwife
# of Unification

> The problem of the metaphorical ("polysemic" or "plurisignative")
> aspect of language is perhaps the most perplexing, vexed, and
> intractable question in the whole of the philosophy of language. It
> brings us to the pivotal center of the distinction between language as
> a "system" and language as "speech-act," language as "illocutio-
> nary" and "perlocutionary," as "logic" and "rhetoric". Here we are
> getting into deep water; everything up to now—even in the quarrels
> we have had with our adversaries—has been comparatively easy.
> Once we enter the realm of "metaphor" we no longer have any true
> "adversaries" for the simple reason that there are no theories of
> metaphor sufficiently developed to be opposed to one another for
> more than a few minutes of reflection at a time.(Edie, 1976, p. 151)

THE precautions indicated in this passage by Edie provide
one with some idea of the formidableness of the question
with which this chapter is engaged. While the interest in the
issue of metaphor has proliferated unbelievably over the past fifty
years (Booth, 1978, p. 47), it remains a fact that the understanding
of metaphor—as of imagination—has advanced only slowly. Nonetheless an understanding has grown—again, as in the case of
imagination—that should not be dismissed as inconsequential.
And it is this understanding that can contribute to the development
of our thought.

## A. PRELUDE: SOME THOUGHTS ON THE INTEGRATIONAL
## PROCESS

The present chapter will focus on the metaphor as a critical
dimension in the area of language and languaging, and as a pivotal

domain in the understanding of the advancement of personal integration. Before undertaking this project head on, we would do well to dwell a while on the subject of personality integration itself. What might it mean, we should ask, to pursue the integration of one's personality? Is such a pursuit meaningful, or is it, in fact, futile? Does it call for a formal decision or is it a pursuit that the human being simply undertakes de facto without ever adverting to the fact as such? Clarifying the matter should aid in disclosing better the role of the metaphor in the process—a role that this chapter has suggested could well be itself metaphorized as midwifery.

Several times thus far the issue of integrating one's personality has been described in terms of one's putting her or his life together. This description, quite apt for the task that it seeks to pursue, calls for some amplification. It is not a description founded upon any particular personality theory, such as that of Freud, Jung, Adler, Skinner, and others. Moreover, if we were to cast it in terms of such theories, then it would be necessary to address the question in terms of the personality ingredients called for by the respective theorists, much as Sigmund Freud did in the passage quoted previously from his New Introductory Lectures. Comparing the psychoanalytic task with that of mysticism, Freud stated clearly:

> Nevertheless it may be admitted that the therapeutic efforts of psychoanalysis have chosen a similar line of approach. Its intention is, indeed, to strengthen the ego, to make it more independent of the superego, to widen its field of perception and enlarge its organization, so that it can appropriate fresh portions of the id. Where id was, there ego shall be. It is a work of culture—not unlike the draining of the Zuider Zee. (1932/1964, V. XXII p. 80)

This is a clear indication that Freud saw the task of psychoanalytic therapy as a draining of the physical Zuider Zee within us: a draining that would result in an integration that he would describe as a strengthening of our ego, a freeing of our ego, a widening of our perceptions, an enlarging of our ego's organization, an appropriating of our ego's inner swampland now reclaimed. In such a description many philosophical and psychological assumptions are embodied in a highly metaphorical picture of the human personality. This should come as no surprise, since every theory of personality presents its own metaphorization, and it is the substance of the

Freudian understanding of the human being that is the issue. Any therapeutic praxis must be pursued in the light of the theoretical picture proposed. If, to cite another example, one were to focus on Jungian theory, the integrational effort would center on the process of individuation, stated in terms now of the Self, the ego, the shadow, the anima-animus, the personal and collective unconscious, and the personal consciousness and the persona. Again, to be sure, philosophical and psychological assumptions are entailed, and these highly metaphorical formulations of Jung would call for considerable explication. The point of our discussion is simple enough: different theoretical understandings call for different integrational processes, and the details of the therapeutic practice can be expected to vary accordingly. Different metaphors highlight different aspects of the person. One could easily imagine the metaphorical disparity that would prevail if we were to compare the Skinnerian understanding of humankind with the interpersonal metaphorizations of a Harry Stack Sullivan, or the field-force metaphors of a Kurt Lewin.

It is evident, then, that no theory captures the entirety of humankind, and each theory represents an ingenious—some more so than others—creation of a theorist's comprehension about human nature. The mere fact that so many theories prevail attests to the rich mystery that is humankind and the impossibility of any metaphorization every capturing human fullness within its structure.

Seeing the process of integrating the human personality as an effort to put life together in a relatively coherent, effective, and satisfying manner, then, is not tied to any particular theoretical understanding. That such may help is apparent enough, but all such understandings are limited and cannot be said to exhaust the human phenomenon. The human mystery ever remains, even though in the process many problems may be resolved and stresses alleviated for the person seeking help.

The truth of it all is the fact that the person himself is the one who is effecting the integration of his life, and the therapist is at most an informed adjunct in the process. This is as it should be. No therapist, any more than a parent, can live life for another. The therapist can, however, and hopefully does, prove to be an invaluable resource for the client, as is the parent, the teacher, the peer, the friend. Obviously the therapist's psychological expertise should render his or her assistance exceptionally qualified for performing the task. But whether this is or is not the case always remains to be seen, for the mystery of the person can escape the professional, however qualified, as it can escape any associate. It is always possible that a significant recovery could be realized by a client, despite the limitations of the individual therapist. The latter, like every teacher, knows that he works with limitations and hopes that, despite those limitations, some movement may be realized and that he or she may succeed in firing the imagination of the client to embark on a journey that will bring him to a happy port.

The "bringing to happy port" is the hope of the therapist, but it is not a carrying to port that is the aim. It is a setting on course that must then be implemented by the person in her or his life situation. Thus the description of integration as a putting of one's life together is precisely the task to be accomplished—a task to be effected by the person, not the therapist. The latter's expertise is invaluable, but the living and the accomplishment must be that of the client.

Let us press this point further. Professional offices are daily being visited by persons who feel themselves falling apart, at loose ends, losing their grip, overwhelmed by life and its demands. Under such circumstances they come for help to put it all together, to gain or regain their hold on things, to manage at least some glimpse of the forest amid the trees of their life. However they may phrase it, their aim is quite clear: to effect some meaningful synthesis amid the pain, turmoil, or chaos of their life. Presumably the professional will enable this to take place. Freud once described the good life in the words "*lieben und arbeiten*" (to love and to work, accomplish). This description, we acknowledge, has its merits, for the person who has truly learned to love and to accomplish meaningfully has indeed found the key for the good life. Likewise the phrase of St. Paul "*facientes veritatem in charitate*" (Ephesians 4:15) (carrying out the truth in a spirit of love) has much of the same quality about it, urging Christians to work meritoriously in the truth and with a spirit of loving relationship. We add, however, that both exhortations are extremely difficult to live out, if and when the person so exhorted finds that the personal world of which he or she is the center is collapsing. Somehow it is necessary that we experience a unity of sorts, however tenuous, before we can hope to love in a relatively selfless way or before we can hope to dedicate ourselves consistently over a period of time to tasks whose realization yields that joy which genuine accomplishment can certainly generate for the person.

Thus the concern of the psychologist (and the client and family) with the human's personal integration, unity, experiential oneness pervading the multiplicity of his everyday living is readily understandable. It cannot be taken cavalierly by the professional, for it is certainly taken quite seriously by the client. To move toward some unity, some feeling of self-possession in one's world, some confidence and experience that one can and is holding one's own in life, at life tasks, in carrying out responsibilities, in making a mark on the world in some small way is paramount. And the integrating of life involves precisely this.

In the process of integrating one's life the person experiences a movement toward wholeness—relative wholeness—and toward the world. Both aspects are important for the individual. We move toward an owning of ourselves, our members, our parts, so to speak. They become more and more "me" or mine. This is part of the process, a process that is ongoing and relative, a more or less experience, not an absolute. One comes to feel more like an integer, much as we might imagine a whole number (1, 2, 3, and so on) feeling like a true integer and not fractionated (such as 1/2, or 2/3, or 3/4). The human being who feels fractionated is one who feels at odds with himself, not all-with-it and not all-it-with-him. Such a person feels unable to meet life courageously and effectively, for his resources do not seem to be at his command. There is no confidence that one will be able to tap the resource that is needed. To be sure, moving toward greater integration does not demand that one feel master of one's world—whatever that might possibly mean—but rather that one feels genuinely able to hold one's own; to carry out one's share of the bargain of life. The process, of course, must allow one time, but it does require that one feels oneself moving ahead and gradually gaining an emotional jump on life, so to speak. And this means that one feels a movement toward the world, not away from it. One begins to sense his or her being on top of things a goodly measure of the time. And our being out in the world engaged somehow looms up as something quite natural and proper and gratifying.

In making mention of an experiential oneness pervading the multiplicity of a person's everyday living, and of this need to feel that we are one with ourselves and the world, there is implied a radical *existential* anthropology. To be more specific, both comments allude to the fact that the human person is a Being-in-the-World (an *In-Der-Welt-Sein*, to use Heidegger's word). This means that a person cannot be understood (whether one focuses on the intellectual life, the sexual life, the emotional life, or whatever) except in terms of that Being-in-the-World that one is. As far as the task of integrating one's life is concerned, this point is paramount. Integration is to be seen as a movement toward oneness with oneself and with one's world. This is at the root of it all. How one stands out, ex-sists, is critical: how one is *in* the world, *with* the world, *at* the world is the key to telling one how one *is*. Radical *existential* thought will not settle for any explanation of the person that would describe him in terms of endopsychic drives or impulses that appear noticeably divorced from his existence in the world. Nor would it settle for any explanation that would study him in terms of objective contingencies over which he presumably has little or nothing to say, but by which his life is allegedly substantially shaped. To see the person as a Being-in-the-World is to see the person as a being of whose very structure the world is a constituent. This being the case, then, to learn about one's world and how one is in-at-with it is to learn about the person.

Needless to say, this is all tied intrinsically to the question of language, the role of which in a person's in-the-world-ness is most unique. It is with and through that language that one creates, shares, handles, and changes his world, and the power of the metaphor in this enterprise is most unique.

There is a final consideration that we would advance: the reluctance of some to accept the significance of integration in the person's life. To some this thinking appears needlessly monotheistic, too Hebraic, as it were, and not sufficiently polytheistic or Hellenic. Such a position would warn of the dangers of ego-tyranny, a tyranny of consciousness that would exclude or excommunicate from the person's life the many so-called secondary personalities that presumably inhabit one's days, but which are allegedly subjected to an egocentric domination by the integrated consciousness of the person. Such a view is that of James Hillman:

> Each of these dream persons influences the habitual personality
> which we too, as did Jung, call "personality Number One". Number
> One usually rules the day world. Number One is rather responsible,

continuous, and socially recognized; when he looks in the mirror, he sees the same familiar body. The secondary personalities are apt to be fragmentary, intermittent, inconsistent, usually without social sanction. The dream is the mirror where they show themselves, and their bodies have many surprising levels of reality. As Number One, we have one name, one vote, one social security number, even though our complete psychic reality is multiple and may be fragmented. We sense these other persons and call them "roles"—mother, mistress, daughter, witch, crone, nurse, wife, child, nymph, innkeeper, slave, queen, whore, dancer, sibyl, muse. But can there be roles without persons to play them? To call them roles and games is itself a game by which Number One may deny the autonomy of these persons and keep them all under his control. . . .

To define my person by my waking state neglects these figures and their influences. I then become tyrannical, reflecting the jealous monotheism of Number One, who will not recognize the existence of independent partial personalities, and through this denial places them outside in the world, where the internal influences of complexes now become paranoid fears of invasions by enemies. On the one hand, we have individual insanity; on the other, insane collective projections upon other people, whole races and nations. (1975, p. 32)

The danger of tyranny by psychic monotheism that, allegedly, would diminish the human personality by its attempted purge of the individual's "little people," can be offset, in the view of Hillman, not by integrating the personality but by liberating these lesser people to advance their own autonomies and enrich the person with their respective contributions to one's psychic polytheism, polycentricity.

At first glance, then, Hillman's analysis would appear to take serious issue with the attempt to integrate a human personality simply because, as has been clearly stated by Hillman, the integrational process would rob the person of his psychic wealth and potentialities. At second glance, however, it becomes evident that the recommendation of psychic polytheism, the return to Hellenism, the liberation of the "little people who inhabit the life of the individual," is but another, though different, proposal for integration. Elsewhere in his work Hillman concedes this fact:

When the monotheism of consciousness is no longer able to deny the existence of fragmentary autonomous systems and no longer able to deal with our actual psychic state, then there arises the fantasy of returning to Greek polytheism. For the "return to Greece" offers a way of coping when our centers cannot hold and things fall apart. The polytheistic alternative does not set up conflicting opposites between beast and Bethlehem, between chaos and unity; it permits the coexistence of all the psychic fragments and gives them patterns of the imagination of Greek mythology. A "return to Greece" was experience in ancient Rome itself, and in the Italian Renaissance, and in the Romantic psyche during the times of revolution. In recent years it has been an intrinsic part of the lives of such artists and thinkers as Stravinsky, Picasso, Heidegger, Joyce, and Freud. The "return to Greece" is a psychological response to the challenge of breakdown; it offers a model of disintegrated integration. (p. 35)

Beginning with a theoretical metaphor of disintegrated integration psychic polytheism would issue forth in a therapeutic metaphor of integrated disintegration. Whatever the merits of his theoretical metaphor, Hillman's proposal would appear to be a de facto polarization from traditional thought that ends up, however, with a new monotheism all its own. As one author recently put it,

Hillman's effort is directed at correcting what he has seen as the one-way traffic moving out of the unconscious toward the subjectivity of the ego. He, on the other hand, has chosen an about-face—hence his concern with the underworld which is itself a one-way movement. . . .

Hillman has a point to make, but in so doing he by-passes or undermines much that has been a valuable contribution to the contemporary study of consciousness—the psychedelic experience, Oriental psychology, and the occult arts which have impacted significantly on the Renaissance psychology by which he is so much intrigued. Still, his description fits the popularization of New Age ideas, and he puts his finger on the idealized pulse of the New Age. (Marlan, 1981, p. 235)

Having ended this detour on the question of personality integration, then, it remains now to return to the study of the metaphor, a creation that has been entitled the midwife of unification and integration for the human personality, a creation of language that stands, as Edie phrased it, at the pivotal center of the distinction between language as a system and language as speech-act, language as illocutionary and perlocutionary, language as logic and rhetoric. Metaphor does indeed stand at the center, but it should be pointed out that it does not stand there alone. It stands there with language and also with imaginative thought. As it should, for language and imaginative thought are its parents. It would be aesthetically pleasing if we could add that, while language and imaginative thinking are its parents, metaphor's own child is the integrational accomplishment, but one is reminded of the old dictum, *Qui probat nimis probat nihil* (He who proves too much proves nothing). Thus we say that the metaphor, while not able to take credit for all the integrating achievements of humankind, has certainly assisted in true midwife fashion at the birth of many, if not most, of them. In the words of Ricoeur:

> Could we not say therefore that the dynamics of metaphor consists in confusing the established logical boundaries for the sake of detecting new similarities which previous categorization prevented our noticing? In other words, the power of metaphor would be to break through previous categorization and to establish new logical boundaries on the ruins of the preceding ones. If we take this last remark seriously, we may wish to draw the ultimate consequence and say that the dynamics of thought which breaks through previous categorization is the same as the one which generated all classifications. In other words, the figure of speech which we classify as metaphor would be at the origin of all semantic fields. (1973, p. 108)

## B. EVERYMAN'S RECOURSE TO METAPHOR

Words, like everything else human, are characterized by finitude. They have their meaning and their limits: that which they mean and that which they do not mean. That which they mean is their denotation: that which is primarily referred to when the word is employed. And they have their connotation—a whole assortment of connotations, some of which may arise from the culture, some from the situation, some from history, some from the speaker himself, and some from the hearer. Words can generate for a hearer or reader connotations that the speaker or writer never anticipated— maybe even wished to avoid. Connotations indeed are a complex issue, being public in some respects, private in others, and highly idiosyncratic is still others. They attend the denotation, so to speak, giving it a fervor, a flavor, a cast all its own. To phrase it another way, one could say that the denotation is that in the word which gives it light, while the connotations are those accoutrements that give it fire, warmth, emotionality, and passion. And both feature actively in the creation of metaphors. Two people can experience the same denotational thrust of a word, but their connotational experiences may be only partially shared. This is true of a culture, a people as well: words which elicit strong responses in one people may prove less effective in another, and vice versa. Thus the virtues and the limitations of a word come gradually to the fore. The finitude characterizes both the denotation and the connotations: no denotation says everything and no connotations does either. Hence a word, being a gathering-together-of-the-gathered, is necessarily restricted, even at its full and best. It lights up a presence, but in a limited, finite way.

To attempt to restrict a word to its denotative ingredient is to rob it of much significative vitality. In one way this can be considered a restriction that clarifies, but in another equally real sense it can be considered an operation that castrates, devitalizes. At best a word is limited, perspectival; de-connotated, however, its finitude is even further finitized. Such a procedure, undertaken for whatever reason, may have its merits, but it also takes its toll. Interestingly enough, history has provided examples of cultures and languages that have attempted this very process, placing their emphasis more or less exclusively on the denotative dimension of language at the expense of the connotative. Thus the search for clear and distinct ideas that characterized the Cartesian world was permeated with a passion for denotative purity, precision. The period of Romanticism, on the other hand, saw the culture, at least in parts of the Western civilization, take on a decidedly connotative turn. By the same token certain languages are more denotative than others, as, for instance, the languages of chemistry and mathematics. In fact most sciences would pride themselves on their denotative simplicity—deliberately aimed at—abjuring almost with a vehemence the connotative aspects of their own terminology. Thomas Kuhn's book, *The Structure of Scientific Revolutions*, is an intriguing account of what happens when the connotative dimensions of language make their presence felt amid the antiseptic atmosphere of denotative science: a revolution in paradigm is sooner or later inevitable.

Thus even in the purity of univocity, denotative clarity, there is inescapable contamination. It is the fate of living language— precisely because it is living, because it is connotative as well as denotative, because it is finite and beckons towards marginal, horizonal, related dimensions of the object or experience that it denotes, highlights—that it undergoes change, development. It is the fate of living language that it moves from the univocal to the analogous to the equivocal, since it is shot through with connotations and the perspectivalness of denotations that make such transitions and metamorphoses the warp and woof of discourse. In short, words, *les mots, logos,* constitute an extraordinary means for people to take hold of their life, their world, and build it anew or renew, to form or reform, to create or recreate. They are in those words as the words are in people, and with them they can engage anything—even problems relating to God Himself. With those same words they can put themselves and their world together. Yet withal, they are beset by the finitude that is the words' and their lot, and their options are reckoned in the light of that finitude. In an undeniable sense people have their language, and in an equally undeniable sense their language has them. But there is another sense in which both people and their language are had by finitude.

Thus it is that mere words, which make presences present, enable people to preside over the birth of beings, the event of reality, the shining forth of what is, and yet, they are not enough.

A person must go beyond, move beyond, if he hopes to unify sufficiently, to integrate his life. Life is simply too big, too huge, too complex to be parceled out in discrete words, however rich they might be, or, to phrase it differently, to be worded discretely. Science, as was stated above, may try to survive with its denotative simplicity, and psychology as a science may attempt to do the same. Whether they succeed or not is debatable. But no individual person or culture can ever hope to restrict its words, his words to their univocity, much less their pure denotations. Even the least creative of persons is too imaginative to settle for that, and no culture could brook the effort for even a day. The cult that permeates a culture would render the attempt futile. Its complex symbolism would undermine the project from the outset. Meanwhile the individuals in that culture would go on uninterruptedly employing language that resonates with connotations and implications that far transcend the pure denoticity of their discourse. They are capturing far more in their words than their sheer denotations, far more than their connotations, far more than their univocal meanings, far more than the retentions that hearken to the past or the protensions that hint towards the future. Thus they go beyond (μετα; beyond;

Φἐϱειν: move, carry) simple wording and enter into the subtleties, the insinuations, the mysterious, invisible, imaginative possibilities inherent in their attempts to deal adequately with the interrelatedness of the real. Pure words are not enough. Leaps beyond are necessary, for life is so demanding on all sides in every person's struggles. Spouses, children, business, schools, finances, health care and everything else—all raise expectations and clamor for attention or resolution, and no one can afford the luxury of endless compartmentalizations even if one wanted it. The realities of life are all intermeshed—a truth that the seeming autonomy of words might lead one to neglect or at least misread. New and more comprehensive formulations are constantly necessary for us to stay atop the intricacies of life demands. Thus, to move toward the articulations needed for life and to effect some kind of workable synthesis for himself, the person cannot settle for staid, staticized, stenotypic language. Nor does he. He moves beyond it; that is to say, he will of necessity metaphoricize it with a new synthesis, minor though it be, an integration that enables him to make larger sense of more of his life. To be sure—and this point is destined to give us pause—if one moves too far or too drastically or too soon in his or her desperation, making integrations that impress others as extreme or irrational, he risks being labeled a schizophrenic or split mind. Short of that, however, he is not only allowed to move; he is expected to do so.

In his *Selected Essays*, T. S. Eliot remarks,

> When a poet's mind is perfectly equipped for his work it is consistently amalgamating disparate experiences; the ordinary man's experience is chaotic, irregular, fragmentary. The latter falls in love, or reads Spinoza, and these two experiences have nothing to do with each other, or with the noise of the typewriter or the smell of cooking; in the mind of the poet these experiences are already forming new whole. (1932, p. 247)

Such a comment helps one understand better how the imaginative syntheses of the genius and the schizophrenic could possibly be akin. Yet both extremes are operating in a manner with which everyone is well acquainted, even from our earliest days. The genious moves beyond with the exuberance of his fullness; the schizophrenic moves with the desperation of imagined double binds or seemingly insurmountable cleavages; the ordinary person moves in the clear recognition of the need to comprehend more of life and to remain equal to this task. Every person will perforce metaphorize somehow, making new amalgamations of her life settings, sometimes quite effectively, sometimes ineffectively. Thus even to metaphorize the chaos as chaos is to make it less chaotic and make possible a search for greater intelligibility. It is no exaggeration to say that in these movements beyond, these metaphorical unifications and leaps of the person, we find the key to his or her ongoing, experiential, phenomenal world: how he is endeavoring to put together areas of life in various syntheses that another person, to be sure, may deem impressive or, on the contrary, self-defeating, ineffective, wild, illogical, and even irrational. We see how he is amalgamating the disparate that looms up before him; how he is imagining, flooding with lateral thought, the real-for-him; how he or she is attempting to get astride. Metaphors for a person's life are not mere aesthetic indulgences. They are one's lifelines, hope for success, embodiment of any anticipations of arriving intact. Indeed, when a person in life, like the client in therapy, is able to metaphorize his situation genuinely and imaginatively, or remetaphorize it anew, it does in fact open up an understanding, a semantic expansion, and provide one with a clearing, wherein he can get his bearings, steady himself, rest a while, think some things through differently, sketch in broader strokes his upcoming future, and then launch forth into life's thickets a renewed and stronger person.

In everyone's life there are countless aspects and details that strike him, that he brings together in meaningful ways, that he conjoins for highly personal reasons, and he is often hard pressed to say how or why he did so. Should we be blessed at such times with the opportunity of genuine dialogue, we may come to realize in the self-articulation and exchange the manner or style in which we have effected these minor syntheses that we now find ourselves living. So often, however, the ordinary person simply lives his minor totalizations out without fully realizing what and how he is doing so. This is not to say that he is operating unconsciously. He simply does not understand all the angles of his life and how erratic or fortuitous so many of his trial-and-error efforts have been. To be bewildered is not to be unconscious; it is to be confused, uncertain, uninformed, playing hunches. We know much about what we are doing; we just do not truly grasp the strengths or weaknesses of our stumbling through. It is much life our breathing or heartbeat, neither of which we really understand even though we assume them all the time. The fact is that we are putting our life together but in a very amateurish fashion; we know we are putting it together, but do not realize how amateurish the effort. Chances are, in the life of most people, that they never come to appreciate that there are qualitative ways of doing so. Certainly, in the life of most people, they never come to appreciate the significance of the metaphorizations that they are effecting and of the manner in which they are living them out.

The point we are making is that our metaphors are mind-filled, not mindless creations. They are imaginative unifications that have helped us make sense of life and its problems—and for these we often express a sigh of relief and even of gratitude to our parents, our friends, our forefathers, our clergy, our religion, our God, our neighbors, or maybe even just to ourselves for having had the good common sense to take it easy, to set aside a few moments of reflection or prayer somewhere along the path of life, to raise our mind and hearts to the better things, to the grander view, to God. The fact is that thanks to such people in our lives and now to our own new imaginative thinking, we have come to see our *marriage*, for example, not as a trap but as a game or a school for learning or a golden opportunity for personal and interpersonal growth; our *job*, not as an impossible drudgery but as a real blessing in disguise that holds far more promise for us than it did when we viewed it in our former light; our *family*, not as burdens that weigh impossibly upon us but as our greatest treasures and most solid source of genuine strength and purpose; our *trials*, not as cruel ordeals visited upon us by a heartless fate or cruel God but as the darkness of midnight that initiates the beginning of a new day, the ebb of the wave that marks the rise of a new one; our *friend*, our *critics*, and so on. Such is the power of these metaphors in our lives—at a given stage—under given circumstances—with given understandings. To be sure, they too will some day be changed, as they should be, and we will later integrate these respective areas of life anew at another time. For the present, however, these are the metaphorization of marriage, job, family, trials, and so on with which we are languaging our life. For the present they constitute our claim to strength, to soundness, to sanity, to peace and we move ahead into life with the buoyancy that they provide.

To speak of these as mindless or unconscious is simply inadequate. To say that they are ridiculous is not born out by the facts. To pretend that they are all thoroughly and flawlessly thought through would be grandiose and untrue. To say, however, that they are highly imaginative creations, metaphorizations, that are helping us create life anew is as true as God Himself.

## C. The Genius of Metaphor: Its Ingeniousness

That such an accomplishment is possible by the use of metaphor attests to the imaginative genius found in the metaphorical act. On the one hand it has entered the construction of words inasmuch as the words of human language are not unrelated to the person's own living and move the person beyond himself to his world where he finds objects, realities that can be best understood in terms of his own body: like head of government, foot of the hill, arms of the clock, bowels of the earth, and so on. So true is this that there are respectable and serious thinkers who feel that all language was metaphorical in origin and that literal language employed in everyday speech is but the cold discard of the once highly imaginative, metaphorical thinking of the past. Second, the metaphor has played the significant role in the extension of ideas, words, categories as new and imaginative understandings and relationships are brought into being and old categorizations extended in previously unimaginable ways. The imaginative thinking of the metaphor has begotten the plurisignifications of polysemy, thanks to which, as Ricoeur has pointed out, there is now possible an almost infinite use of very finite verbal creations. And finally, it is the imaginative genius of metaphorical thinking that enables a thinker to perceive in differences an element of sameness that allows a deeper appreciation of the unity of beings and the Oneness of Being, fostering greater intelligibility on all sides and unbelievable fecundity in the presumably barren.

To understand this all better, we shall at this point return to chapter two, section C,: Field indeterminacies and the integrating effort. There it was shown that the effecting of personal integration on a greater or lesser scale called for an imaginative synthesis of the perceptual and felt components of one's life: its constituents and their emotional ingredients in some given area or areas of living. And it was especially noted that our consciousness functions in an autochthonous manner, meaning that it tends to structure or organize our experience such as it is. Experience thus shows itself forth as an organizational whole, a field with its theme(s), thematic field(s) and marginal dimensions, all of which are marked by some measure of clarity and a considerable measure of vagueness or ambiguity: indeterminacies, to use the word of Gurwitsch. The theme and its noema are characterized by the greatest degree of clarity. The thematic field is less striking with a measure of vagueness, while that portion of the perceptual field termed marginal is the most vague of all even though it is present, framing the experience and giving its tone to the whole. At the same time each area of the perceptual field has some measure of indeterminacies, features that attend the experience but which fade in comparison with the centeredness of the theme itself, dropping as it were between the cracks of the experience. Even the theme has its limitations, since the noema or specified profile to which one is attending is perspectival, adumbrating the object in a limited way, but providing enough seductive clarity in its perspectivalness to entice the percipient to contemplate the profile and to pursue the beyond, to follow through in reality or in imagination toward other profiles that are there to be had or imaginatively created. Such is the perceptual experience of everyone, an experience that is highly cognitive, highly imaginative, and highly, provocatively affective.

Perhaps this abstract description of the conscious experience could be illustrated with an example. A very thoughtful one can be taken from Heidegger's essay on *The Origin of the Work of Art* in which he meditates on Vincent Van Gogh's painting of a peasant's shoes. Through the eyes of Heidegger one comes to see a very definite theme as well as its field, but also considerations that are certainly marginal, however valuable their presence might be for the particular percipient.

> As long as we only imagine a pair of shoes in general, or simply look the empty, unused shoes as they merely stand there in the picture, we shall never discover what the equipmental being of the equipment in truth is. From Van Gogh's painting we cannot even tell where these shoes stand. There is nothing surrounding this pair of peasant shoes in or to which they might belong—only an undefined space. There are not even clods of soil from the field or the field-path sticking to them, which would at least hint at their use. A pair of peasant shoes and nothing more. And yet—

From the dark opening of the worn insides of the shoes the toilsome tread of the worker stares forth. In the stiffly rugged heaviness of the shoes there is the accumulated tenacity of her slow trudge through the far-spreading and ever-uniform furrows of the field swept by a raw wind. On the leather lie the dampness and richness of the soil. Under the soles slides the loneliness of the fieldpath as evening falls. In the shoes vibrates the silent call of the earth, its quiet gift of the ripening grain and its unexplained self-refusal in the fallow desolation of the wintry field. This equipment is pervaded by uncomplaining worry as to the uncertainty of bread, the wordless joy of having once more withstood want, the trembling before the impending childbed and shivering at the surrounding menace of death. This equipment belongs to the *earth*, and it is protected in the *world* of the peasant woman. From out of this protected belonging the equipment itself rises to its resting-within-itself. (1977, p. 163)

Heidegger's description, of which this is but a short excerpt, speaks eloquently for itself. The shoes are obviously thematic, and the thematic field looms up before one as Heidegger's reflection continues, while off to the margin are many subtleties whose presence makes a difference but whose presence must be divined or simply felt, like as not. The picture includes them all as would a symphony, too, with its theme, and field and marginal riches that are all but forgotten in the hearing, but features whose absence would render the opus quite different. The point is clear enough. Using the thoughtful descriptive analysis of Gurwitsch, then, one comes to understand that in every perception the totality, however perspectival it be as object of our perception, is a richly structured experience; and in every phase of the totality, beginning with the striking and unmistakable major theme of the perception and continuing through to the farthest margin of consciousness during the experience, there are gradients of consciousness in which indeterminacies abound, making their present felt, far less than the preceptual noema of the theme, to be sure, but felt nonetheless.

It is to these indeterminacies, then, that one turns to discover the genius of the metaphorical experience. Obviously thematic dimensions of any and every experience stand forth and call for one's attention, and frequently on the basis of such thematic noemata, or profiles, one can move toward a metaphorical unity of sorts. But such examples of thematic metaphors are obvious and the metaphors arising amid such circumstances, however worthy, often lack the creative power and striking impact to bring into being that unexpected creation that stands, in the words of Ricoeur, at the origin of a sematic field or at an originary formulation of *parole parlante*, truly vital discourse. Such as these find their base less in the purely thematized portion of the perceptual experiences than in the much less thematized, more field or marginal dimensions of the experience. It is here that the secrets of the metaphor are to be found, or, to phrase it more accurately, the secrets of great metaphorical leaps.

These comments should not be misunderstood as a denigration of the many metaphorical creations that spring from the study and recognition of resemblances that obtain among the apparently disparate experiences of life. As will be seen in the following section of this chapter, such resemblances do generate meaningful metaphorical creations in everyday life as well as in art and literature. Rather, we are calling attention to the fact that one does not always find in such metaphorical formulations the magic and genuine ingeniousness that mark the creation of truly great metaphors. The inspiration for the latter originates, not in the obvious resemblances, not even in the patent themes of perception, but more in the profound and subtle indeterminacies with all that cognitive, imaginative, and emotional depth that grace perception and provide it with the powerful explosiveness that distinguishes a truly great metaphor and enables it to effect an incredible fusion analogous to that of hydrogen fusion. Vital metaphors do not necessarily grow out of the experience of thematic sameness amid thematic differences. Often obvious sameness prevents the experience of new perceptual sameness. The reverberations of the indeterminacies, on the other hand, can set off the experience of affinity and identity long before the metaphorical creation is actually and accurately formulated. On occasion one can experience the metaphor before it is formulated, much less explicated. We can imaginatively unite the reverberations prior to the metaphorical formation, much as Wolfgang Amadeus Mozart said that he had imaginatively composed many a symphony or even opera without even hearing a note. When T. S. Eliot spoke about the poet amalgamating the disparate of life, he was speaking less about the disparity of themes as noemata—everyone can more or less do that on occasion—than themes that lie ripening or beckoning in the thematic fields and even margins of consciousness for those who are imaginatively attuned to their possible presence. This would be the domain of the great poets and the great metaphor makers of history.

Herein lies the metaphor's ingeniousness. And once one understands this, then it becomes readily comprehensible why thinkers of the stature of an Albert Einstein would be allowed the time to walk in the woods, idle by the stream, stroll aimlessly at will, not certainly to squeeze out by purely logical deductive processes the implications of a given theorem or argument or formula, but to let happen those imaginative fusions that can occur in great minds once they allow the indeterminacies of countless perceptions to rise up from within their depths while they attend in wonder and awe at the entire transpiration. And we can also understand the great value that every human places on those moments of solitude and contemplation that she or he treasures in some very special corner of the earth, be it a garden, a swing, a chapel, a sunset. In moments such as these we all listen to the calls of the siren, the promptings of the spirit, the Voice of God. And one emerges from such experiences reborn, renewed, uplifted, or quietly calmed. Incipient metaphorizations are taking form and even though all do not see the light of day, some few do, sooner or later. Life then takes on a difference. One does not forget such moments or such places, and there remains a longing to return to them.

> even as the trees
> that whisper round a temple become soon
> Dear as the temple's self, so does the moon,
> The passion poesy, glories infinite,
> Haunt us till they become a cheering light
> Unto our souls, and bound to us so fast,
> That, whether there be shine, or gloom o'ercast
> They always must be with us, or we die.
>
> John Keats, "Endymion"

Amid the power of such an imaginative experience, there is no telling what semantic field may realize its origin, its birth.


## D. THE THEORETICAL CONFLICT SURROUNDING METAPHOR

It was stated previously that the study of metaphor has proliferated in recent years. If in 1927 John Middleton Murray could complain about the paucity and superficiality of discussions on metaphor, the same could hardly be said today. Wayne C. Booth of University of Chicago wagers that the year 1977 saw more titles on metaphor than the entire history of thought produced prior to 1940 (p. 47). Be this as it may, it remains a fact that the last decade has witnessed a growing appreciation of the genuine significance of metaphor, not only in discourse and literature, but in human thought and invention (Gordon, 1961). As one might anticipate, the rebirth of interest has led to a reconsideration of the nature of the metaphorical act, a reconsideration that took great impetus from the work of I. A. Richards and Max Black among others.

## 1. Substitution Theory

Traditionally metaphor has been approached from the viewpoint of rhetoric. The viewpoint, dating back to the time of Aristotle and subsequently developed over the years, saw the metaphor as an artistic device designed to enhance or embellish the aesthetic significance of a word. As Ricoeur has pointed out, it was traditionally considered one of the figures of speech called *tropes* because they proceeded from a deviating use of the meaning of words. Tropes affected just the names and the giving of names. This treatment of metaphor has been termed a substitution theory, for the writer chooses not to use the literal word in its proper sense but to replace it with another word which seems to be more pleasant. Understanding a metaphor, then, requires that we restitute the term which has been substituted. Hence it is easy to understand that these two operations—substitution and restitution—are equivalent. Thus, paraphrasing a given metaphor presents no special difficulties, for the metaphor, seen in this theoretical understanding, offers no new information. It teaches nothing. It is a mere decorative device, with no informative value. Simply adorning language in order to please, it gives color to speech, providing a garment to cover the nudity of common usage. Such, in brief, is the substitution theory of metaphor (Ricoeur, 1973, p. 106).

## 2. Tension Theory

Since the work of I. A. Richards in his *Philosophy of Rhetoric* an entirely new appreciation of metaphor has been developed (1936). If the traditional approach could be termed a substitution theory,

as explained above, the contemporary approach can more properly
be termed a tension theory. Basically it focuses, not on the word
which can be substituted for and eventually restituted, but on the
entire sentence. Thus it sees the metaphor as something that is
contained not in a word, but in the entire sentence, even if the
sentence should perchance contain only one word. In short, in the
tension theory, only a proposition can be considered to be metaphorical, and it is metaphorical principally because it captures a
predication in which inheres a semantic impertinence, a purposeful
creation of a semantic discrepancy. Thus the problem arises as to
the manner in which one can make sense of self-contradictory
statements. Since the semantic impertinence institutes a tension,
described by different theorists in different ways, this ultimately
means that the metaphor enunciates a sameness amid differences.
The heat of the tension, as it were, melts the walls or boundaries of
the previous categorizations and leads them to run into each other,
so to speak. Out of this arises a new sameness hitherto unseen or
even suspected. Thus it can be said in all accuracy that the
metaphor does not settle for the mere substitution of one word for
another, but actually leads to the creation of new information about
the subjects. It is in truth informative, having genuine cognitive
value, and not purely aesthetic. Thus too it can be said to possess a
truth value and have an objective impact. It issues forth in a
redescription of reality. In the words of Ricoeur:

> If this analysis is sound, we should have to say that metaphor not
> only shatters the previous structures of our language, but also the
> previous structures of what we call reality. When we ask whether
> metaphorical language reaches reality, we presuppose that we
> already know what reality is. But if we assume that metaphor
> redescribes reality, we must then assume that this reality as rede-
> scribed is itself novel reality. My conclusion is that the strategy of
> discourse implied in metaphorical language is neither to improve
> communication nor to insure univocity in argumentation, but to
> shatter and to increase our sense of reality by shattering and
> increasing our language. The strategy of metaphor is heuristic
> fiction, for the sake of redescribing reality. With metaphor we
> experience the metamorphosis of both language and reality. (1973,
> p. 111)

As seen by Ricoeur, a threefold paradox permeates the metaphorical experience. That experience, of course, is shot through

with ambiguity, despite whatever clarity may be present in the noematic dimension. Such is the lot of finitude: it begets the clash of perspectives, even to the point of contradiction. That ambiguity, that altercation of perspectives, that vital contradiction are all captured—and preserved—in the paradox of the metaphor. The subtleties of paradox invade the metaphorical atmosphere, in as much as it (the atmosphere) seems to call, on the one hand, for an immediate, direct intuition of likenesses and/or sameness and, on the other, for a discursive, round-about detour that beclouds the issue at hand. Thus Ricoeur sees the paradox occurring on a threefold level: psychological, semantic, and logical. On the psychological level, the new insight begets a new structure that springs out of the collapsing old one. On the semantic level, the subject embraces a predicate that it also repudiates. On the logical level, the sameness and differences inherent in the metaphor remain opposed while joined in their likeness. The tension inevitable in all this centers in the copula, the is, which at the one and the same time is and is not. Thus the metaphor can itself be described metaphorically as a lie that tells the truth, a confusion that clarifies, a detour that puts one directly on the road, a blindness that enables one to see all the better. (Murray, 1975, p. 281)

It is thus apparent that the tension theory, which originated with Richards and has subsequently influenced variant theories, sees the manufactured tension as the quintessential feature, whatever form that tension may take. In some instances it obtains between the subject and its modifier in the sentence, and in others between the subject and its modifier in the phrase (as in Wittgenstein's phrase "logical space"). Something is amiss, awry, and the statement is challengeable if understood literally. Withal, it remains intelligible, thanks to its metaphorical twist.

The discussion thus far makes it clear that the metaphor is much more than a mere decorative device, and that it has indeed—if seen as significant strategy of language—an epistemological and even ontological role to play in the human scheme of things. As the tension theorists point out, however, it can in no way be truly plumbed for its riches if it is seen in isolation from discourse. As such, it partakes of the diacritical features of the sentence as does every word in the discourse. No word in the sentence stands alone; it is part and parcel of the enunciation and must receive its meaning in the context of the whole sentence. Words are chameleons taking on the coloration of their context, and they in turn are transformers, affecting each other in and by their uttering. Thus their meaning emerges, not in the enunciation of each word, much less syllable, but in the unification of the totality, be it the totality of the sentence, the paragraph, the article, or the book. The same is true of the metaphor. It, too, emerges in its meaning from the predication of the sentence, the paragraph, the work. In a very real sense one could even say that the metaphor emerges from the context of the person's life. One metaphorizes as he lives, but he also lives as he metaphorizes. They both belong to his existence-in-the-world. Hence, in addition to its epistemological and ontological role, the metaphor has a decided psychological role to fill in the human life as well.

It would appear from this highly concentrated presentation on metaphorical theory that metaphors may arise from the experience of resemblances in virtue of which one denomination may be substituted for another in true epiphoric fashion; or that they may arise from the experience of contradictions, impertinences, twists in which the tension is unmistakably present in the mutually annihilating predications. This occurs in what Wheelwright has termed diaphoric metaphors. (1968, ch. 4) If so, then it would seem that metaphors can be placed on a continuum ranging from sweet similarities through dissimilarities to sour contradictions, at every stage of which some sameness is perceived, some discrepancy is detected and some tension is felt. The more the similarity, of course, the less the tension, until eventually an identity is proclaimed that leaves the metaphorical element lifeless and buried in what now stands forth as cold literalness. On the other hand, the less the similarity, the greater the tension and the more vital the metaphor. Everyone's life has its share of both and needs even more.

### 3. The Metaphor and Literalness

There is one more approach to this issue that should be pursued before we bring to close this consideration of the theoretical conflict surrounding metaphor: the issue of literalness and its force in the metaphorical creation.

The argument has been made that the preceding attempts to understand some of the theory underlying metaphors are futile efforts to focus on the use and interpretation of metaphors rather than on the primary concern: the experience of metaphors. Were we to forget theory and follow the experience, we would presumably uncover that the secret of the metaphor does not lie in any special metaphorical sense, in any metaphorical twist, in any tension, but rather in the pure literal sense that the word brings to bear on its object. According to this view, the words in metaphor literally signify what their words ordinarily signify, and the speaker's attempt or suggestion is made to have the hearer conceive or imagine something as something else. There is no special metaphorical meaning in any word—much less in the sentence—and no more is meant in the metaphorical use than would be meant in a literal use of the word in question. Thus making a metaphor is admittedly a creative act, but no more so than is the understanding creative. If a metaphor is present in a statement, it is there not because of the words and their meaning but because of the special use to which they have been put. Literalness dominates even in the metaphor and is in fact the source of the metaphorical power. The metaphor shocks one into sitting up and taking notice. Far from there being a definite metaphorical content to be grasped, the metaphor actually has no limit to what it might choose to call to our mind. Hence, to try and say what a metaphor "means" is to try to give limits to something that has none.

Donald Davidson phrases the issue this way:

> What I deny is that metaphor does its work by having a special meaning, a specific cognitive content. . . . The central error about metaphor is most easily attacked when it takes the form of a theory of metaphorical meaning, but behind that theory, and stateable independently, is the thesis that associated with a metaphor is a cognitive content that its author wishes to convey and that the interpreter must grasp if he is to get the message. (1978, p. 41)

This position is substantially that of Yoos, who approaches the matter more phenomenologically, taking issue primarily with the claim of any special metaphorical meaning other than that which is to be found in the ordinary signification of the words. The latter make possible, he contends, that $x$ be imposed on $y$, not that $x$ is like $y$ or *similar to $y$*, but as $y$. Thus a duality is apprehended, and that constitutes the metaphor, for the person experiences two ideas interacting with each other in regard to the same object. There is no tertiary quality in the metaphor, and our interpretations are an afterthought. The metaphor in fact preceded them. Using the same example of Max Black ("The poor are the Negroes of Europe"), Yoos goes on to say,

> We conceive of one thing under the aspect of something else. We think of the poor of Europe *as* Negroes, not *like* Negroes; and in as far as we do so, we are thinking of Negroes under the aspect of the poor of Europe. Of course we can think of the poor of Europe *as like* Negroes but the important point is that this apprehension is different from the apprehension *as* Negroes.

He then contrasts this thinking with the work of Richards and Black:

> This analysis in part corresponds to Richard's and Black's inter-action theory, but it differs in that what is literally expressed as interacting are ideas not secondary connotations or associations of words. What Beardsley's and Black's theories fail to recognize is that metaphors literally signify what their words ordinarily signify. . . . What is literally expressed are the two thoughts brought together in the constitution of one under the aspect of the other. Thus, in the verbal expression of live metaphors, such as in our example, we have two ideas "the poor of Europe" and "Negroes" literally expressed. The subject "the poor of Europe" is constituted under the aspect of "Negroes". We conceive or imagine the poor of Europe as Negroes. Just as in personification when we think of something abstract or inanimate as a person, so in metaphor as in our example we conceive or imagine the poor of Europe as Negroes. Thus, one important essential feature of *live metaphor* is the conceiving imagining of something as something. (1971, p. 78ff)

The views just described cause one to reassess the theoretical dispute currently in vogue on the nature of metaphorical thought. In some ways one could term the position of Davidson, as Max Black himself does, as an update on comparison theory, which is it self a variation of substitution theory. On the other hand, Yoos describes himself as an interactionist, much like Richards and Black. This school of thought, however labeled, is singular in as much as it stresses the literalness of the metaphorical words and denies the so-called metaphorical meaning that the words are supposed to contain. It would appear, however, to be attempting to prove too much. There is no disagreeing with the fact that any use of words in metaphor starts out assuming the awareness of the ordinary literal meaning, and there is no major theorist claiming that words used in a metaphorical remark thereby acquire some new meaning, or that standard literal meanings are lacking. There is no figurative meaning hovering over the words, which is then invoked for the occasion. It remains a fact, however, that words are being used, and seriously so, in situations where the explanatory power of the standard sense is obviously inadequate. In such situations it is imperative that the hearer realize that a special extended sense is being employed by the speaker for whatever purpose.

Thus, while no special figurative meaning is invoked by the hearer, it is most proper and necessary that, when the standard sense of the literalness is obviously inappropriate, the listener imaginatively invokes what the speaker might mean when he speaks metaphorically. There is no special metaphorical sense hovering over, but there is a special meaning that the speaker is giving his words in the context and which his audience attempts to comprehend. Obviously a metaphor says something striking with ordinary, literal words, and hopefully an audience understands it, but inevitably there is in a metaphor a good deal that must be supplied by the reader or audience itself. As Black has pointed out, to say something with suggestive indefiniteness is not to say nothing. Neither, of course, is it to say everything. It says something, starting off a new suggestive train of thought and letting the hearer take over from there. The speaker has taken the literal and gone beyond it; the hearer takes that beyond and in turn goes with or beyond it.

The problem remains as to how in the one predication a statement can be both right and wrong at the same time; and, more remarkably still, everyone knows it. Indeed, one sees in the would-be absurdity an engaging, maybe even profound, statement which in some instances is tantamount to a significant, major breakthrough in human thought.

Black's comments on his own interaction theorizing are sobering:

> In my opinion, the chief weakness of the "interaction" theory, which I still regard as better than its alternatives, is lack of clarification of what it means to say that in metaphor one thing is thought of (or

viewed) *as* another thing. Here, if I am not mistaken, is to be found a prime reason why unregenerate users of appropriate metaphors may properly reject any view that seeks to reduce metaphors to literal statements of the comparisons or the structural analogies which *ground* the metaphorical insight. To think of God *as* love and to take the further step of identifying the two is emphatically to do something more than to *compare* them as merely being alike in certain respects. But what that "something more" is remains tantalizingly elusive: we lack an adequate account of metaphorical thought. (1978, p. 189 ff)

This excursion into metaphorical theory has proven a worthwhile trip, opening up as it did a deeper appreciation of the genuine respect that serious thinkers hold for metaphorical thought, and providing some understanding of the efforts that have been expended in the attempt to understand its intricacies. Obviously one is dealing in the metaphor with a highly imaginative mode of thought, or, to phrase it differently, with a unique mode of imaginative thinking. And it is imaginative to the core. In metaphorical thinking one holds up an object, so to speak, for viewing, fully aware of what it is and of what the literal predicate expresses. One does not focus on the words alone; he focuses on the presences that they effect. Both presences are understood perspectivally, adumbrating their respective objects but by no means saying everything that can be said. Besides that, each object is experienced in a field of consciousness in which the theme, thematic field, and marginal aspects attending the object are all embodied. Indeterminacies abound in all areas. In wording, experiential reverberations are set off, some shared with others, some idiosyncratic. If the respective themes are consonant and more or less congruent in bonafide ways, the magnetism of the resemblance or analogy draws them together, and an epiphoric metaphor is in the making. Even though literally different, they move gracefully toward each other. One predication is unsaid, being suspended, while the second is said, being imaginatively entertained. Thus one knows that life is not a merry-go-round but this remains unsaid, imaginatively suspended; and it is stated that life is a merry-go-round, an imaginatively intriguing predication that the first imaginative suspension allows us to make. If, on the other hand, the respective themes are obviously disparate if not contradictory, their polarization keeps them vigorously apart. Yet the imaginative speaker asks us to suspend judgment again in our imagination and to entertain the possibility imaginatively that these impossibilities are compossible. To be sure, it is risky, tentative, but imaginatively engaging. He moves toward his imaginative predication, and a diaphoric metaphor is now in the making. We see our collapse as our end; he is suggesting that it is our beginning. We see our weakness as our forthcoming demise; he is suggesting that it is actually our strength. At this stage perhaps only the speaker or thinker may see that imaginative possibility; it may take the rest of us years to share his vision. Diaphoric metaphors ask much of our imagination; but because they do, they are challenging, vigorous, and exhilarating.

It is apparent from the foregoing that the metaphor is a unique and significant creation. Yet without the literal (whatever the origin of that literal), there could be no movement beyond, no metaphorization. This is true even when one metaphorizes a metaphor. The president, for example, may well be the head of the government, but, once assuming office, he quickly becomes everyone's target or possible doormat. For this to happen, the first metaphor takes on a certain measure of stability, a certain literalness, if you will, enough at least that one can meaningfully move beyond it and see it in yet another way. There would seem to be no dispensing with the literal aspect of things, with even the remetaphorized metaphor taking on a relative literalness so that new imaginative movement can occur. But the literal is simply not enough. For the metaphor to be created, the imaginative must enter the picture. Now we may employ a base in similarity, contrast, contradiction, or perhaps pure irrelevance, and on that base experience reverberation enough to predicate imaginatively anew. To do this, however, we have imagined a sameness in the differences that others also can imagine, or maybe cannot imagine. Ours may be a metaphor that many can appreciate or few or maybe no one except ourselves.

The entire metaphorical enterprise is shot through with the imaginative and with the literal, but the use of the imaginative transforms the literal. It is characterized by a movement that is centrifugal, a leap outward from a base that is literal or quasi-literal. Being mired in the base, however important that base may be, will not give us the metaphorical. It is the movement beyond that does that.

## E. The Metaphor as Trailblazer, not Window Dressing

In the previous section the observation was made that in a very real sense it could be said that the metaphor emerges from the context of one's life: that one metaphorizes as he lives.

> Have you ever felt yourself between the rocks of Scylla and Charybdis regarding a particular decision? Or attracted to a siren whom you somehow knew would lead you to destruction? Or perhaps some particular experience our of your past is an Achilles heel for you? Such parallels between fable and human experience are often so consistent and widespread that they are assimilated into language as idioms. In one form or another each of us deals daily with Pandora's box, Serpents proffering apples, Sleeping Beauties and Prince Charmings. (Gordon, 1978, p. 7)

The metaphors that one constructs do not come out of nowhere. They spring from one's life, from one's experiences, from one's perceptions, from the indeterminacies that grace one's field of consciousness. They owe much to one's education, one's life challenges, one's learning. They take significant root in our culture, our ethnicity, our religious faith. They are not unrelated to our exposure in life to people of talent, of stature, of quality. They are affected by one's own understanding of literature, of art, of culture, of history. They show the impact of our heroes. In brief, our metaphorizations take root in our life, and the powerful effect of one's life permeates his or her metaphorical creations. These considerations show clearly that all those factors and influences that feed the imagination also feed one's metaphors. This comes as no surprise; it is just as one might expect. We metaphorize as we live.

Conversely, we live as we metaphorize. This is another way of saying that our life shows the powerful influence of our imaginative thinking. It is not necessary here to decide which—the metaphor or living—is the chicken and which the egg. The fact is, it doesn't matter. Both affect both. Our principal point is the easily overlooked fact that the metaphorizations are not mere window dressings in life, niceties of language, verbal facades that we construct about the realities of our everyday existence. If anything is to be learned from the recently increased interest in metaphors, it is the realization that one's imaginative thinking plays a far more significant role in one's life than we have previously realized. It is not dreams that are the royal road to one's consciousness, for dreams are but one kind of imaginative experience. It is imaginative thought itself which calls for study.

Metaphors are especially critical inasmuch as they are an imaginative creation that has to do with one's perceptions, one's consciousness, and one's constituted realities in life. The literal dimensions in metaphors bring a person into close contact with the realities of the everyday world. And the imaginative thinking of the person plays a central role in the creation of new metaphors and the co-constitution of new realities. Thus the study of our metaphors introduces us into vital dimensions of the life that we are living, as well as the expectancies that await us as we live out our metaphors. For we do live them out in one way or another.

Having seen that everyone's recourse to metaphors is a necessary dimension of living, and that our metaphors are not mere aesthetic niceties, but are in fact our lifeline, life raft, bid for survival, hope for success, the embodiment of our anticipations of arriving intact, it begins to become apparent that these imaginative creations are in a real sense one's anticipations of the future. The metaphor is an imaginative leap that enables a person to arrive at a destination, so to speak, even before setting forth. The metaphor cuts a swath or path for the person. It blazes a trail for us, opening up a way of imagining our lives in some sphere or other in a manner that was hitherto unspeakable—unspeakable because it was hitherto unimaginable. Now, however, it is both imaginable and imagined, and one finds oneself already being transported. This by no means infers that one has to deny the reality that one knows, any more than it means that one must predicate that which one knows is untrue. It means rather than one can face up to the harshness of whatever confronts one and imagine it anew. In so doing he can now affirm the hitherto unaffirmable, say the hitherto unsayable, move toward the hitherto unreachable, think the hitherto unthinkable, and begin to do the hitherto undoable. In this way he is staking his claim on a new way of imaginizing, flooding his life with imaginative thinking. It is not that he is living and, while doing so, trying to find a clever word to describe it all. In his imaginative and metaphorical languaging of his life he is laying out the existence that he is or will live.

It is in the light of these realizations that one can aptly say that the metaphor is not the cart of artistic tabs or stickers that one drags through life and periodically places upon some act or other. The metaphors are rather the horse that leads the way, and upon which we ride into the future with all that we possess. The life that opens up and the way that it opens up are the artistic creation of the metaphorical genius that we have brought to bear upon the enterprise. The poet in the person leads the way, and the life that we have to show for our efforts bespeaks the poetic achievement that we have made of it. Once that poetic achievement has sedimented, a way of living is established. Such is the power of the trailblazing metaphor—but such too can be its danger.

Colin Turbayne addressed himself to this matter in his work, *The Myth of Metaphor*, a treatise on the manner in which a metaphor, itself a trailblazer, can become sedimented, stagnating, and imprisoning. As he sees it, there are three main stages in the life of a metaphor: The first is the inappropriate use, or the misuse, of a word giving a thing a name that belongs to something else. The second stage occurs, however, when the once inappropriate name becomes a metaphor. It has its moment of triumph. We accept the metaphor by acquiescing in the make believe. The third stage is the long period when the metaphor is accepted as commonplace. Now it is that the metaphor is no longer recognized as such, but actually dominates thinking as though it were a nonmetaphor. At this stage, says Turbane, it has become a myth, victimizing its inventors:

> Whether I describe these two attitudes as using metaphor and being used by it, or as awareness of metaphor and lack of awareness of it; or whether the metaphor involved is to be called myth, model, fable , or allegory; it is certain that the two attitudes exist. The history of science and philosophy records many instances of both, but many more of the latter. One is the attitude of the Wizard of Oz himself for whom "The Emerald City" is but a name and the green glasses but a color screen to heighten the make-believe. The other is the attitude of his duped subjects for whom the Emerald City is really green. Forgetful of their green glasses, they believe they contemplate nothing but the un-made-up face of the truth. While, on the one hand, the use of metaphor to illuminate dark areas—the price of which us is constant vigilance—is not to confuse a device of procedure with elements of the process, on the other hand, being used by metaphor involves the addition to the process of features of proce-

dure that are the products of invention or speculation. The victim of metaphor accepts the way of sorting or bundling or allocating the facts as the only way to sort, bundle, or allocate them. The victim not only has a special view of the world but regards it as the only view, or rather, he confuses a special view of the world with the world. (1962/1970, p. 24ff)

That Turbayne is highlighting a real danger cannot be denied. He illustrates the truth from the history of science, citing the cases of Descartes and Newton in particular, both of whom were physicists and philosophers of science as well. It could be illustrated from other areas of study also, particularly that of anthropology. Cultural stereotypes are a classic example in which ethnic or cultural typifications are no longer realized for what they are: imagined styles of existence established by a people but now assumed to be nature's dictates. One can be victimized by his own metaphors, as can an entire people.

The most significant aspect of this truth, however, is not the victimization as much as the power of the metaphor in the person's or the people's tradition. That the kind of formulation makes a difference, that the anticipations inherent in the metaphor have their effect, that the expectations toward the future awakened by the metaphor espoused will vary accordingly—these are the critical realizations so germane for our present work. It is not a case of the metaphor serving as mere window dressing. It is not a matter of the metaphor coming along for the ride in the cart. It is not a question of just substituting one label for another. It is indeed quite different. The metaphor trailblazes for the person or the people. It provides the stamina for the enterprise, or the alteration sought. It is the imaginative projection in a given area of life and as such it puts its stamp or mark on the entire effort. Tradition is the explanation given to any inquiry, and tradition it is. But that tradition is not the genetic achievement so many might think it is. It is rather the metaphorical triumph of a people that is now long hallowed and henceforth imagined as unchangeable. Only a prophetic voice could intervene now. And if it did, it would have to convince others that a new metaphorization is possible. Even then, it would remain a formidable task to persuade others to allow sufficient time for the new metaphor to work its own wonders. Metaphors are not quickly abandoned.

F. AFTERTHOUGHTS

### CLIMB DOWN, O LORDLY MIND

Climb down, O lordly mind.
O eagle of the mind, alas, you are more like a buzzard.

Come down now, from your pre-eminence, O mind, O lofty spirit!
Your hour has struck
your unique day is over.
Absolutism is finished, in the human consciousness too.

A man is many things, he is not only a mind.
But in his consciousness, he is two-fold at least:
he is cerebral, intellectual, mental, spiritual,
but also he is instinctive, intuitive, and in touch.
The mind, that needs to know all things
must needs at last come to know its own limits,
even its own nullity, beyond a certain point.

Know thyself, and that thou art mortal,
and therefore, that thou art forever unknowable;
the mind can never reach thee.

Thou art like the moon,
and the white mind shines on one side of thee
but the other side is dark forever,

and the dark moon draws the tides also.

Thou art like the day
but thou art also like the night,
and thy darkness is forever invisible,
for the strongest light throws also the darkest shadow.

The blood knows in darkness, and forever dark,
in touch, by intuition, instinctively.
The blood also knows religiously,
and of this the mind is incapable.
The mind is non-religious.

To my dark heart, gods *are*.
In my dark heart, love is and is not.

But to my white mind
gods and love alike are but an idea,
a kind of fiction.

Man is an alternating consciousness.
Man is an alternating consciousness.

Only that exists which exists in my own consciousness.
Cogito, ergo sum.
Only that exists which exists dynamically and un
    mentalized, in my blood.

Non cogito, ergo sum.
I am, I do not think I am.

D. H. Lawrence

We are accustomed to considering logical thought as that kind of thinking most characteristic of the human we are, of the human at its finest. Only in the realm of clear and rational thought do we meet the unique human quality that is our mark. Such a position, as we have seen, is highly prejudiced and misleading. It takes no cognizance of the primacy that is everywhere enjoyed on the human level by the poetic, the imaginative, the analogical, the emotive, the whimsical, the affective. It is bewildered, if not frightened, by the cogency of desire, if for no other reason than that the latter will not honor the niceties of distinctions or respect the confinement of categories. It seems unaware that the reflective and the ultracognitive are themselves abstractive achievements, and can make the valuable contributions they do only when those contributions are embedded in a context that is comprised of many human components other than the purely logical. Freud pointed this out in dramatic fashion, but the same basic lesson was taught by Vico. As he saw it, the human being enters into intercourse with life not only on the rational level; he enters into an understanding of life on a level that is at once sensible without being brutish, and intellectual without being angelic.

*Homo intelligendo fit omnia* (Man by knowing becomes all things) was transformed by Vico into *Homo non intelligendo fit omnia* (Man by his unknowing becomes all things) for the simple reason that he saw human beings giving birth to meaning on a primordial level that was actually earthy and imaginative, not abstract and conceptual, but for all that not a whit less human or profound. Thus the recourse to metaphor that characterizes human thought is no coincidence.

> The mind, that needs to know all things
> must needs at last come to know its own limits,
> even its own nullity, beyond a certain point.

Turning as we do to the metaphor in an effort to effect and to communicate experiences is as natural to us as our breathing. And turning as we do to the metaphor in an effort to understand our experience is likewise natural. But turning to the metaphor in an effort to open up, to allow, to experience in anticipation by unique unifications and integrations—this is our genius. The dark moon that draws the tides, the black night that speaks of the brilliant sun, the ignorant heart that knows of gods and love are metaphorical disclosures about the mysteries of being human that can escape us in our concentrated studies. But these metaphors that move human beings toward experiences of disclosure and unity at both the cognitive and affective levels of our being deserve to be taken seriously. By his own admission Ricoeur is convinced that the metaphor lies at the origin of all semantic fields. This speaks for the power of the metaphor in the realm of human living and study, and brings to light a deeper understanding of nature's interrelatedness. Holderlin, too, while acknowledging meritorious human achievements on earth, insists that the truly human sojourn is not only one full of merit but also replete with the poetic. Here is lauded the power that the poetic wields in the realm of the *lebenswelt*, the lived world. To capture the human experience by focusing on humankind's objective achievements is an engaging enterprise, but, left to itself, it is destined to fall short. If it does not allow for the poetic and the analogical in people, this effort will miss that which is most distinctly human in it all. For even the most prosaic of moments, when experienced in life, is somehow being imaginatively touched at the same time. And when the imaginative is there, can the metaphor be far behind?

# CHAPTER V

# Symbols: Multum in Parvo

A T the beginning of the previous chapter it was stated that the metaphorical aspect of language was one of, and perhaps the most, perplexing and intractable questions in the whole of the philosophy of language. The study presented in that chapter indicated why this was the case, and how our understanding of the metaphor has advanced slowly over the centuries, as has the study of imagination. The same, however, cannot be said in the same way about the symbol. It has received more than its share of attention, but, paradoxically enough, our understanding of it still leaves much to be desired. Moreover in some circles, up to recent years, the symbol has been held somewhat suspect. While appreciated and used considerably by Protestant scholars, it was given only diminished attention by Catholic thinkers, who saw the symbol as a possible vehicle for explaining away dogmatic formulations. Protestant thinkers, on the other hand, held at bay the Catholic enthusiasm for analogy, a device that they in turn questioned as misleading. Today, of course, with the renewed focus on language study, this situation has changed considerably, and both Catholic and Protestant scholars are engaged in the study of the symbol as well as the analogy (MacQuarrie, 1967, p. 214).

## A. SYMBOLS AND SYMBOLS

### 1. The Proliferation of Symbols

In his work *Interpretation Theory* Paul Ricoeur pointed out some of the problems attending the study of the double meaning inherent in

---

*Multum in Parvo:* Much in a little.

symbols. He indicated, for example, that symbols belong to too many and too diverse fields of research. He himself had considered three such fields in his earlier writings: Psychoanalysis, with its treatment of symptoms, dreams, and cultural objects; poetics, in the broad sense of the term, which sees symptoms as images of a poem, or images that dominated the work of an author, or school or culture; and finally the history of religion, as illustrated by the work of Mircea Eliade, who deems such concrete entities as trees, labyrinths, and mountains as symbols insofar as they represent space, flight or transcendence, and point beyond themselves to something wholly other. In essence, the problem, as Ricoeur sees it, is scattered over many fields of research and so divided among them that it tends to become lost in the process. (1976, p. 53)

One need only study the many analyses of symbol to grasp the truth of these comments. To many, the symbol is something that stands for something else. According to this school of thought, a word is representative of a concept, and is thus its symbolic expression. At the same time the word stands for the thing that it designates and can thus be called its symbol. The thing itself, if it be a red traffic light, or a red lantern, symbolizes the halting of traffic that the street intersection demands or the danger that lies behind a barracade. Any and all of these are symbolic creations. By the same token a flag symbolizes a country, or a stamped seal the institution that employs the seal on its stationary. Or a phrase, such as John Donne's "No man is an island" becomes a philosophical symbol for the human condition, much as a crown or tiara symbolizes royalty, or the White House the presidency. Examples abound on all sides—all illustrating the same thesis: that a symbol is something that stands for something else.

These symbols are built into the human situation. Suzanne Langer has phrased it well:

> Most of our words are not signs in the sense of signals. They are used to talk *about* things, not to direct our eyes and ears and noses toward them. Instead of announcers of things, they are reminders. They have been called "substitute signs," for in our present experience they take the place of things that we have perceived in the past, or even that we can merely imagine by combining memories, things that *might* be in past or future experience. Of course such "signs" do not usually serve as vicarious stimuli to actions that would be appropriate to their meanings; where the objects are quite normally

not present, that would result in a complete chaos of behavior. They serve, rather, to let us develop a characteristic attitude towards objects *in absentia*, which is called "thinking of" or "referring to" what is not here. "Signs" used in this capacity are not *symptoms* of things, but *symbols*. (1942/1951, p. 37)

Already, it should be noted, our discussion has made reference to symbols, to analogies, to signs, to signals. The list continues, when we turn to the natural sciences or to mathematics; to their nomenclature, formulae, abbreviations, operations. If one introduces then the world of the computer into our discussion, a host of new symbols and symbolic transformations is now at our fingertips. It is apparent that symbols do indeed belong to too many and to too diverse fields of research, and the problem of symbols does tend to become lost.

If, in the midst of these efforts to decipher our understanding of symbols, we now turn to the field of anthropology and sociology, to say nothing of political science, an entirely new world awaits our finding. The world of the ritual, the taboo, the magical—symbolic gestures and values all—awaits our exploration. The world of ceremony, sacrifices, aspersions, cleansing, blessings, healings is there to be studied. The significance of human work, creations, buildings, arts, music remains to be explicated. It is the same with the field of economics and of government, bureaucracy, and legalism in the courtroom, and all the intricacies of the business world. At every turn humankind finds itself engaged in pursuits that are highly symbolized, whose development in turn is intimately connected with the kind and quality of the symbolization that is employed. At all levels of human existence there are its happenings: events that are taking place effecting social change and affecting human history.

It would appear from what has been mentioned thus far that human beings are truly an *animal symbolicum*, beings that live and die, succeed and fail, delight and suffer, work and play, with, by and through their symbols. Indeed it is impossible to conceive of the human individual or a human society surviving without such symbols sustaining it. And sustain they do, for with our symbols we humans not only create our world, but create ourselves in the same process. We not only find ourselves always already in a world, but also establish ourselves, find our place, in that world that has been of our making. Change—social change and symbolic change—is inevitable in this process; it is at the heart of our becoming. And symbols, old and new, are needed at every turn. Without them everything would grind to a halt. Putting a new world together, for a society as for the individual, calls for new images and new symbolism.

## 2. Toward a Clarification of the Notion of Symbols

The need to clarify the notion of symbol is evident. It lies at the heart of so much that is human that a clearer understanding of its nature is paramount. And to hope to understand the manner in which the symbol is employed by human beings in their efforts to integrate their lives makes that clarification doubly necessary.

While various authors have made attempts to classify the various kinds of symbols, few have seriously sought to explicate its structure. Suzanne Langer's work was a significant move in that direction. Her *Philosophy in a New Key* acknowledged the power with which the symbol had become invested, particularly in the field of mathematics. Having pointed out that the edifice of human knowledge stands before us as a structure of facts that are symbols and laws that are their meanings, the cue to which is the power of symbols just as the cue to a former era was the finality of sense data, she states that a new key note has been struck not only in philosophy, but especially in two main technical fields, thanks to the discovery of the all-importance of symbol using and symbol reading. These fields are widely separate with problems and procedures that do not seem to belong together—yet they do. Those fields are modern psychology and modern logic. In her words:

> One conception of symbolism leads to logic, and meets the new problems in theory of knowledge; and so it inspired an evaluation of science and a quest for certainty. The other takes us in the opposite direction—to psychiatry, the study of emotions, religion, fantasy, and everything but knowledge. Yet in both we have a central theme: the *human response*, as a constructive, not a passive thing. Epistemologists and psychologists agree that symbolization is the key to that constructive process, though they may be ready to kill each other over the issue of what a symbol is and how it functions. One studies the structure of science, the other of dreams; each has its own assumptions—that is all they are—regarding the nature of symbolism itself. (p. 29)

Langer's reference to a symbolism that leads to psychiatry, the study of emotions, religion, fantasy, and so on is a reference to that symbolism that characterizes human living in the *lebenswelt*. This is a symbolism that is beset by plurisignification, multiple meanings, concentrated references, and not by the artificiality of logical symbols which can be written and read but not spoken. It is the symbolism of orality, spoken symbolism, that dominates the daily life of us all and calls for the clarification of which we have spoken.

Ricoeur's analysis of the controversy surrounding the definition of oral symbolism, found in his work, *Freud and Philosophy: An Essay on Interpretation* (1970), is extremely helpful. He distinguishes two positions on the matter, one of which favors a broad definition of symbol and the other of which adopts a narrow definiton. The former, first formulated by Cassirer in his *Philosophy of Symbolic Forms*, see symbolism as the mediating function between the mind and reality. Symbols, in this view, would apply to all those cultural instruments involved in our apprehension of reality: religion, language, science, art. All discourse and perception are conducted in terms of these symbolic forms. In brief, it would appear that symbol in this sense would be as broad and extensive as culture and reality. In Ricoeur's view, however, these mediating functions and forms might more happily be described as signs or signifying functions. Such a notion can do justice to that which Cassirer intended and at the same time preserve that singular element or characteristic which uniquely features the symbol: its duality of meanings, its plurality of meanings. Many signs and cultural creations do not have such a uniqueness, but every symbol does. The latter have both a direct meaning and an indirect one that is revealed in and through the direct meaning. Thus to speak of these as mere signs is to lose that feature which differentiates the symbol from the many other kinds of signs that do not possess it. In short, Cassirer's definition is much too broad and actually endangers the distinction between univocity and plurivocity that is at the heart of the symbol itself. We would speak of the symbol as a sign of a special kind: a sign that features a duality of meanings in a unique structure.

At the other end of the spectrum from Cassirer, as Ricoeur's analysis sees it, is a school of thought that understands the symbol in a very restricted, narrow sense. According to it, the symbol would link meaning to meaning, the direct meaning to the indirect, but it would limit itself to those that are related by analogy. Thus one could speak of the symbolic meaning of the heavens in reference to infinity and base the symbol on the analogy of endlessness that befits them both. So too any other sign could be called such, once there was established an analogical base for the designation. Unfortunately there are many other signs that admit of a duality of meaning—hence would qualify as genuine symbols—the interpretation of which is not based on analogy. This can be found in the interpretation of dreams, for example, where the latent and manifest content of the dream may be constituted, not on an analogy, but on some other foundation, such as distortion. In these cases the manifest content of the dream is properly considered a symbol of the latent content which it has distorted, but not analogized. Hence, if we were to restrict the concept of symbol to meanings that are linked only by way of an analogy, there would be many instances of genuine symbolic duality of meanings left aside. The position, in brief, in contrast to that of Cassirer, is much too narrow. It would appear, then, that the richest concept of all requires that we limit the concept of Cassirer on the one hand and widen the concept of symbolism based solely on analogy on the other.

Having sketched out these two extreme positions in regard to the notion of symbol, Ricoeur suggests a possible clarification, limiting the notion of symbol to the specificity of interpretation. As he sees it, then, a symbol would exist, where linguistic expression lends itself by its double or multiple meanings to a work of interpretation (p. 18). This view would thus see in the symbol an architecture of meaning, in which meaning is built to meaning, is built to meaning, is built to meaning, and the structure is such that an interpretation, or hermeneutic, must be performed in virtue of which the second or third meaning are related to the first or primary meaning, whether that interpretation be based on analogy or not, whether the first meaning reveals (as in analogy) or disguises (as in distortion) the second and subsequent meanings. Thus a circle, which in its primary meaning is a figure all points on whose circumference remain equidistant from the center, is often considered as a symbol for eternity—this on the basis of its having neither beginning nor end. Hence it is this texture, which becomes clear in the process of interpretation, that makes the interpretation possible in the first place. Thus it is evident that this analysis has protected the

uniqueness of the symbol (its duality of meanings, its plurisignification) while recognizing that the plurisignification may be
founded on bases that include but are not limited to mere analogy.

There is a final aspect of the symbolic structure that Ricoeur has
highlighted in a later work, *Interpretation Theory* (1976). He sees in
the symbol, not only the semantic dimension about which we have
been speaking thus far, but also a nonsemantic dimension, in as
much as the symbol always seems to cry out for some kind of bind
or tie to the cosmic, to the earthy, to the biological. One sees this in
the symbolism of the poet whose powerful moodedness permeates
his creation with feelings and affect that serve to disclose new
understandings of human existence. We see it in the study of
religions where the symbols capture an entire dimension of existence, and the numinous and the sacred are ritualistically encountered in truly experiential ways. We see it in the domain of the
psychological where symbolic experiences can be seen overcoming,
permeating, mesmerizing the βιοσ, the bios in humans whose
imaginative experience of the logos of their symbols becomes for
them an awesome moment. These nonsemantic aspects of the
symbol provide it with a further uniqueness that merits more
consideration than we shall give it at this time. In brief, the symbol
would appear to be distinguished by a semantic duality that links
primary meaning to secondary meaning and a nonsemantic duality
that links language (logos) in a highly imaginative way to their
cosmic and earthy self (their βιος, their bios).

## B. DEPTH SYMBOLS

### 1. *Grades of Comprehension among Symbols*

Having explored somewhat the problem of clarification that was
necessitated by the proliferation of symbols in almost every conceivable field and arrived at an understanding of symbols that are
distinguished, on the one hand, from the plurality of signs that
abound everywhere and, on the other, from the exclusivity of
analogous symbolization, we have prepared ourselves for a more
profound reflection on the symbol as it is experienced at the deeper
levels of our living. Such a reflection is needed if we are to appreciate the manner in which the symbol exerts its presence at the more
profound reaches of the personality. The fact is, that among genu-

ine symbols there is a gradient, so to speak. That is to say, that they exhibit a gradation, different levels of impact, on the personal functioning of the individual. Some symbols are immediately apparent, some much less so. Some can be discerned in the imaginative complex of life only in stages. For all that, their impact is no less; on the contrary, it can be far greater, but the contextualization of the symbol obscures it from our focused awareness and its presence and power are only slowly detected.

In his work, *Metaphor and Reality*(1968), Wheelwright speaks to the various levels at which the symbol can be discerned. He refers to these levels as main grades of comprehensiveness, or breadth of appeal. In his analysis he would distinguish five such grades:

1. The grade at which a symbol functions as the presiding image of a single poem. In such an instance the symbol would emerge from a given poem as the dominant image that bestows a certain cohesiveness to the work. One such example that Wheelwright cites with fondness is Hart Crane's "Brooklyn Bridge", which impacts powerfully upon the poet's work.

2. The stage at which a symbol manifests its strong personal appeal to the author—one that he or she has invested with considerable personal value. Here he would speak of symbols that obviously hold significant meaning for the poet throughout many of his writings. Such a symbol possesses what Wheelwright calls a continuing vitality and relevance for a poet's imagination and perhaps even his actual life. Hence it may be expected to crop up from time to time in his writings. His example is Crane's penchant for the Atlantis symbol. He could just as easily have cited examples from the work of D. H. Lawrence and others.

3. This stage would include symbols of ancestral or traditional vitality. In this instance Wheelwright refers to those particular symbols that have appealed to various authors over time and which are subsequently employed precisely because they do wield a unique power by virtue of their overlapping history. His examples include the harlot as she appears in "The Waste Land" of T. S. Eliot and before him in the "Cleopatra" of Shakespeare; the chess game as it figures in "The Waste Land" and in Act V of *The Tempest*. A third example is the cock which commands such attention in "The Waste Land", in Kyd's "Cornelia", in sacred scripture at the time of Christ's trial, and elsewhere. Such symbols are singular and have a significance that is inescapable. They carry

with them their unique cast and they emerge, submerge, and emerge again and again over the centuries.

4. These are symbols of cultural range. They are images that permeate an entire culture or community or people. Wheelwright cites some of those found in Eliot's *Four Quartets*: the wounded surgeon, the dying nurse, the dripping blood, the dove. He also mentions many of the shared symbolic materials found in the Bible, Christian poetry, the New Testament: the door, the vine, the word, bread and wine. Such symbols transcend the individual poem as well as the author. They transcend too their own unique history. They are of a social tradition, a society, or community, and they speak of and to that tradition in unmistakable ways. Obviously such symbols would be empowered to effect transformations in the individual or the community that can be attributed, not merely to their own uniqueness, but just as well to the reverberations that the tradition bequeathes ‚them, and to the contextualization that the particular community has provided for their experience. They are of a cultural range, to use his phrase.

5. The archetypal symbols, or archetypes. Such are symbols that have an identical or similar meaning for a large part of humankind. Here Wheelwright speaks to the symbolic meaning and power that accrue to such meanings as up or down, water, earth, light, circle, center. Symbols such as these have a tremendous appeal and speak to people all over the globe. No nation is without some version of them, no people is totally beyond them, no individual is completely untouched by them in some way. To be sure, different people and different symbols are found together—a people has its own variation—but the general theme is discernible in some way almost everywhere. As Wheelwright has put it:

> Like many other archetypal symbol the Wheel is potentially ambivalent. It may have either a positive or a negative significance, and occasionally both. Negatively the Wheel can symbolize in the West the hazardous play of fortune, and in the East the persistent cycle of deaths and rebirths from which release is sought. . . . In Tibet the idea of the perfection and sincerity of universal law can be symbolized by so simple a gesture as joining the thumb with the middle finger. The Tibetan prayer wheel had originally the same meaning, and perhaps still retains it for informed worshipers, despite the crude magical uses to which it has later been put. (p. 110)

Each people has its own way of capturing the symbol and thus enabling it to speak to the community, to inspire the community, to bring about the community's rebirth. But withal, the symbol in some form is found to be there—simply because it has a basic simplicity that cannot but stir the imaginative thought of everyone. These are the archetypes made so famous through the writings of Carl Jung.

Wheelwright concludes his analysis of symbols with a profound passage:

> Thought is not possible to any significant degree without language, nor language without metaphoric activity whether open or concealed; the stabilization of certain metaphors into tensive symbols is a natural phase of the process. While any given symbol—the Cross, or the Flag, or the Divine Father, or the act of genuflection—can be examined skeptically and can be rejected as outworn, or as superfluous, or an involving idea and attitudes to which the critic is antipathetic, a rejection of all symbols would be, in the last resort, a rejection of language and thought themselves. When a straightforward thinker sets out to free himself from symbolic and metaphorical thinking, what he actually means to do is limit himself to those symbols and rigidified metaphors which have become habitual stereotypes in everyday life. This issue is not between symbolic and non-symbolic thinking, but between limiting one's thought and sensitivities to the plain meanings denoted by conventional symbols and learning to think with a more tensive alertness (p. 126)

This analysis of Wheelwright provides us, as it were, a handle with which to grasp this complex field. It is apparent that imaginative thinking is present throughout the whole of human existence, serving at once to enrich the human perceptions, to provide verve and vitality to human logical operation, and to illuminate with its own new articulations the human experience of existence. In his study he has shown that in the imaginative thought that we described as symbolic we bequeath to a work, to our personal existence, to our community living, to our basic being-in-the-world, a depth, a quality, a capacity that no other kind of thinking can equal or surpass. At times, obviously, it is more fleeting than at others—more on the superficies or surface of life—and this can be expected. It is no putdown; it is simply the truth that the reverberations of imaginative thought at some levels and in some areas are less momentous than at others, but they remain valuable just for what they are and the ambience, the unique ambience, that they supply. At other times such thought, such imaginative symbolism, can be far more profound, touching deeper reaches of our existence, and resonating with experiences that have had and still do have far greater significance for us as individuals or us as a people. At these times we seem to find ourselves caught up in truly basic dimensions of life that seem to echo in our very psychic basements.

Such is the power of the symbol at whatever level or manner in which it may appear. To phrase it another way, such is our humanly imaginative way of bringing life together and furnishing it with an affective tone and resonance that redound to ourselves in such a way that our experience is truly stabilizing and wondrous: symbolic in the finest sense of the word.

Let us pause here to consider a poem by Robert Frost, an example that we might at first glance be prone to place in Wheelwright's first category. Thoughtful reflection, however, will soon convince us that it belongs at least in the third or fourth—and maybe even in the fifth—category, so deep is the depth of its utterance.

MENDING WALL

Something there is that doesn't love a wall,
That sends the frozen ground-swell under it,
And spills the upper boulders in the sun;
And makes gaps even two can pass abreast.
The work of hunters is another thing:
I have come after them and made repair
Where they have left not one stone on a stone,
But they would have the rabbit out of hiding,
To please the yelping dogs. The gaps I mean,
No one has seen them made or heard them made,
But at spring mending-time we find them there.
I let my neighbor know beyond the hill;
And on a day we meet to walk the line
And set the wall between us once again.
We keep the wall between us as we go.
To each the boulders that have fallen to each.
And some are loaves and some so nearly balls
We have to use a spell to make them balance:
"Stay where you are until our backs are turned!"

We wear our fingers rough with handling them.
Oh, just another kind of outdoor game
one on a side. It comes to little more:
There where it is we do not need the wall:
He is all pine and I am apple orchard.
My apple trees will never get across
And eat the cones under his pines, I tell him.
He only says, "Good fences make good neighbors."
Spring is the mischief in me, and I wonder
If I could put a notion in his head:
"Why do they make good neighbors? Isn't it
Where there are cows: But here there are no cows.
Before I built a wall I'd ask to know
What I was walling in or walling out,
And to whom I was like to give offense.
Something there is that doesn't love a wall
That wants it down." I could say "Elves" to him,
But it's not elves exactly, and I'd rather
He said it for himself, I see him there
Bringing a stone grasped firmly by the top
In each hand, like an old stone-savage armed.
He moves in darkness as it seems to me,
Not of woods only and the shade of trees.
He will not go behind his father's saying,
And he likes having thought of it so well
He says again, "Good fences make good neighbors."

Robert Frost

This is an excellent example of a work whose primary meaning is quite clear, but whose secondary meanings, springing from the first, far eclipse the first and so dominate our attention that the wall itself becomes insignificant. We see Frost trying to convince us that Nature itself is working to get rid of it, quietly but inevitably and constantly. Every year Nature intervenes: the gaps are there. But the two men start over to erect the barricade. Much care and effort are invested in the operation, and both cooperate meticulously in furthering their mutual isolation. It is as though they were seeking to bury each other, so that both might live happily ever after. Then we see Frost marshalling his arguments and pleading for his neighbor's companionship. All, of course, to no avail, as they continue on their course. Finally, Frost shakes his head in disbelief and realizes that his neighbor is imagining his life just as his father had imagined it before him. Frost despairs at the darkness of thought that has engulfed the man. And indeed Frost's only consolation at this point is the realization that Nature somehow agrees with him. Someday, he says to himself, we may come to realize what we mean to each other and how our annual cooperative venture is actually keeping us apart.

The wall, which quickly has become not a wall but an entire philosophical position, permeates the entire poem. It makes us laugh, it makes us sad, it makes us want to cry, it makes us shout out loud, it makes us pensive, it makes us hope almost against hope. And yet it is not the wall at all; it is the entire understanding of the human condition with which we are confronted. In every line it weaves in and out, and yet it never obscures our vision of what the poet is trying to say. And its message, once we see it, will never leave us. We shall be quoting it time and time again, just as we experience its truth in life over and over again. Such is the power of the symbol—in this case, that of the mending wall. And such is the way a symbol makes its presence felt in a given work and then spills over into our lives.

At this point we are ready to resume our reflection on the depth symbols and their power in life. It should be pointed out that the classification of symbols that Wheelwright advanced should not be interpreted rigidly. Even in his own analysis, he warns that a given symbol may function differently in different contexts, and at time thus come to have more power, force, breadth, and depth than at other times. Even the distinction between live and dead symbols, as live and dead metaphors, must be taken with a certain measure of flexibility. A so-called dead metaphor may indeed be so over-worked by everyone that it deserves to be called dead (as the foot of the mountain). Yet to a given person at a given moment in her life, that dead metaphor could come very much alive. The same is true of the symbol. The flag erected by the soldier on Iwo Jima was not the same flag that they had seen at home when they were school-boys. It was, of course, but then it was not. At Iwo Jima it had all the reverberations of the truly sacred. Thus, while we can and must make distinctions as did Wheelwright in the interest of furthering our understandings of symbols, it must be kept in mind that a given symbol can be experienced now at this level and later at another one. Hence the reflections on depth symbols, which at first glance appear to apply to symbols of the fifth, fourth, and maybe the third category, may in fact apply to any of them at a given moment, since any symbol under unique circumstances can function with the power of an archetype.

## 2. *Pursuing our Reflection on Symbolic Depth*

*a. Horizontally expansive, vertically rooted.* There is something of a paradox in the symbol. We have suggested by our title of this chapter, Multum in Parvo, that the symbol is much in a little. This is to say that in the symbol we can expect to find many dimensions where we might normally expect to find none. There is no special reason why, in a given symbol, that it should take on these dimensions. A hill is a hill, a cloud a cloud, a wall a wall, a homestead a homestead. That they should be what they are is reason enough for rejoicing. When such becomes a symbol, however, it takes on a horizontal expanse and a vertical depth that were simply unanticipated.

When we pause to consider what is happening when the symbol is symbolized, we should expect some kind of imaginative transformation. The symbol is, after all, an imaginative creation and it is impossible to say what that symbol will encompass once the transformation begins. It may taper off quickly, to be sure, but may very well undergo continuous or at least continued expanse. The second meaning given to the first meaning may itself be imaginatively embellished by a third. That is to say that the symbolic meaning given to an object may itself undergo in time further symbolic transformation. In such an instance the first meaning comes to support not only a second, but also a third and perhaps a fourth. The circle, for instance, may symbolize eternity or maybe the sun in the heavens. The sun in its warmth may symbolize life, growth, sustenace, and joy. The endlessness of the circle, the eternity that knows neither beginning nor end, may symbolize before long the omnipotence and power of the gods. And thus in time, a new network of meanings can grow in the imagination of a person or a people, and the circle ere long means ever so much to the community. To build its churches in the round; to introduce the circle into its ritual or liturgy; to build the concept into its music; to employ the circle as an artistic embellishment—these and countless other appointments of life might well capture in a living way the basic symbolism that is identified with the original meaning. One cannot hope to ever exhaust the fullness of the horizontal expanse that even the most unassuming of symbols may conceivably entail. Of course, one need not compulsively do so either, settling for some less than exhaustive understanding of the horizontal expanse; but one can respect the many possibilities that lie within the image.

By the same token the symbol takes on a depth, some more so than others, but all taking on some. This would mean, then, that the symbol in its imaginative largess could dig deeply into the person or people, perhaps because of the affective dimensions inherent in the construction of the symbol or perhaps because of the historical significance that a given dimension may have for those involved. Whatever the case, it is conceivable that a symbol could be rooted so deeply in the people that it thus becomes identified with their very selves. That such could occur, especially in the area of religion or basic maternal and paternal sounds, is almost to be expected.

In his writings Jung gives an account of a symbolic rite that he himself witnessed in his researches. It illustrates well the depth that symbols can manifest in a people's life:

> I will illustrate this by an experience I once had with the primitives of Mount Elgon in Africa. Every morning at dawn, they leave their huts and breathe or spit into their hands, which they then stretch out to the first rays of the sun, as if they were offering either their breath or their spittle to the rising god—to *mungu*. (This Swahili word, which they used in explaining the ritual act, is derived from a Polynesian root equivalent to *mana* or *mulungu*. These and similar terms designate a "power" of extraordinary efficiency and pervasiveness, which we should call divine. Thus the word *mungu* is their equivalent for Allah or God.) When I asked them what they meant by this act, or why they did it, they were completely baffled. They could only say: "We have always done it. It has always been done when the sun rises." They laughed at the obvious conclusion that the sun is *mungu*. The sun indeed is not *mungu* when it is above horizon; *mungu* is the actual moment of the sunrise.
>
> What they were doing was obvious to me, but not to them; they just did it, never reflecting on what they did. They were consequently unable to explain themselves. I concluded that they were offering their souls to *mungu*, because the breath (of life) and the spittle mean "soul-substance." To breath or spit upon something

conveys a "magical" effect, as, for instance, when Christ used spittle to cure the blind, or where a son inhales his dying father's last breath in order to take over the father's soul. It is most unlikely that these Africans ever, even in the remote past, knew any more about the meaning of their ceremony. (1964, p. 70)

*b. Synchronous and diachronous.* There is in the symbol a synchronic and a diachronic significance. This is to say that in the symbol one can anchor himself in the current scheme of things such as they are being lived. He can through his symbolization become part of that which is currently transpiring, and it is important that one be able to do so, whatever the imaginative leap. One must be able to experience himself as part of the cross section of life. By buying into the symbolization that is prevailing, so to speak, one becomes identified in an experiential way and within limits with the present and its enterprises. This is the symbol's synchronic effect. Both its logos (meaning) and bios (affective, incarnational) reverberations are made available to the person who participates sympathetically and reverently in the culturally approved symbolizations. She or he has at her or his command a vehicle of unification that is very real in life, and it is made available through imaginative participation. He can embrace it as he wills. Something akin to this is spelled out by Berger in his work, *Sacred Canopy*:

> Looked at from the viewpoint of individual subjective consciousness, the cosmization of the institutions permits the individual to have an ultimate sense of rightness, both cognitively and normatively, in the role he is expected to play in society. Human role-playing is always dependent upon the recognition of others. The individual can identify himself with a role only insofar as others have identified him with it. When roles, and the institutions to which they belong, are endowed with cosmic significance, the individual's self-identification with them attains a further dimension. For now it is not only human others who recognize him in the manner appropriate to the role, but those suprahuman others with which the cosmic legitimations populate the universe. His self-identification with the role becomes correspondingly deeper and more stable (1969, p. 37)

Thus the symbol is not to be taken lightly, particularly if it is one of proportions such that neither the individual nor the society deems insignificant. His imaginative embracing of the symbol redounds to his own and his culture's advantage.

There is, however, another aspect of the symbol. It not only links the person to his contemporaries, but it also ties him into history. The symbol that he has created, but particularly if he has created it for himself by electing to embrace the culturally and perhaps religiously revered symbol, is his pledge for the future. In the deep symbol with all its sacredness the person experiences himself transported to the beyond, the future, the heavenly, the cosmic. He no longer remains solely with the contemporaneous, but has become part of that which reaches back to those who antedate him and ahead to that which beckons him. The symbol, once truly appropriated and revered, has the power to lift one out of himself to others and out of the present to the past and the future. The imaginative transportation is a very real experience. Eliade's observation about the myth can be said with equal justification about the depth symbol, such as that of the lost Paradise, or the Eucharist or the cross. It takes a person out of his own time, into the Great Time.

> Enough to remind ourselves that the myth takes man out of his own time—his individual, chronological, "historic" time—and projects him, symbolically at least, into Great Time, into a paradoxical instant which cannot be measured because it does not consist of duration. This is as much as to say that the myth implies a break-away from Time and the surrounding world; it opens up a way into the sacred Great Time. (1952/1961, p. 58)

*c. Substantive at heart.* The depth symbol is substantive. To say this may appear to say the obvious, but it is worth the saying nonetheless. Symbols may come and go in a person's or people's life. They have their purpose, their day, and then, like a wave in the ocean, go back to the ocean. But there are symbols in life that do not return to relative nothingness so easily, for they speak to the great treasures of life that one values most. Such symbols can be said to be substantive, just as the values for which they speak are substantive. Every person knows that his or her life encompasses many items of passing interest. Its needs must be this way in life, for one cannot give the self seriously to endless details, just as he cannot give his undivided attention to every single person whom he meets. Human finitude makes his limits inevitable. Thus one opts for that which is more meaningful in his life. It is said to take on value for him, and the living of one's life in the light of such values makes living truly meaningful and rewarding.

The symbol that is of depth encompasses that which is of value. It encompasses that which is of substance, providing to the person an ingenious and highly imaginative creation that calls forth memories, moments, movements of the heart that have touched one profoundly and rendered a contribution to his person that will not quickly or easily be forgotten. Such experiences and all that they stand for have been caught up in the symbol and to abandon it would be tantamount to abandoning life itself. Such, for example, would be a prayer that one learned as a child and which one continues to whisper to himself in old age; or a ritual (such as visiting the ancestral graves) that takes one back to his earliest days with his parents and to all that he truly loved. To have such a symbol at one's command is to be truly blessed. If one did not have such moments in life to capture in this way one would be forced to create them, for such moments buoy one up amid the vicissitudes of life and enable him to rise above the disturbances that mark our quotidian lives. Only the substantive can lend itself to such symbolization, and one can drink from this source and quench spiritual thirst as from no other. Keats has captured this remarkable truth in the passage quoted in the first chapter. It is worth repeating. Speaking of the power of the thing of beauty in human life, he states

> Nor do we merely feel these essences
> For one short hour; no, even as the trees
> That whisper round a temple become soon
> Dear as the temple's self, so does the moon,
> The passion poesy, glories infinite,
> Haunt us till they become a cheering light
> Unto our souls, and bound to us so fast,
> That, whether there be shine, or gloom o'ercast,
> They always must be with us, or we die.
>
> John Keats, "Endymion"

This same truth is captured by Shakespeare in his Sonnet XXIX, where we experience the substance and the power of the symbolism surrounding one's love for a beloved:

> When, in disgrace with Fortune and men's eyes,
> I all alone beweep my outcast state,
> And trouble deaf heaven with my bootless cries,

And look upon myself and curse my fate,
Wishing me like to one more rich in hope,
Featur'd like him, like him with friends possess'd,
Desiring this man's art, and that man's scope,
With what I most enjoy contended least;
Yet in these thoughts myself almost despising,
Haply I think on thee; and then my state,
Like to the lark at break of day arising
From sullen earth, sings hymns at heaven's date;
　For thy sweet love rememb'red such wealth brings
　That then I scorn to change my state with kings.

*d. Metaphorical in origin.* If at heart the depth symbol is substantive, then we must hasten to add that in origin it is metaphorical. These observations are no mere happenstance, nor is their relationship incidental.

We have seen in previous chapters that the metaphorical is, contrary to what many might think, truly substantive. And we would add now that it is that metaphorical origin that can be said to bequeath to the symbol its own substance. This can come as a surprise, to be sure, to one who has never come to see that imaginative thinking is anything other than ornamental. Indeed it is but a short step for such a critic to wonder whether it deserves to be termed thinking at all. We find such sentiments in no less an artist that T. S. Eliot himself. Taking issue with Wyndham Lewis's remark that Shakespeare, with the exception of Chapman, was the only thinker one meets with among the Elizabethan dramatists, Eliot goes on to say:

> It is the general notion of "thinking" that I would challenge. One has the difficulty of having to use the same words for different things. We say, in a vague way, that Shakespeare, or Dante, or Lucretius, is a poet who thinks, and that Swinburne is a poet who does not think, even that Tennyson is a poet who does not think. But what we really mean is not a difference in quality of thought, but a difference in quality of emotion. The poet who "thinks" is merely the poet who can express the emotional equivalent of thought. But he is not necessarily interested in the thought itself. . . . But by "thinking" I mean something very different from anything that I find in Shakespeare. Mr. Lewis, and other champions of Shakespeare as a great philosopher, have a great deal to say about Shakespeare's power of thought, but they fail to show that he thought to any purpose; that

he had any coherent view of life, or that he recommended any procedure to follow. . . .

I would suggest that one of the plays of Shakespeare has a "meaning," although it would be equally false to say that a play of Shakespeare is meaningless. All great poetry gives the illusion of a view life. (1932, p. 115)

We have acknowledged that imaginative thinking is of a different quality and style than purely rational, logical thinking; but we have also pointed out that it is thinking every bit as intent, creative, and serious as logical thought. In fact it is the imaginative thought behind logical thought that uncovers for the latter that treasure that it does bring to light; and we have seen that the genius of imaginative thought is its ability to redescribe reality itself. As John Middleton Murray put it, the metaphor should not be considered as a simple comparison between two terms, but rather as "almost a mode of apprehension." (Dorfles, 1969, p. 582)

Hence the substantiality that lies at the heart of the depth symbol owes much of its being to the metaphor or imaginative thought that brought it into being in the first place. And yet there is some distinction that must be drawn between the two, particularly if we are speaking about depth symbols. Every symbol could rightly be termed a metaphor at origin, but every metaphor could hardly be termed a symbol. The symbol is characterized by greater stability and permanence, although it must be granted that these qualities are more pronounced in some symbols than in others.

It has been seen, too, that the metaphor grew out of the metaphorical twist given to the literalness of the first predicated meaning, and that the symbol did much the same. In this sense they can both be said to have a double meaning structure in virtue of which a second meaning finds its own unique force and power, however great, subtly or not so subtly tied up by way of resemblance, contrast, polarization, or perhaps even irrelevancy with that of the first meaning. It is the setting provided for the second meaning and predication by the first meaning and its literalness that gives rise to the unexpected incongruence of the second predication. To be sure, if the metaphor and symbol are based on resemblance and/or analogy, the incongruence will be lessened. Should the basis of predication be that of polarization, however, the diaphoric metaphor that results will, or at least can, be quite striking and vital. If, then, the basis for the predication is not resemblance, or even contradiction or polarization, but rather sheer irrelevancy, it is not inconceivable that the metaphor and symbol could prove most remarkable of all. After all, a contradiction, even though dramatically polarized from an original, literal predication, still lies within the same genre. An irrelevancy appears out of nowhere and may prove the most fruitful of all. For example, the lion could well be metaphorized as the king of the forest. He could also, by way of contrast, be termed the slave of the forest. Both metaphors could generate fruitful meaning, with the latter meaning (that of slave) provoking a more challenging demand on the imagination than the former (that of king). Suppose, however, employing irrelevancy, one were to metaphorize the lion as the computer of the forest or the pencil of the forest, the imaginative thinking could be thrown totally back on itself with little or no recourse. This, of course, may appear inane, but actually it isn't.

It is metaphors such as these that one meets with in severely disturbed persons. R. D. Laing, in his work, *Politics of Experience* (1967, p. 172 ff), has written a chapter at the end of the book entitled "The bird of paradise." This chapter represents an ingenious attempt to lead the reader by the hand, as it were, through the world of the schizophrenic with the intention of providing the reader with an opportunity to experience what the world of that patient might be like. We shall take a few excerpts and would encourage the reader to read them out loud. Appealing to the imagination of you, the reader, I would ask you to imagine yourself as the person of whom Laing is writing and to say aloud slowly and meaningfully the following passages. While reading, notice how the imaginative leaps spring upon you. They come out of nowhere, and you are stunned by the loud clash. We are dealing here, not with resemblances or even contrasts. We are dealing with irrelevancies which the patient, however, has deemed proper to conjoin.

> Each night I meet him. King with Crown. Each night we fight. Why must he kill me? No. I shall not die. I can be smaller than a pinhead, harder than a diamond. Suddenly, how gentle he is. One of his tricks. Off with his Crown! Strike. Bash in his skull. Face Streams of blood. Tears? Perhaps. Too late. Off with his head. Pith the Spine! Die now, O king!

We see here how the would-be sweetheart looks on her beloved: as a King. Suddenly he is a murderer threatening her life. She then sees herself become almost invisible—as invisible as a pinhead, invulnerable as a diamond. Her assassin is again her lover. Then he is a deceiver. Now is an enemy. She attacks him. Blood and tears touch her and she begin to regret. Then just as quickly he is again the enemy and must die. Such metaphorizations come like a stream of consciousness, one after the other, until she moves to kill her lover-now-enemy. Laing gives another instance of the same:

> Spider crab moves slowly across bedroom wall. Not horrible, not evil. Acceptance. Another one appears and another. Ugh! No, too much. Kill. Suddenly it was always a bird, so frail, so beautiful; now, twitching in death agony. What have I done? But why play such a game on me? Why appear so ugly? It's your fault, your fault.

Both of the above examples are the metaphorizations, symbolizations of a highly disturbed person, as has been said. But they do give one a taste of the metaphorizations that characterize the schizophrenic world. On the other hand one can metaphorize with irrelevancies that might conceivably prove most fruitful and productive. Or at least they might provide one with a wholly new experience of life—an experience that in turn can lead to a redescription of reality unheard of previously. Brainstorming sessions, for example, are designed to do precisely that, and the question is raised as to what new reality might emerge into view once a company is metaphorized as a baseball, or an administrator as an ink bottle, or a car as an encyclopedia. Metaphors such as these are not based on resemblances, obviously, nor on contrast. They are based on sheer irrelevancy, but they still are designed to further our human understanding of the unity of beings.

The above examples were not intended as digressions. They were designed as illustrations that imaginative, metaphorical, symbolical thinking is rich with possibilities of rethinking, redescribing, and recreating the world. In all such instances, but particularly in the metaphor and symbol, we are dealing with double meaning structures that call for reflections and interpretations. This is particularly true in the case of the symbol, for the second meanings can themselves becomes the basis for further symbolization: a third meaning, which in turn could lead to a fourth meaning—until a veritable network is gradually built up that gives the symbol a girth, a stature, a solidity that sets it apart from the mere metaphor with which it commenced. One could say, in fact, that the symbol does indeed take on a stability or solidity and a permanence, as Wheelwright has described it. One could say more: we could refer to the symbol as a ganglion of metaphors around which, indeed, families of metaphors might cluster.

At this point let us make mention of root metaphors—a concept that has taken on considerable meaning the last few decades, and which has proved to be extremely meaningful for hermeneutical ventures in the areas of anthropology, religion, theology, and literature. Root metaphors are those that constitute, as it were, families, much as ancestors, great grandparents and great, great grandparents are said to do. Ricoeur refers to such root metaphors as "the dominant metaphors capable of both engendering and organizing a network that servers as a junction between the symbolic level with its slow evolution and the more volatile metaphorical level." (1976, p. 64) In brief, one can progress slowly down from the dynamic metaphors about which we spoke in the previous chapter through the root metaphors that have brought together many families of metaphors over the years and down still further to the powerful depth symbols. All of this network would exhibit double meaning structures, but some—the depth symbols—would exhibit at least double if not triple meaning structures to which would accrue the cosmic, earthy, and biological overtones of which we have spoken previously. Not only would they exhibit such complex structures as well as powerful affective overtones and reverberations, they would also serve as the ganglia for countless imaginative and affective experiences. In their own way they would be available to the person for mustering up profound resources that he needs not only for the redescriptions of life for which he is seeking but also for the strength required to enable him to undertake and implement whatever projects upon which he has at long last embarked.

*e. Centripetal in operation.* The depth symbol is primarily centripetal in its operation. This statement may appear at variance with our observation previously that the symbol is characterized by a horizontal breadth or expanse. The difference is readily resolved if we keep in mind that the horizontal expanse referred to speaks to the fact that the meanings that attach to a symbol may increase, that it may reach out, as it were, to other meanings in whatever way. The imaginative thinking of the person or a people can incorporate new meanings into the symbolic structure if they are deemed significant enough to the individual or the community. Such meanings, however, once imagined into the symbolic picture of the primary meaning, tend to gather around the primary symbol. It acts as a magnet, so to speak, and draws them into a larger whole. Unlike the metaphor, which is primarily functioning centrifugally, going beyond the primary, would-be literal meaning, and chartering a new course, opening up a new appreciation, suggesting a new and powerful redescription of reality, the symbolic movement of the person or people tends toward the center, the ganglion, the primary meaning. Thus it is that the symbolic structure becomes a veritable labyrinth whose intricacies are never truly obvious and whose possibilities for awakening the inner person are never exhausted.

In his *Images and Symbol* Eliade, considered by many as one of the outstanding religionists in the world, notes the gathering power of the symbol, particularly as it is manifested in the realm of religious studies:

> Finally, the study of religions will shed light upon one fact that until now has been insufficiently noted, namely, that there is a logic of the symbol. Certain groups of symbols, at least, prove to be coherent, logically connected with one another; in a word, they can be systematically formulated, translated into rational terms. This internal logic of symbols raises a problem with far-reaching consequences: are certain zones of the individual or collective consciousness dominated by the logos, or are we concerned here with manifestations of a "transconscious"? That problem cannot be resolved by depth-psychology alone, for the symbolisms which decipher the latter are for the most part made up of scattered fragments and of the manifestations of a psyche in crises, if not in a state of pathological regression. To grasp the authentic structures and functions of symbols, one must turn to the inexhaustible indices of the history of religion. (1961, p. 37)

In this passage Eliade, who was here discussing the logic of the symbol, ascertains that there is rich meaning, not bizarre meaning, in the symbolic architecture that is exhibited in the study of the symbolisms of world religions. Certain symbols prove to cohere, coalesce, draw together, move toward the center. Unlike the metaphor, which is primarily centrifugal, they are primarily centripetal. Thus the affective power of their nonsemantic moments, their cosmic and biological accroutrements, can be tremendous and moving. The same semantic indeterminacies of all perceptions and those of the metaphorical creations are locked into the symbolic architecture. It takes little imagination to surmise the force which such symbols can exert in human lives once a person or a people has come to understand, respect, and reverence their worth in our lives.

*f. Numinous and sacred.* There is about the symbol of depth a numinosity and a sacredness. In saying this we are venturing into an area that has traditionally been treated in the realms of religion. The word "numinosity" is itself the creation of Rudolph Otto, to be found in his work, *The Idea of the Holy.* Our present concentration, however, will emphasize less the religious than the sacred aspects of the symbol. It has been stated several times already that the symbol coalesces, draws together in higher unities much that is to be found in discrete experiences. The very etymology of the word "symbol" speaks to that aspect of the image: sym (together, as in sympathy, symphony, assimilate) and ballein (the Greek word for throw: ballistics would be an English derivative). Thus the symbol throws together, hurls together, brings together in whatever way that which is coalesced. It is an image that takes its uniqueness from the fact that it brings together in an awing way the multiplicities, or at least some of the multiplicities, that characterize our lives. And this feat is one worthy of the human.

We can get a feel for the power of this realization when we contrast the word "symbol" with the word that is its contrary: "diabolic." Rather than the "sym" (with, together) we speak of "dia" (through or apart, as in diatribe, diabetes). This notion of "dia" as "apart" along with the Greek word "ballein" (throw) gives us the idea of throwing or ripping apart, scattering. Thus the idea contained in symbolic (hurling together) is contrasted with the idea contained in diabolic (ripping apart). In brief, the symbolic is opposed to the diabolic: the coalescing together is opposed to the ripping apart. In addition to that, the diabolic also has ugly or vicious connotations: that which is diabolic is that which is of the Devil, or evil. In other words, in speaking of the symbolic we are speaking to the manner in which persons or the community uses its resources, personal or communal, to bring together the resources of the person and the community to further the goals of the person and the commune, as distinct from the way in which a person or a community is ripped apart—thus deadened. Obviously the diabolic is destructive while the symbolic is unifying. In thus bringing together, the symbol bequeathes soundness, solidity, status, stature, sanity and renders the original meaning more awing and awesome, inspiring and overwhelming, enlightening, and even bewildering. The symbol takes on a complexity that commands respect and reverence, for it has brought about an experience of a sacredness that humbles and numbs the beholder, while inspiring and uplifting him at the same time. If the diabolic is of evil, of the Devil, then the symbolic is of good, of the gods, of God. And in the presence of the truly symbolic one experiences some such transformation, if not transportation.

It does not follow from this that the symbol, for all its power to uplift and transform, is devoid of the ambiguous. Quite the contrary, the mystery is not diminished, much less eliminated. In speaking of the symbolic as sacred and numinous we are acknowledging that it borders on the holy in one's life, but at the same time it has about it an element of the uncertain and the uneasy. *Mysterium fascinans et terribile* is the phrase of which Otto is fond, for it takes cognizance of the fact that the symbol is at once a mystery that is fascinating but awing, not to be tampered with, so to speak. The element of the terrible is present because its sacredness eschews the cheap or the vulgar. It commands of us that which is of our best.

*g. The interpersonal dimension.* The symbol has about it the ambience of intersubjectivity. That is to say that the symbol cannot be understood as a purely impersonal event or creation. Not only is it of people, for people, and by people, in its origin and power: it is toward people in its function. Every symbolic creation brings us into the presence of the interpersonal past: our ancestors, our immediate forefathers, our family, our peers, our heritage. It might be the select heroes of our preference in our own lives. That which is sacred, that which is awing, that which is captivating to us is that which was considered or made sacred, awing or captivating by the great ones in our tradition, or at least the ones whose judgment we saw as extraordinary and praiseworthy. Thus in the symbol we have remarkable and unique access to our own heroes and people as well as their feelings. We are one with them in the possession of the symbol and we are one with them in the experience of that same symbol. In brief, the symbol makes me, enlarges me with the blessing of my and our significant past. I become more than I am simply because the symbol is more than it is. It is my people and so am I. I have the strength of identity that they have bequeathed me and which I have appropriated. In a highly imaginative way I am my tradition in the experience, the imaginative experience, of the symbol we all possess together, even when I am alone in a situation seemingly abandoned. Thus the symbol opens me and us up to our people and, through them, to their God, for the symbol so often was employed by the people to bring about a God experience.

Mirceau Eliade has a rich passage in which he addresses the openness that inheres to the image, the symbol, and the manner in which that openness was respected as many of the ancient rites and symbols were translated into the Christian setting and idiom:

> Much has been said about the unification of Europe by Christianity: and is never better attested than when we see how Christianity coordinated the popular religious traditions. . . . It is, above all, through the creation of a new mythological language common to all the populations who remained attached to their soil—and therefore in the greater danger of becoming insulated in their own ancestral traditions—that the civilising mission of Christianity has been so remarkable. For, by Christianising the ancient European religious heritage, it not only purified the latter, but took up, into the new spiritual dispensation of mankind, all that deserved to be "saved" of the old practices, beliefs and hopes of pre-Christian man. Even today, in popular Christianity, there are rites and beliefs surviving from the neolithic: the boiled grain in honor of the dead, for instance (the *coliva* of Eastern and Aegean Europe). The Christianisation of the peasant levels of Europe was effected thanks above all to the Images: everywhere they were rediscovered, and had only to be revalorised, reintegrated and given new names. (1961, p. 174)

This is a provocative passage. It deals with an historical phenomenon, to be sure, but it provides distinct illumination of the efficacy of that phenomenon. It illustrates powerfully the force of the symbol and image in the transformation of a people and peoples. The image was at the heart of the phenomenon, and the images and symbols of the people were recontextualized in such a way that the people of a nation or tribe never felt that they were losing their ancestors or betraying their forefathers. The retention of images and symbols provided living proof to them all that they were still one with their people even though they were as a nation moving into the new context provided by the Christian faith. Had the conversion been seen as a betrayal of their ancestors, the conversion would have been repudiated. As it was, their Christianization was not seen as a betrayal, and the retention of their symbols provided them the living and emotional guarantee that made the conversion possible.

*h. The symbol as self-revelatory.* The symbol provides the person and the community with a revelation of themselves. In saying this, we are not reiterating that the symbol, like every other act of a person, bespeaks one's stance in the world. We mean that but we mean more. The symbol has grown out of a history. It is rooted in the past and has gained over the years of a person or people's life a benediction or blessing from those who embody the culture. Thus it reveals, not only the values that were manifested in the creation of the symbol, but also the continued echoing of those values and that election over the years. Thus, in moving through the world of a symbol, we are moving through the treasured and blessed world of a given people. Hence we are beholding a people's revelation of itself, a person's disclosing of himself. In brief, it is self-revelatory, and that revelation can be seen in many of the artifacts and creations of a nation. It can show forth in the poetry, the architecture, the literature, the music, and the art in general. We are introduced to their history, obviously, but also to their dreams. We gain some understanding of their concept of what it means to be human and what their idea of human existence is all about.

It would be folly to think that, in virtue of this fact, we can hope to reconstruct the entire thinking of a person or nation. It would be folly simply because we can never hope to master the subtleties that enter the making of a symbol. And it is unnecessary, for we do not need to uncover every dimension in order to gain a respectful appreciation. At best we can learn something, and from that something grow in respectful reverence for the group. Even in the study of one's own symbolism we gain but limited understanding of our own mystery, our own genius, our own humanity. At no point is the subject exhausted, or the matter mastered. On the one hand that might be the despair of it all—the pursuit seems too hopeless. On the other hand, however, that might well be the joy of it all: there is seemingly no limit to the world of further discovery and increased understanding.

*i. The symbol gives rise to reflection.* The symbol calls for an interpretation, a hermeneutic. This is a poor paraphrase of Ricoeur's statement, first expressed in his work, *The Symbolism of Evil*, but later repeated in many of his works. His statement was, "The symbol gives rise to thought." As he states it himself, this sentence really says two things: that the symbol gives and that what it gives calls for thought, is something to think about (1961/1967, p. 348).

That a symbol gives is apparent by this time. That the symbol should give rise to thought is something else. It requires first of all that one construct some kind of interpretation of the symbol, a hermeneutics, since in the symbol we are dealing with a double meaning structure that must be deciphered. But then, in addition to the interpretation, one is pressed to go beyond the mere interpretation and set it forth in some kind of a theme bigger than the symbol. Thus we are moving toward a reflection of sorts. When, then, one moves from the theme and seeks to understand it in the larger picture of life, human existence, one has entered into the full-blown experience of reflection, profound and labored thought. In this sense one can say that the symbol has given rise to thought, has provoked us to have recourse to profound thought on the human situation. Indeed we can say with no hesitation that the apparently simple symbol has provided genuine nourishment for the profound reflection on the meaning of being human.

But, by the same token, the effort at interpretation or reflection is not totally unencumbered. It encounters its own problems, for a genuine interpretation is aimed at giving us a deeper understanding of our efforts at existing, our own engagement in the human enterprise. In Ricoeur's phrase, the reflection in which we engage as we attempt to understand the full meaning of symbolization is itself intended to gather up, to retrieve, to reassemble our effort at existing, our desire to be—all in the attempt to understand better our own humanity and its place in creation. To do this requires that we take up the study of those human works that bear witness to that effort to exist. Thus, since those works are themselves the symbolizations about which we have been speaking from the outset, it follows, paradoxically enough, that the reflection leads us to a better understanding of life—but only through the world of the symbol.

All this means, in effect, that we move from our symbol to our reflection, and during the latter we return to the symbols with which we started. Only now, thanks to the reflection and its fruit, we find ourselves back at the beginning, but with an enrichment that we did not possess when we commenced our effort. Thus the symbol has led us to reflection and the reflection has led us back to the symbol. Such is the way, the price and the achievement of human finitude.


## C. Symbols and the Integrating of Personality


In previous chapters we have come to see the significant role that imaginative thinking plays in the movement toward integrating our lives and personalities. The entire process entails a thinking that is logical and rational in many respects, but which is by no means exclusively so. Hence the absence of clear and distinct ideation necessitates the employment of many imaginative images and movements that are only analogously rational. Indeed the significance of lateral movement in this process is considerable. Everyone, even in the absence of any thorough understanding of life and its mysteries, undertakes some such integration and manages, more or less successfully on his or her own, to effect some unification of existence. In this process, as we have also seen, the importance of metaphorical leaps and unifications looms up most strikingly. Thanks to these endeavors the person effects unifications that enable him to deal with relative success with the countless situations with which he is beset. Thus the totality of life for most people, however trying at times, is not overwhelming, at least not constantly; and despite the disparities that abound on all sides, we are able to bring them into some kind of intelligible and manageable whole. Complexities of life still confront us, and to meet them it is necessary that we effect larger amalgamations, syntheses than the metaphors allowed. At this point we have recourse to symbolizations.

In a certain sense the symbol takes up the challenge and builds on the achievement of our metaphorizations. We could say, to begin with, that the symbol is and does much the same for us as does the metaphor; but in saying that, we dare not press our point too far. The metaphorical thinking functions at what Ricoeur has called a more volatile level and does not capture the tremendous historicity that is the person's or the community's. This is the function of our symbolic thinking, thanks to which we are able to tap the interpersonal, sacred, and historical depths of our lives in greater and more meaningful syntheses of life issues. It is in these symbolic moments and achievements of our lives that our personalities manage to cut across the boundaries with which mere metaphorical thinking cannot cope. These make it possible for us to deal at once with the present situations as well as the historical antecedents that have preceded our situation, and orient ourselves toward the futurities that are our lot, indeed our principal lot. For whatever else we may be engaged in, we humans are caught up principally in the thrust toward the future; and the measure in which we are able to grasp understandingly the possibilities of life for the future, is the measure in which we are satisfied that our integrational achievement to date has met with some success.

What is necessary at this point is that we move forward into the ambiguities and perplexities of our lives, whatever form they take, and that we deal with them to the best of our ability. To do so requires that we bring into the picture of our lives a unity or oneness within limits, to be sure, that still enables us to gain the self-possession and composure that are required to rise above it all. At times this is required on a lesser scale, and at other times on a grand scale. In either instance the symbolizations that we employ—religious or otherwise—prove invaluable, for they allow for irregularities in our understandings and still provide us with needed comprehension and strength for implementation.

Symbols must take cognizance of our particular selves, whether we speak of the individual self or our people. It must speak to me, or to us. In addition it must speak to the presence of the others in my life. It must also show reverence for the values that I or we esteem: our traditional values, our present ones or those of our dreams. It has to manifest consideration for those significant places, locations that have featured and do feature in our lives, and which take on special meaning to us and our people. It must partake of our unique time, those temporal unifications of life which have come to mean so much to me or us. All these categories a symbol must touch if it is to take on in my or our life a stature that befits an image worthy of being called symbol. The "throwing together" that is the symbol must reverberate in all such respects; failing to do so, the event or scene will lack symbolic stature and prove incapable of effectively moving us toward an experience of wholeness and sacredness.

As we have stated before, every culture forms such symbolizations, and they do effect their wonders for the individual and the collectivity. However it often happens that we are heedless of their powerful ramifications, since so much of our life is a life unexamined. Nonetheless we are not totally nescient and are reasonably aware of our preferences: we know our strong likes and dislikes and that a given event or locale triggers off dynamics that cannot be ignored. We are aware of much of this without understanding all or many of its dimensions. We do not know the full significance of what transpires, do not appreciate the complex roots of our impulsivities toward certitude and finalizations. And yet, we know and feel that that which engages us commands our attention, deserves our respect, elicits our sympathy, and may even merit our reverent obedience.

To look more closely at this matter, let us return to the basic double meaning structure of the symbol, and watch its development into a full-fledged symbol of status, one that partakes of the status that we have attributed to depth symbols. In the second chapter, speaking of perception, we pointed out the unique relationship between the self or co-constituting subject and the co-constituting object. Let us represent it diagrammatically as follows:

*Figure 1.*      Self⟨---------------------------------------------------- ⟩Object

During the present chapter we have spoken of the double meaning structure of the metaphor (which is at the origin of the symbol) and symbol. Let us represent that in this manner:

                                                            Other

*Figure 2.*      Self ⟨---------------------------- ⟩ Object (now Symbol)

Now the object, which had its own meaning in Figure 1 has come to have a second signification (other) in Figure 2. It has this second signification however, in virtue of the first signification and finds its meaning somehow in virtue of that. Thus we no longer speak of it as object, but as symbol. It now symbolizes the second signification. It is this duality of meanings that makes it symbolic. We have seen further, however, that the element of this duality must have certain qualities for this to be a true depth symbol. It must be substantive; the elements must be elements of value to me or to us. It must speak to the presence of others, meaning that it must bear some relationship to the others of our life; that is to say, to our national history, our personal or collective experience that was noteworthy, our family ancestors, heroes, parents, and so on. Depth symbols must speak significantly to me and to others, even if they are only my own personal symbols. It must somehow be worthy of my parental or ancestral benediction, even if my parents never knew of it. I need only be convinced that it would have won their respect and blessing had they known it as I do.

And there are other qualities or references that must surround the depth symbol. It must address itself to human activity in some way. It may refer to a people's heroic dying in virtue of which they triumphed over evil or brought about the salvation of a nation (as in Gettysburg); or their ingenious craftsmanship or artistry (as at the Acropolis or the pyramids); or, on a personal level, fundamental human acts like gardening, working in the fields, cleaning, playing, studying, praying, and so on. Fundamental human activity must be captured in it to give it fundamental human significance. Even a great mountain which has come to symbolize God himself, as did Sinai, was seen as the meeting place for Moses and his people to commune with the Lord.

Place is an important quality about the symbol, lending it a setting for the significant activity to occur. Thus we think of the symbolic possibilities of the mountain, as we have just said, but also of the home or homestead, the garden, field, cellar, ballfield, school, church, barn, hideaways: all those areas that Bachelard has captured in his treatise on the *Poetics of Space*. And there is the quality of time, that most unique characteristic of the human experience: the way-back-when, the period of greatness that the symbol recalls. Thus there is the story-telling time, the praying time, the golden age, the time of the famine, the great depression years, the death of Camelot when the world stood still, in shock and disbelief. No symbol is without its time. If it were, it would not speak to people, for no one can live, or even conceive of living, without assuming some binding time. The symbol must respect this unique feature of our existence.

Thus we have seen that the duality of significances, whereby a depth symbol is created gradually for a person or a community, must capture in the architecture of the symbol human activity, significant meaning for others, something of value and substance, and referentials to time and space. This we would represent in Figure 3:

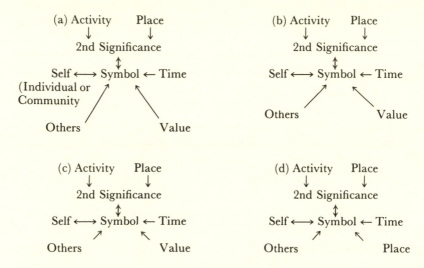

In this diagram we have presented four different symbols with their respective architectures. What we have not shown, however, is the way in which such symbols may become interrelated to each other—a development that would eventually lead one or the other of such symbols to become symbols of major proportions. It can easily be imagined, given time and circumstances. If such should come to pass, we would anticipate for understandable reasons why they would be characterized by great matriarchal and patriarchal themes.

A final point. We should point out that the symbol is imaginatively formed by the person or people themselves. Symbols cannot be forced upon one—if they are to be heroic symbols. They are not imposed; they are picked up and appropriated, just as one's heroes are. To be sure, a culture or a nation anticipates this process by selecting its own and passing them on to its children. But the child, to experience the stature, the reverberations, the uplift of the symbol in his or her life, must in turn appropriate that symbol to and for himself. As Shakespeare phrased it, "My state and glory thou cans't dispose, but not my griefs. Still am I king of those." Each of us is his or her own king in this respect, and reserves for the self the right to select those whom we would knight.

## D. AFTERTHOUGHTS

Thinking about the above, one might wonder how to uncover the symbols that speak to one's own life. A worthy question indeed, and a fruitful pursuit. Many do uncover such symbols while engaged in personal and professional therapy. Many, however, never have that therapeutic experience, and are curious nonetheless about their own symbolizations. Such can be uncovered by attending to one's own experiences, and the process is worth the effort in our lives.

Reflect for a while on your living. Attend to some of your finer experiences, your finer moments, or if you will, your more dreaded moments. Let the heart go out to such experiences and see where they lead you. Listen attentively and especially to dimensions of your life that are most meaningful, persons in your life who feature prominently in it, scenes old and new that have about them an elegance or beauty that arrests you, pursuits that touch you and linger, questions that rise up frequently to haunt you, experiences that take you back to the golden and great days to inspire you, melodies and memories that bring to your heart an uplift, an ease, a smile. In all such recollections you will be touching upon profound dimensions of your life and person. Taking these and relating them to your *self* (as in the above diagrams of the symbolic architecture), meditating on the *persons* who figure prominently and frequently in them, finding the *values* and *worth* that such memories embody for you, recalling the *scenes*, the *places* and the *times* they allow to rise up before you, gazing upon the *activities* the memory of which is near and dear to you—doing all this in quiet and meditative moments can bring you ever so close to your own profound symbolizations. Staying with such over a period of time will gradually enable you to feel some of the depth that such symbols can reveal, provided they are not rushed, hurried, or rudely and impatiently treated. They are treasures that will yield their bounty if they are but allowed to do so. The imaginative poet within us who created these symbolizations over the years will now help us to understand them imaginatively. And we can move toward realizing for ourselves in ways that no therapist could possibly emulate the marvelous manner in which such symbols have often helped us to put it all together over the years.

A magnificent poem that addresses itself to this dimension of our lives and bids us to make the effort to retrieve our personal wealth is that of the Greek poet, C. P. Cavafy. His is a beautiful treatise on the journey to Ithaca, our true home. It speaks to every person's homecoming.

## ITHACA

When you start on your journey to Ithaca,
then pray that the road is long,
full of adventure, full of knowledge.
Do not fear the Lestrygonians
and the Cyclopes and the angry Poseidon.
You will never meet such as these on your path,
if your thoughts remain lofty, if a fine
emotion touches your body and your spirit.
You will never meet the Lestrygonians,
The Cyclopes and the fierce Poseidon,
if you do not carry them within your soul,
if your soul does not raise them up before you.

Then pray that the road is long.
That the summer mornings are many,
that you will enter ports seen for the first time
with such pleasure, with such joy.
Stop at Phoenician markets,
and purchase fine merchandise,
mother-of-pearl and corals, amber and ebony,
and pleasurable perfumes of all kinds,
buy as many pleasurable perfumes as you can;
visit hosts of Egyptian cities,
to learn and learn from those who have knowledge.

Always keep Ithaca fixed in your mind.
To arrive there is your ultimate goal.
But do not hurry the voyage at all.
It is better to let it last for long years;
and even to anchor at the isle when you are old,
rich with all that you have gained on the way,
not expecting that Ithaca will offer you riches.

Ithaca has given you the beautiful voyage.

Without her you would never have taken the road.
But she has nothing more to give you

And if you find her poor, Ithaca has not defrauded you.
With the great wisdom you have gained, with so much experience,
you must surely have understood what Ithacas mean.

C. P. Cavafy

# CHAPTER VI

# *The Myth: Authoring Our Own Life's Story*

We find it easier to say what myth is not than to say what it is. Myth is not mere metaphor; myth so understood has no identity of its own. Nor is myth mere poetry, poetic apprehension and expression. Myth is not history, even in the sense in which we use the word history of ancient literature; nor is it the story, popular tradition in the usual sense of the word.

Myth is not logical discursive thought; hence it is not strictly true to say that myth is a philosophy or a theology. Neither is myth a substitute or an alternate for discursive thought. It does not really do the work of discursive thought, the work of analysis, organization and synthesis. (McKenzie, 1963, p. 185)

IN embarking on a discussion of myth, and its relevance for the pursuit of personality integration, we are entering into a domain marked, paradoxically enough, with the utmost clarity on the one hand, and, on the other, with endless confusion. And we are dealing with an aspect of existence whose value would seem to be minimal in the scientific technological world of the late twentieth century; but which, as a matter of fact, has commanded growing attention in many serious thought circles and touched ordinary people in powerful and unmistakable ways in their religious and nationalistic outcries in the contemporary world scene. Thus our attention must focus on the significance of the myth as it is manifested at both the communal and personal levels, that is, if we could understand better the impact of imaginative thinking in one of its most significant and striking forms in the human enterprise of living. The topic is shrouded in obscurities, however, and it is to this aspect of the subject that we must first turn in an attempt to enrich our understanding.

## A. When Authorities Cannot Agree

As the opening passage from McKenzie indicates well, the discussion surrounding the question of myth has run the gamut, and the debate that emerged has proved devastating and confusing. Saying what a myth is not, to McKenzie, is easier than saying what it is. But the realizations that a myth is not this or that originated in the prolonged and serious study of the many contentions that a myth was that or this. It is only the subsequent critiques of previous claims that have given us an understanding of what a myth might conceivably be, and such critiques continue to the present day. As early as the sixth century before Christ theories concerning the meaning of myths were advanced on different sides, and the efforts of current scholars have had many bases upon which to build. During the present century the trends were set by J. G. Frazer, whose *Golden Bough* set the pattern for myth theorizing. His theories, based on the studies of many different cultures, were considered somewhat arbitrary and to many superficial. It was left to men like Malinowski and Radcliffe-Browne to challenge the legitimacy of considering matters like myth and cult without due consideration being given to the need to study the social complex as a whole and to see myth as imbedded in said complexes. The criticism leveled at Malinowski in turn centered around his emphasis on the practical implications of myths as providing legitimations and validations of various social institutions with little attention devoted to their possible speculative implications. To many who acknowledged Malinowski's contribution to the field of anthropology as enormous, his failure to see the intelligible and meaningful content of myth was a serious limitation in his work. In holding that abstract ideas were entirely absent from myths in every savage community, including those of Melanesia, his views seemed too restricted by the conditions found in a particular culture. That myths could mirror customs and beliefs as well as institutions is an understanding that proved valuable; that they were restricted to those sacred tales that accompany rituals, however, is a view not born out by subsequent research (Kirk, 1970/1973, p. 22ff).

The belief that there is a close affinity between myth and ritual is one of long standing. In earlier studies it took the form of considering myth to be the legomenon, or thing said, in contrast to the dromenon, or thing performed. In essence, this was Kluckhohn's thought, who saw a delicate interdependence between the two. His work with the Navaho Indians established this conclusion for him, but his work forced him to concede that myths were employed for purposes of entertainment and intellectual stimulation as well as ritual. It is the opinion of some contemporary thinkers that the relationship between myth and ritual can readily be acknowledged in some instances, but cannot be advanced as a valid general principle for every culture, much less every case. One such author is Kirk, who puts it this way:

> Where ritual is conspicuous, it is a function of many other aspects of social life. A powerful priesthood can sometimes develop for reasons other than an ethnic predisposition to ritualism; but there rituals will follow. Enforced leisure can be a factor in the proliferation of rituals, as it certainly has been in Australia; and the nature and concentration of settlements is another factor. Certain relatively secular cultures, like those of the ancient Greeks, the early medieval Teutons, the African Bushmen, or the Brazilian Indians, do in fact possess as many myths as the more hieratic cultures. In the latter case it is natural that many, perhaps most, myths are associated with rituals, or more generally with religious practices and occasions; in the former, that relatively few will be so associated. (p. 29)

This thumbnail sketch gives some indication of the range of the debate that has centered around the topic of myth. It has been seen as a phenomenon related to peoples' lives, obviously, but more particularly to some deeper aspects of the culture and social system. It is related also to the system's mores and values, as well as its ideation and reflection. It holds some bearing in regard to a community's ritualism, at least in some respects. And it has been seen by some, particularly by Cassirer, as indisolubly connected with a people's religion (1944, p. 87).

This view of myth, while having powerful appeal to some thinkers, has drawn considerable criticism from others. It is readily acknowledged by most that myths feature prominently in many religious enterprises, primitive and nonprimitive, but the identification of the two for whatever reason is called into question by some. Kirk, for example, feels that myth and religion can no more be considered twin aspects of the same subject any more than myths and rituals can be. He would not deny their de facto relatedness in many anthropological report, but he would likewise point out their unrelatedness in many another report.

MacQuarrie, in his study *God-Talk*, takes up the subject of the part played in the mythical dramas by supernatural agencies. Yet he too admits that myths presupposed a cosmology which scientific investigation has long since led us to abandon, but he is reluctant to dismiss their spiritual input. Having developed his point at some length, MacQuarrie then says,

> When we bear these points in mind, we do indeed see that the mythological way of representing the supernatural conflicts with both theology and science, as we understand them today. Yet we also see that the conception of the supernatural, even as we find it in myth, cannot just be swept aside. Unsatisfactory though it may have been, it pointed to aspects of man's being-in-the-world which we must either find ways to reinterpret or else frankly acknowledge that we have lapsed into a positivism in which any kind of religious faith, and, in particular, any recognizable form of Christianity have become impossible. (1967, p. 176)

MacQuarrie, of course, is pointing to the religious influence that is to be found in many a myth, and this must be conceded. The point at issue, however, is whether or not the myth is intrinsically religious as Cassirer seemed to imply, and that is another matter. It would appear that this is not necessarily the case, if we are to judge by the findings of Claude Lévi-Strauss' studies on the savage mind. These appear to call effectively into question whether Cassirer's analysis of the myth and the mythmaker is wholly accurate. He seemingly built his theory on the intensity of emotional experiences shared by myth and religion, and the absence of analytical acumen in the primitive mind. Lévi-Strauss's work would not appear to bear Cassirer out. Thus we again confront a serious position on the subject of myth that in turn has met with serious rebuttal. Seemingly the subject defies resolution, and the authorities continue their quarrel.

As seen by Kirk, writing in the 1970s, there would appear to be three principal developments in the modern study of myths. The first would feature Tylor, Frazer, and Durkheim, all of whom saw the myth as a significant aspect of primitive societies and one that called for serious study if we are to comprehend the respective societies under scrutiny. The second development would be the work of Sigmund Freud, who saw in the myth and in dreams a vital key for the understanding of the unconscious mind as it was proposed by Freud in his many writings. The third stage in the present understanding is the work of Claude Lévi-Strauss, whose emphasis on the structural theory of myth has become well known.

In presenting his theory on the structural nature of the myth Lévi-Strauss draws a linguistic analogy, as would be expected in a structural analysis. To him the myth is a product of language, a mode of human communication. That it has its contents is obvious; but the contents themselves are not relevant, feels Lévi-Strauss. What is critical is the elements of the myth—the narrative elements, the persons, the various objects—and the relationships that obtain among those elements. Even the formulation of the narrative is not critical, and the real meaning of the myth is not to be found in the narrative but in the structural interrelationships. Thus one might find many variations at the surface level of a myth while at the deeper levels the structure itself remains invariant, much as one might find many ways in a language to state a given position while the position underlying the words remains ever the same.

As one might expect, much debate has ranged about the structuralist position. Ricoeur, for one, has taken issue with several aspects and maintained, in effect, that Lévi-Strauss's explanations of myth might well apply to more primitive, totemistic cultures but not to the more advanced civilizations of the West. Others, such as Kirk, claim that the structuralist analysis purports to ignore all content and to focus on the relationships of elements within the mythic system or structure, basing its position on the language analogy. Yet it remains a fact that the purpose of the language structures and surface formulations is the communication of ideas from one to another. Language structure does not find its fulfillment in the language structure; it finds it in the communication. By the same token the myth, like language, does not settle for conveying its own structures to another; it must convey, like language, a message other than itself, a message for which it is the vehicle. And in practice Lévi-Strauss does appeal often to the specific content of a myth for its ultimate interpretation. Indeed, as he sees it, it is in the resolution of the content antinomies or polar positions that the central characteristic of a myth is to be found. In brief, myth is intended to effect some kind of reconciliation of these polar contradictions evidenced in the content of the narration. Content, then, or so it would appear, is not totally irrelevant in any attempt to understand a myth or the mythic experience. This, to be sure, would not imply that the structure was inconsequential; it would simply show that the structure, however meaningful, finds its own full meaning outside itself and in the communication of mythical meaning and content.

In this regard it will be profitable to insert here a discussion on the growing interest in the topic of parable. It has been contrasted by some authors with the myth, particularly as understood by the Lévi-Strauss school, but it is seen as the binary opposite of myth, functioning in literature and life as a polarization of myth while making its own unique contribution to human life and understanding. As presented in the work of John D. Crossan, the parable is to be found at the extreme end of a continuum that begins with myth and follows through apology, action, and satire, concluding then with the parable. Integrating into his analysis Sheldon Sacks's theory that prose fiction can be organized according to three mutually exclusive types (satire, apologue, action), Crossan sets up a binary picture along with Sacks's story spectrum. Bearing in mind that the Greek word for story is muthos, we can see the relevance of his endeavor. If myth and parable can be assumed to be the two extremes of the spectrum, and the story classification can be admitted to be threefold, one is presented with the following figure:

*Myth     Apologue     Action     Satire     Parable*

Crossan reminds us that each part of this spectrum must be understood in relation to world. The story in whatever form depicts the world as related-to in the narrative. Thus the world is the world which story in one manner or other creates and defines (1975, p. 58).

In the myth a world is established. Literature then deals with that created world in one way or other. In the apologue we find that world defended somehow. The truth that the world presents is set forth in its worth and desirability; the story of an apologue can serve to intensify the admiration and further the emulation. The satire, on the other hand, does precisely the opposite. It attacks, ridicules, demeans that world and its purported truth. In this its every part is conjoined in the effort, just as in the apologue every part is conjoined to provide unity and ultimate inspiration to the reader. In an action story, finally, we are presented with people, characters, whose lives interest us, whose stories are complicated by inevitable and unsettling intricacies, and whose perplexities are ultimately resolved. Such is the task of the action story. At the extreme of the spectrum is the parable. It too is a story that creates its world, but it is not a myth in the full sense, and it presents a subversion of the mythical world in some dramatic fashion. For its effect it depends upon the myth; without the latter, it can have no point or effect. The myth in other words, does not need a parable, but the parable does need the myth. The parable in turn operates within the tension set up between the myth and the parable, not as an antimyth, but as a story that would focus on the limitations of the myth world. In so doing, it subverts without destroying the world of the myth. The parable's power lies in its presentation of the surprise, the antihero, so to speak, who challenges the limitations of the myth and tradition and highlights its need for change, reform, dissolution, and so on. It is a story deliberately calculated to show the limitations of myth, to shatter world so that its relativity becomes apparent. It does not, *as parable*, replace one myth with another. It is in fact the dark night of story, that prepares us for the experience of transcendence. With this Crossan goes on to illustrate this analysis of story in terms of comic strip characters.

> The best way I can think of to exemplify these five modes of story in a unified way is to take up the comic pages of the newspaper and illustrate all five types of story from among the comic strips. *Myth* is represented by "Rick O'Shay," which continues the venerable Western myth of the virtuous gunslinger whose gun is fastest because his heart is purest. *Apologue* is rather blatant in "Dick Tracy," where law and order is advocated by such immortal saying as "Yes, INEVITABLY a criminal's mind cracks first, then with reason perverted he fashions his own finish." You can usually see the "message" (apologue) coming because Tracy, or whoever, will announce it, looking straight out of the strip at the reader. *Action* is found in the adventures of "Brenda Starr." We are made to care about Brenda through the course of interminable episodes because there is a basic "instability of relationship" introduced in the story by the fact that her boyfriend is always off in the jungle trying to stay alive on black orchid serum ("Home from the airport, Brenda falls on her bed in a flood of tears"). *Satire* is now very ably represented by "Doonesbury," with, for example, Mrs. Richardson asking her

husband, "Elliot, don't you think it's about time you started looking for a job?" *Parable* is present, at times, in the recently arrived "Basil." Quite often this strip moves between whimsy and fantasy, but just as often there is a strong element of parable asking why things might not be just as well some other way rather than the way we expected and presumed. (p. 61)

The interlude on myth and parable illustrates the binary principle so near and dear to the structuralist views, but also serves to highlight the role of the myth in the spectrum of the story. The myth is the story par excellence, and the story, while having a structure of its own with which one must contend, is first and foremost content-oriented. The point is not a minor one, and this truth will become increasingly important as the role of the myth in personality integration moves more to our fore.

Returning to the issue of myth itself, it is apparent by now that the concept itself is at once beset with difficulties on all sides and yet truly meaningful when used to describe the rich, often sacred, sometimes very serious, and always imaginative stories of the early origins of a given people or the human race as seen in various traditions. Attempting to classify or categorize myths, then, is acknowledged by all as a rather hopeless task. Yet withal, it is not a useless endeavor. However inadequate, a classification of some kind is preferred to none, for it at least gives one an assist toward comprehension.

In an effort to render a classification we could turn to that often employed in treatises: myths of the cosmogonic type, theogonic type, and anthropogonic type, each of which in turn deals with the origins of the cosmos, the gods, or mankind. Then to these we could add myths dealing with the primitive state of the cosmos and mankind, such as the Paradise myths; the soteriological myths dealing with the savior gods; and the eschatological myths, dealing with the destruction of the cosmos and the arrival of the hero-god at the time of final judgment. Such a classification, however, with its subsequent subclassifications quickly becomes unwieldy.

A very meaningful classification or typology has been suggested by G. S. Kirk of the University of Bristol, who proffers one that emphasizes the narrative and speculative aspects of myth rather than their practical and ceremonial ones (1970, p. 253ff.). It has the additional merit of avoiding those problems that arise when emphasis is placed upon items of less consequence. Kirk would suggest that myths be classified in three categories allied with their respective mythical functions.

The first of these divisions is the type that deals with primarily narrative and entertaining aspects; the second with operative, iterative, and validatory functions; and the third with the more speculative, explanatory functions. In the first category, the emphasis centers on myths that are heavily narrative with little or no speculative or operative content. In this class would be included those that build upon legendary myths that are preserved through their appeal as simple tales or as elaborated relics of the past. Such would include parts of the Homeric *Iliad* or Hesiod's poem *Ehoeae*. The second class, that of the operative, iterative, and validatory type, would include those that tend to be repeated regularly on ritual or ceremonial occasions and whose repetition is part of their value and meaning. Such are the many fertility myths or rituals and the kinds of myths celebrated by the findings and reflections of Mirceau Eliade. Such myths would confirm, preserve the memory of, and provide authority for tribal customs and institutions, such as the clan system or the institution of kingship and succession. These we would find highlighted in the work of Malinowski dealing with the Trobriand Islanders. On occasion, this class would lend itself to some overlap with the first category, but often their content shows little in the way of narrative and more in the emphasis of mythical relations, wherein, for example, the moon is seen as the wife or child of the sun. The third or speculative variety—myths that are extremely significant by any standards—serve an explanatory function and often tend to be highly imaginative and fantastic. They purport, as it were, to offer solutions, or at least possible solutions, for human problems, although those solutions are at times unreal or highly mythical. Such would be the *Myth of Gilgamesh*, a quasi-divinity whose humanity on his father's side leads him to grapple with the problem of his own mortality, a fate that was not to his liking but which he eventually came to accept. This theme also features in the Greek myth of Orpheus and Eurydice. Such myths hold considerable fascination even for modern readers who find themselves dealing with the same basic human problems, none of which admits of easy answers and all of which pose weighty problems for the humanity that we all share.

This classification, by Kirk's own admission, is not unflawed. It has, however, the merit of holding out some measure of understanding for the modern thinker, allows for an overlap in its analysis, and yet claims for itself no more than a reasonable plausibility of establishing some grasp of a subject that is truly complex and at times overwhelming. Thus we are led to a growing respect for the heroic efforts of the mythical imagination of our ancient forebears. The plenitude of their achievement provided them with considerable sustenance. What is even more astounding is the fact that it likewise speaks, fascinates, intrigues, and seriously impresses the person of the contemporary scene.

## B. THREE SIGNIFICANT CONSIDERATIONS

Ever since the time of Bultmann the notion of demythologizing has commanded serious attention. It manifest the efforts of Bultmann and others to cut the myth down to size, so to speak, to rid it of its excesses and to set it forth in its proper glory. There was in the myth much pseudo-knowledge, accretions that had gathered over the ages, and the truth-seeking expression in the myths was covered over like a palimpsest. To demythologize is to attempt to arrive at the rich kernel of truth inherent in the myth. Its effort should not be understood as an attack on the myth itself. This is why Ricoeur suggests that we speak, not of demythization, but of demythologizing. The human race has always had its myths and continues to have them; to demythologize is to make the effort to preserve the genuine in the myth and to share it with one's fellow human.

The previous section indicated in brief form the great problems associated with the question of understanding precisely what a myth is and, some such understanding assumed, the need to separate the chaff from the wheat, setting the myth forth in its genuine glory as a rich and sacred story. Unfortunately, as we have seen, this is not an easy task.

That much having been granted, it still remains that certain features of myths have begun to emerge from the many studies of the experts over the past century. We say the past century, for it has been during that time that the myth as myth has come into its own, or at least begun to do so. Thus it is no exaggeration to say that it is only in the relatively modern period that we have come to recognize the myth as myth—which is one way of saying that we have learned to distinguish it from authentic history on the one hand and from genuine explanation on the other. Yet it makes its appeal to the days of yore—*in illo tempore*—and to a basic wisdom of sorts that it embodies.

Three particular considerations about myth would now be advanced. They emerge from a careful perusal of our previous discussion and a thoughtful meditation on the myth as we are coming to know it. First of all there is the basic fact that the myth is highly languaged and cannot be understood apart from languages. Whether one focuses on the details of the unfolding myth itself, or attends to the metaphors and symbols that permeate it, or seeks to trace within a given myth the archetype that it appears to mirror, one is engaged with language. Even if we were to favor the view that the myth originates in some instances in a ritual that is carefully and periodically enacted, the issue of language remains paramount. The ritual, for all its emphasis on acts, is a studied enactment of a people and one that is itself thoroughly languaged. The truth is that any cultural achievement of a people is a languaged achievement, even if it be carried out in silence. It speaks to and for all just as loudly as do archeological finds. Thus the myth manifests a style of languaging, a way of speaking about life, a depiction of a people's thought, as surely as rituals and ceremonies declaim the inner man and his sentiments. Nothing, for example, is more spoken, and spoken with keener expertise, than is mime. The ritual is akin to mime, and the myth is at one with the ritual.

It is in the unfolding of the languaging that one meets up with the metaphors and symbols that permeate the myth. We have seen previously that the metaphor, which would transport us beyond in some manner or other, is at the origin of the symbol. It is apparent from the respective myths that they are replete with symbols of many kinds, be they symbols of action, ritual, or mere formal words. And it is in the understanding of the many symbolic manifestations in the myth that one comes to grasp the powerful meaning and significant depths that the myth may actually contain for the initiated. Whether one chooses to explain the significant depths in terms of a presumed archetype upon which myths are allegedly based, or prefers to explain them in terms of a basic human structure (as Harry Stack Sullivan has phrased it, we are all very human and thus will be found to act in basic human ways), it still remains that the myth at this level is a human creation and represents a highly imaginative, languaged achievement.

A second critical consideration we would note is the narrative form that the myth always takes. As stated previously in our discussion on Crossan's work, the myth constitutes a story endowed with its own unique time and place and extended over some stretch of primordial time in drama fashion. It comes to grips with the human situation, the human issues, by throwing them back into a primordial time and casting them into the larger-than-life *dramatis personae*, if not would-be gods, and moves by many plots, subplots, and detours toward minor and major resolutions that would seem to offer mankind the sought-for plenitude or wholeness that is missing from the lived human life. To say that it always seeks to offer a reconciliation may be to say too much, for many of the reconciliations seem anything but that. It does, however, often provide a semblance of resolution and provides those concerned with a depiction of a struggle engaged and the possibility of an acceptable resolve.

In so doing the myth is capturing the drama that the human experience of life actually is, with all its inevitabilities. Nothing for the human is ever finished once and for all. No great decision brings everything to the longed-for closure. Dissonance accompanies decision after decision and must be lived with. Thus the entire narrative, which every human is ever enduring, should be depicted as just that: an ongoing drama of endless dimensions, none of which is ever put to final rest, and decisions that can still haunt one long after they have ceased to be important. In short, the myth expresses dramatically ambiguous drama that is the human life. As Ricoeur has phrased it,

> Hence, the narrative form is neither secondary nor accidental, but primitive and essential. The myth performs its symbolic function by the specific means of narration because what it wants to express is already a drama. It is this primordial drama that opens up and discloses the hidden meaning of human experience; and so the myth that recounts it assumed the irreplaceable function of narration. (1960, p. 170)

Human beings love their stories if for no other reason than that they are always living one. We are at home, from the inside, with the drama, the play, the novel, the anecdote, because we are living them constantly. And it takes but little for us to recognize something of our own story in even the most bizarre of narratives, for the most tranquil of lives has more than its share of the bizarre. As we commonly phrase it, truth is stranger than fiction. Thus we can allow for considerable exaggeration, if need be, for we have all known such exaggerated moments at close range. Strange as it may seem, we can even allow for the impossible, unlikely resolution, for it enables us to taste for a while that wholeness that is at the base of the mythical endeavor. "And they lived happily ever after" we say with an affirming nod of the head, knowing full well that they really did not. Thus the reconciliations proposed by many myth narratives are not reconciliations at all. But neither do they have to be, for the myth to realize its purpose. We know, as we see the myth coming to its would be happy close, that a new struggle looms on the horizons and soon will be engaging the gods or the heroes. It is the unspoken agreement to let it suffice for the moment that there was the possibility, however unlikely, of resolution, and that suffices for the myth to have served its purpose. Human beings can understand that, and it is even reassuring that they learn that the gods, too, found answers that were not perfect. Humans love their stories, and they never tire of dreaming about Camelot.

A third consideration would be advanced, and this is much to the heart of our topic. The myth is a story, and, like every story, it is the fruit of our creative imagination. We have seen that it is certainly not history, and, though we have mentioned that it attempts to share understandings of sorts, it is not philosophy or science. Nonetheless, it takes us back to primordial time, and introduces us to the actions and antics of the gods and heroes of yore. Imaginative thought is of its very essence. We enter the thinking and musings of the heroes, the struggles with which they were engaged, the feelings that seized them amid their struggles, the machinations in which they indulged, the idealism that they were wont to personify, the broodings in which they were caught, the pettiness that beset them on occasion, and the manner in which they sought to work out their perplexities. All this taps the imaginative genius of the people, their bards, their storytellers, their troubadors. In the myth we see the real and powerful force of imaginative thinking at work, and we can with ease understand the appeal that such stories held out to the ancients. They were imaginative creations designed to appeal to the imaginative thought of the populace.

But the myth did more. In its embodiment of the narrative it reflected within limits the lives of the people themselves. It depicted in exaggerated form the thoughts, questions, suspicions, wonderings of the people. The gods and heroes, if you will, were the people written large with extravagances and grandiosity. It is never a question of truthfully and accurately portraying the doings of the people and the gods; it is a question of imaginatively raising to heroic proportions for human consumption the issues of life with which people were confronted. Thus the myth tells us much about the people in their humanity, but it deals with that humanity from a distance, in terms of the gods and heroes.

In the light of all this, it is understandable how the very ancient myths could give rise to a Homer, to use the case of the Greeks. Applying his genius to the artistic assembling of the stories of yore set the stage for the *Iliad* and the *Odyssey* where we meet the myths once again, but now in a more disciplined and restrained form. From there it was but a small step from Homer to Aeschylus, from the *Iliad* to the *Oresteia*, from the myth to the drama, both of which are stories which spoke to the people ultimately about themselves, just as they ultimately speak to us now about the people. The myth, like the drama, calls for an imaginative engagement with and appropriation of the story by the hearer or the audience. It bids us follow the god or the hero over a series of life movements imaginatively depicted. It shares with the hearer another's life (however large that other, however large that life) in the hopes that the audience itself, in and through its appropriation of the issues dwelt upon, may move into its own life somehow affected by the experience inspired. From every angle, be it that of the creation of the myth, or the narration of the myth, or the hearing and appropriation of the myth, the appeal is to imaginative thought imaginatively enlivened.

That the mythical depiction should make use of metaphors and symbols in countless forms is not surprising. It is precisely what we would expect. On all sides we find their impact being felt in our lives, so much so that it is impossible to conceive of a human life being lived without them. By the same token it is to be expected that the narrative about life should manifest that same predilection. It is true of our stories; it was true of their stories.

It is becoming clearer, then, that the story is an item of no little consequence to the human person, not only because the person is ever and eagerly responsive to the imaginative appeal of a story when narrated, but also, and maybe primarily, because the person is himself living out a story of his own creation, proceeding imaginatively through his or her own life. We have seen that Malinowski disputed the idea that the myth is always explanatory, at least in tribal myth. We might add that neither is the story always explanatory. Kluckhohn saw it in fact as having some entertaining value. We can claim the same for the story; its entertainment value is obvious, but its thought-provoking contribution to life should not be underestimated. A significant story can bring new, important and much needed heroes into everyone's life.

These three aspects of the myth just indicated—its languaged nature, it narrative form, and its imaginative coloration, permeation—give us occasion to pause. For these are precisely three critical dimensions of our own human lives. In each individual, as well as community of peoples, we find a narration of some kind being enacted. Every people to be vital, must experience itself moving in some directions. Its ideals, its dreams, its hopes—its narrative, if you will—provides that direction in broad terms: A person's narrative is the movement in which he, she, they are engaged.

We find at the same time the important fact that every narrative of a person or people is languaged. In saying this we are not adverting to the fact that each speaks its own tongue, although that, to be sure, is implied in the statement. Our attention, on the contrary, is addressed to the fact that the wording of life is intrinsic to its being lived, and our human institutions of whatever kind— hospitals, schools, churches, government, policies, laws, courts, and the rest—have come into being through the instrumentality of human languaging. Had word broken off, no thing of any kind would ever have been. Thus our lives, like the myths that describe them, must have their narrative and be languaged through and through.

Finally, the human narrative is not only described imaginatively as in the myth, it is lived that way as well. It is imaginative thought—thought saturated with the imaginative—that is found animating, invigorating, exciting, urging, intriguing human life, even at times obsessing it to the degree that it is conceivably endangering the human enterprise. To hope to eradicate the imaginative from the human, however, is futile. Moreover it is undesirable to do so, for it would eliminate that in the human which founds

his freedom, furthers his sensitivity to his fellow person, and floods
the logical, rational talent in each of us with an infinity of possibilities. It should never be our intent to deprive the person of imaginative creativity, for that would be to seek the death of the human.
Rather it is the human goal to employ the imaginative potential
and the rational endowment of the person and place them both in
the service of our worthiest dreams.

Thus our reflections on the myth and the story with their unique
triad of language, narrative, and imagination have brought us face
to face with the profound realization that the myth is in effect the
mirror of the languaged and imaginative narrative that is our lived
life. Small wonder that we humans love our stories.

## C. The Impact of Myth and Story at the Societal Level

Having traversed some difficult terrain in which we sought to
look for a comprehension of the myth as it has come to be understood through modern studies, and then focused on some unique
features of the myth, now seen as story, which qualify it to be the
paradigm par excellence for the human endeavor, we shall now
seek to find how the myth-story as such has figured in the human
picture. The present section will explore that topic at the community level, while the following will allow us to consider the myth-
story at the more personal level. It is here, of course, where we shall
see its immense relevance for the individual in his quest at integrating life.

Many examples could be cited to illustrate the societal impact
the myth-story can exercise. We shall focus on two, one illustrating
the societal hearkening to the ancient Teutonic myths endorsed by
the National Socialist party of Germany during the rise and power
of Hitler, and the other focusing on the myth-story that furthered
the spread of slavery in the United States and fostered its de facto
effects long after the abolition of slavery in 1863.

### 1. National Socialist Rise in Germany

The rise of Nazism in Germany centers around Adolph Hitler
himself, whose own artistic interests suffered badly in his early
years and whose political efforts at a coup d'etat against the

Republic in 1923 saw him jailed. His own personal strength derived much from his enthusiastic appreciation of Wagner's operas, Nietzsche's philosophy of the superman, and the anti-Semitic writings of Stewart Chamberlain, the Teutonized Britisher, who was the son-in-law of Richard Wagner and the author of a work *Foundations of the Nineteenth Century*, which advanced the thesis that virtue and civilization are the product of the Aryan race and are ever threatened by the Semitic people. Although an Austrian citizen, Hitler enlisted in the German army during the First World War and received an iron cross for valor. The subsequent German defeat and the republican revolution in Germany left him ashamed and embittered. At this point he decided to enter a political career.

In 1919 he joined army acquaintances to form the National Socialist (Nazi) party. They adopted a radical platform, denouncing the Peace of Paris, demanding unification of all Germans in a Greater Germany, the restoration of German colonies, the rearming of Germany, the denunciation of Jews in Germany as "aliens," and the denial of German citizenship to Jews with the threat of exile. In 1923 at the failure of the coup, as we have said, Hitler was sent to jail and spent the year writing his *Mein Kampf*, an exciting narration of his life and ideas. For the next five years he and his lieutenants strengthened the party organization, staged more and bigger demonstrations against the Republic, organized headquarters and cells in Munich for adults as well as societies for youth and children, set up a special police force and a corps of storm troopers. The former were clothed in brown shirts with the Aryan emblem of the Swastika in black on a red arm-band, while the latter had a uniform of black shirt with a skull as a badge. These provided protection for the Nazi leaders and meetings, while wreaking havoc on the meetings of their enemies. By the spring 1932 Hitler chose to run against President von Hindenburg but lost. In January 1933, however, the senile president was, through circumstances, forced to appoint Hitler to the chancellorship. It took only six months for Hitler to establish himself as the practical dictator of Germany. Hindenburg remained titular president, but the republic was dead, and Hindenburg himself was seriously ill.

The vote of the Reichstag to delegate its powers to the Hitler government on April 1, 1933, marked the formal demise of the German Republic and the birth of the Third German Empire, the first having been the Holy Roman Empire (962 to 1806) and the second the Hohenzollern Empire (1871 to 1918). Intense popular enthusiasm reigned everywhere, exploited by Hitler's propagandists. The press, radio, and cinema were used for patriotic purposes. Demonstrations abounded: brown-shirt troopers paraded and saluted; young folk sang and cheered; inflammatory speeches were the order of the day; swastika flags waved constantly. Joseph Goebbels, with his genius for showmanship, staged demonstration after demonstration, whipping up a whirlwind of hysteria that swept throughout the entire country. Amid all this were the vicious attacks against Jews and Marxists, who were made scapegoats for all the country's misfortunes since the World War.

On that same April 1, 1933, it was decreed that only Aryans (German citizens who were not Jews and whose parents and grandparents were not Jews) could occupy civil or military posts or serve as judges, policemen, school teachers, or university professors, and with this followed a wholesale dismissal of Jews and Christians with Jewish blood from all state institutions and public offices, as well as manufactured discriminations against them in professions and businesses. Then came periodic attacks on them individually and collectively—all designed to further national unity and patriotic fervor. A clean sweep was made of all elements who had opposed the Nazis during recent years. Obviously Jews suffered, as did Marxists, but so did many other German citizens who opposed the inhumanity of the government. Dissenters were either exiled or put into concentration camps. By November 1933 a new Reichstag was elected. Some 39.5 million cast ballots for the National Socialist candidates, and some 3.5 million ballots were left blank or spoiled. By the end of the year Hitler had destroyed the autonomy of Prussia, and that of every other historic German state—an achievement that the Hohenzollern empire never even dared to attempt. When, after the infamous purges of the 1934 summer, Hindenburg died, Hitler decreed that he would be chancellor and president. A popular ratification followed, and Hitler's new title became that of the imperial leader (*Reichsfuhrer*).

In all this, German National Socialism became the avowed foe of liberalism, democracy, Marxian socialism, pacifism, internationalism, and the Christian virtues of humility, meekness, and charity. It upheld the racial superiority of the Germans as "pure Aryans" who were considered inherently superior in moral virtue and military prowess to all Slavic and Latin neighbors, as well as the contaminating "Semitic" Jews at home. The followers of the party were inflamed with these teachings, while extremists among them cried out for a national repudiation of Christianity as well as a revival of the pre-Christian tribal and pagan religion of the ancient Germans, with at least symbolic worship of Thor and Woden and the veneration of the warrior-heroes of Valhalla. Among such extremists was the philosopher of National Socialism, Alfred Rosenberg, the Russian Jew, whose book of 1930, *The Myth of the Twentieth Century*, was an explication of the philosophy of the Nazi movement. Rosenberg had become the most ardent anti-Russian leader in the party.

During this ordeal, many upright and conscientious Germans, Jews as well as non-Jews, repudiated these doctrines and policies. Ultimately their choices were to escape into exile elsewhere in the world if they could, to suffer in silence at home, or to die in prison camps.

By March 1939—only six months after the famous Munich Pact—German nationalism had given rise to German imperialism. A short time later the Second World War began, a war that devastated the countries of Europe, led to the gutting of the entire German nation, saw the inhuman slaughter of some 6 million Jewish people, and ended in Europe with Hitler dying amid a blaze of smoke in his burning bunker.

This incredible history of the National Socialist movement in Germany cannot be properly understood unless one takes into account many factors that have not been mentioned in this sketch. That should be obvious. But at the same time it cannot be understood without considering the powerful role that the ancient Teutonic myths, as taken up by the Nazi movement, played throughout its history. It is a fact that Hitler himself took seriously the racist beliefs of the Teutonic past, particularly their anti-Semitic ones. And, as has been pointed out, these were at the heart of Rosenberg's philosophy. And they were at the heart of Teutonic thought long before Rosenberg. There is no doubt that Hitler owed much to the financial support he received from the Rhur barons and the East Prussian landowners. They were instrumental in bringing him into power. But he owed much to the Gotterdammerung and the heroes of old—not only for the epidemic spread of his teachings, but also for his own defeat and the destruction of his own country.

In the early eighteenth century the pre-Romantics among the Germans had supported the aspirations of rising ethnic groups and were sympathetic to their longings for some kind of independent nation or culture. Novalis, for example, in his *Christendom or Europe* (1799) extols the Middle Ages but also finds reasons to defend the French Revolution. Most of his contemporaries, however, were nonpolitical, although some Heidelberg intellectuals exhibited a German Romanticism that Henry Hatfield terms "pre-Nazi" (1960, p. 203). After the defeat of the Prussians by Napoleon in 1806, the interest of the German intellectuals in matters political grew remarkably. Younger writers were deeply stirred, and the myth of a medieval Germany charged with the poetic, the romantic took on a real political turn. The glories of Prussian military valor, the notions of northern superiority, the heroic figures of the forest, the empire of old became meaningful themes by the mid-century and thereafter.

> Broadly speaking, the German Romanticists display two related tendencies of much interest: the almost Faustian search for the original, the "*Ur*"; and the habit of thinking mythically, rather than in more or less precise, logical terms. In the search for origins, the Grimm Brothers, Friedrich Schlegel, Gorres, and Fichte are dominant figures. This enterprise combined a great deal of patient, scholarly work—one thinks of the fabulous industry of the Grimm Brothers, Friedrich Schlegel, Gorres, and Fichte are dominant figures. This enterprise combined a great deal of patient, scholarly work—one thinks of the fabulous industry of the Grimms— with reckless speculation, some of it highly chauvinistic. The Romantic scholar searched for the "*Ur*" myth, folk tale, language, and nation. Even the Grimms, conscientious scholars though they were, were often moved by a prejudice in favor of all things Germanic. The philosopher Fichte, like Gorres a lapsed liberal, proclaimed that the Germans were the *Urvolk*, and German the "*Ur*" Language. (Hatfield, 1960 p. 204)

One cannot help but think of the work of Friedrich Nietzsche. Some of his ideas, that of the superman, the blond beast, the will to power, speak certainly to the thought later developed by National Socialism. It is true that there are those who would allow for his metaphors and interpret him more sympathetically, but it remains a fact that his later works do speak loudly in praise of war, brutality, and power. And it also remains a fact that he held considerable appeal for many of the Nazi propagandists, and that his ideas wielded strong influence upon Hitler himself. Indeed there were few German intellectuals who were untouched by his thought.

Many other significant writers took up the same themes that were later embodied in the Nazi culture: the alleged superiority of the Germanic and Aryan people; the presumed distinction between the primitive Semites and the later "degenerate" Jews of the contemporary world; the evils of liberal thought; the glories of the northern heroes. None of them, however, compared to the figure of Richard Wagner, whose imaginative and musical genius and whose ability to attract and influence his contemporaries were truly remarkable. And his powerful anti-Semitism was unmistakably patent. As Hatfield expressed it,

> The virulence of Wagner's anti-Semitism is frightening. Towards the end of *Jewishness in Music* he speculates on the possibility of "casting out by force the decomposing alien element," but adds with apparent regret that he does not know whether forces exist to perform this task. Rather grudgingly, he concedes in the next sentence that the assimilation of the Jews may be possible, but the intention of the whole passage is such that one must agree with the epigram that Wagner "forged the uncreated conscience of the Third Reich." (Hatfield, p. 210)

The appeal of Wagner's thought and music to Hitler is well known, as was the thought of Wagner's son-in-law, Houston Stewart Chamberlain. His work, *The Foundations of the Nineteenth Century*, published in 1899, stressed the same basic ideas that were shared by German writers throughout the century: the superiority of race, the national hero, and the dangers of the Semitic influence. His work, less antagonistic than that of Wagner, was still influential and served the Nazi propaganda machine well. Indeed in *Parsifal*, Wagner had prepared the concept of Aryan Christianity that his future son-in-law would subsequently bequeath to Alfred Rosenberg and the Nazi movement. The traditions that reached into the past and which offered so much hope for the future were seized upon as needed. The idea of a leader as the Fuhrer, endowed almost with godlike qualities of omnipotence, omniscience, and infallibility was ideal for the Nazi purposes. The sense of national superiority that needed to be fostered to offset the remnants of past failure that dated even to the Thirty Years War was there to be stimulated, and it was during Hitler's rise to power. Then with the growing importance of the myth of Nazism, the repudiation of nineteenth-century softness, modern art, humanistic culture, and humanitarianism followed as night the day. The Prussian cult of hardness reared its head in the student duels and the "education for barbarism" practised by the SS in its *Ordensburgen*. Finally, as Hatfield remarks,

> Nazism marked a climax of the revolt against Christianity which has been such an important part of German (and European) intellectual life since the mid-eighteenth century . . . "Nordic" neopaganism, leading from relatively innocuous beginnings through Wagner to Rosenberg, is obviously an important factor. It ended in the most unrestrained endorsement of hardness, brutality, and the extermination of other races. (p. 218) 1960

Enough has been said to illustrate our point: that the myth-story has had its impact on human life at the societal level. Unlike the myths of old, the Nazi story is history, but it is a history in which mythical elements played a powerful and sinister role. To explain the entire historical phenomenon of Nazism in terms of the myth-story alone would be extravagant and exaggerated. He who proves too much proves nothing. But to say that this phenomenon had its demonic elements and that they originated in part and fed upon the Teutonic myth-stories is to say no more than the truth.

### 2. *Myth of Racism in the United States*

The previous section dealt with an historical development that was tied in with ancient and powerful Teutonic myths, whose impact on the unfolding of history was incredible. We would now treat briefly of another historical development whose underlying myth, while having possible remote mythical ties, is actually of more modern origin. We shall be speaking of the myth of slavery, in which one race is seen by another race, not as inferior, but as dehumanized. They were seen to be people who did not possess human rights and were thus to be considered as chattle. In presenting this myth-story we shall again briefly sketch the historical picture, and then look to see the presence and power of the myth that sustained it.

By the year 1500 slavery had long disappeared from Europe, but it had been practiced by the Portuguese and Spaniards in the West Indies, Mexico, Peru, and Brazil, who forced the native Indians to hard labor in field and mine. These non-European slaves were not used simply because of the need for labor, but also because of the debilitating climate in the tropics that the Europeans themselves were unable to withstand. Before many years, it became apparent that the natives themselves were in danger of extermination for the same reasons. By 1517 a plea was sent to the king of Spain that blacks from tropical Africa were better adapted than native Americans to forced labor in the West Indies. That year the king granted a patent to one of his subjects in the Netherlands, authorizing him to supply 4,000 blacks annually to the West Indies. The patent was sold in turn to some Genoese merchants, who then bought the slaves from the Portuguese. This was the beginning of the first systematized slave trade between Portuguese Africa and Spanish America. Once legitimated, it grew rapidly, and slave catching in Africa became an intrinsic element to plantation growing in America. Europeans were enriched by slave labor in a way that they could never have been enriched by free labor at home.

The English landed at Jamestown in 1607, and brought in blacks in 1619. At first these were indentured servants. In time, however, slavery was introduced into the British colonies, and by the middle of the eighteenth century slavery had become an important part of the economic life in colonial America. There were protests. Quakers and some other Christians inveighed against it, but the vast majority accepted it as unavoidable and even highly desirable. As one might expect, the issue became embarrassing when, in time, the colonists began accusing England of oppressing them. In 1764 James Otis in his *Rights of the British Colonies* acknowledged the black's inalienable right to freedom. Ten years later, in 1774, several blacks addressed the Massachusetts General Court, asserting their natural right to freedom. In the meantime, at the Boston Massacre in 1770, there emerged the shocking fact that the first person to die in the fight for freedom was a black patriot, Crispus Attucks. Finally, when Thomas Jefferson submitted his early draft of the Declaration of Independence to the Continental Congress, it was unacceptable to the Southern delegation to include his reference to sacred rights which were being violated by carrying people into slavery. The reference was omitted from the document. When the War of Independence did break out, blacks were not allowed to fight for the colonies. That changed quickly, however, when the English offered freedom to those blacks who would fight with them against the colonies. By the end of the hostilities, some 5,000 blacks were fighting for the colonies.

Despite the growing opposition to the institution of slavery, the Constitutional Convention of 1787 upheld it. Indeed it was decided that for purposes of representation in Congress, a slave should be counted as three-fifths of other persons and that any slave caught running away should be returned by the states to the rightful owner. This provision was written into the new Constitution, thus not only recognizing slavery but also putting the resources of the country behind the institution. It flourished. In 1790 there were approximately 700,000 slaves in the country; by 1860 there were almost 4 million.

In addition to all this, to protect the owners and their possessions, the respective states drew up slave codes. In substance these codes decreed that slaves could not be away from their owner's premises without written permission; that they were incompetent to make contracts, including that of marriage; that their testimony was inadmissible in any litigation with a white person; that they were not to own property; that they could not be taught to read or write; that they were not permitted to assemble without the presence of a white person. Needless to say, enforcement of all such codes was often impossible, but the laws remained in existence nonetheless. On the other hand, the slaves' task and purpose for living was defined as the duty to provide income and comfort for their owners. Even those blacks who were free (approximately a half million by 1860), it should be noted, were subject to proscriptive laws as severe as those governing the slaves. Limited education, socializing, and religious organization were allowed them, but their contact with slaves was discouraged, and their competition with whites for jobs was circumscribed.

The Civil War started in April 1861. Blacks rushed to offer their services to the North, but they were sent back home. They then gave money, goods, and other kinds of support: as cooks, teamsters, hospital attendants, scouts, and so on. They were not welcome, however, to fight side by side with the white soldiers. Only after the Emancipation Proclamation went into effect on January 1, 1963, were they invited to enlist; and by the end, some 186,000 had done so. Of that number some 38,000 gave their lives, and many a black soldier was cited for gallantry.

The next hundred years saw the blacks go through the Reconstruction period and post-reconstruction with their conditions steadily deteriorating. Their only hope lay in education, and they expended constant effort in that direction. The First World War saw over a third of a million serve in the armed forces and brought new hopes to the race as its people participated vigorously in the national crisis. After the war their new hopes were dashed quickly as riots, lynchings, and burnings became commonplace. The Second World War saw some million blacks in service, and, despite the persistence of segregation and discrimination, they served in all branches of the armed forces. President Truman ended discrimination in the service, but it was the Supreme Court of the United States that stepped in to advance the question of civil rights. Thus the winds of change blew forcefully during the 1950s and continued during the 1960s and 1970s, but not without much fighting, suffering, and dying. And the struggle is by no means ended even yet.

Looking at the race question as sketched above, it becomes apparent that we are dealing, not with a mere view or cultural bias on the part of a few closed Americans, but with a kind of mythical thinking—a strange and highly emotional story that goes way back in the history of the continent—that was appropriated by the descendants of the early colonists on this land. Obviously slavery did not originate in the colonies. It was found everywhere and even in antiquity. Indeed when the first settlers—the Spanish and Portuguese—arrived, they found the concept of slavery in practice among the natives. Slaves were the booty of wars even among the tribes. Thus the colonialists did not hesitate to exploit the situation, knowing full well that it would be impossible to do so if one were dealing with Europeans. Somehow, however, the importation of non-Christian blacks from Africa gave the practice a legitimacy it might not otherwise have maintained.

We have seen, of course, that in the colonies the practice was challenged, but it continued despite the challenges. In 1764 James Otis saw and admitted its wrong: that the colonists' lives were giving the lie to their protests to the king. It was hypocrisy to accuse the king of wrong when he was doing to the colonists the very thing they were doing to the blacks. Jefferson and many other delegates to the Continental Congress also knew and admitted the evil of their ways. The members of the Constitutional Convention eleven years later were aware of the movements in Philadelphia, New York, Massachusetts, and New Jersey to abolish slavery, but they continued in bitter battle over the issue nonetheless. When the convention ended, its decision allowed them to count the slave as three-fifths of a person, and to return fugitives to their owners; but it also had agreed, after acrimonious debate, that the slave trade, if prohibited it must be, would not be prohibited for some twenty more years: 1808.

About this same time, on April 12, 1787, George Washington wrote a letter to Robert Morris of Philadelphia expressing his feelings about slavery:

> I hope it will not be conceived from these observations, that it is my wish to hold the unhappy people, who are the subject of this letter, in slavery. I can only say that there is not a man living who wishes more sincerely than I do, to see a plan adopted for the abolition of it—but there is only one proper and effectual mode by which it can be accomplished, and that is by legislative authority. (1972, p. 276)

In 1808 the African slave trade was formally closed. Traders continued to smuggle in thousands of slaves to a ready market from the Carribean as well as Africa, and from many parts of the domestic scene as well. In brief, the young nation, however dedicated to freedom for the human being, moved without qualms of conscience to deny that same freedom to human beings—and the principal justification for their charged emotionalism was the fact that the slaves were black. That fact was considered sufficient to explain all the limitations that the enslaved people manifested; and in substance the skin color has remained the basis for the discrimination and injustice inflicted upon them ever since.

The race myth holds that the racial differences were normal and natural, and that the black American was a classical example of an inferior people. During the Reconstruction William G. Sumner even expressed the notion that Reconstruction was an attempt to reverse the natural course of things in which superior whites ruled over inferior blacks. And he was not alone in his espousal of this myth. Says Franklin,

> The most respected literary journals of the country reflected the view that the Negro was inferior and did not possess rights which

should be protected by the government. Articles made them appear ludicrous by bestowing absurd titles on them and describing them as superstitious, dull, stupid, imitative, ignorant, happy-go-lucky, improvident, lazy, immoral, and criminal. The leading writers seemed to want to justify almost any degradation of Negroes at the hands of their white superiors. (v. 16, p. 190)

This myth did not die easily, and in many parts of the United States it has yet to die. But it is only when one considers the power of the myth that one can understand the history of the question since the Emancipation Proclamation went into effect on January 1, 1863. With that document slavery as an institution in the United States did indeed die; but the racial myth that gave rise to the institution and maintained it against all rational and human arguments did not die. It is only in the last two decades that the myth as such has been forthrightly challenged, and much more effort will need to be expended before the myth is laid to rest for good.

These two examples of the impact of myth at the societal level could well constitute books of their own. In both instances intelligent, moral, Christian peoples were caught up in a frenzy, a hideous and cruel frenzy against another people, and their obsession blinded them against seeing the truth that would have shown them the evil of their ways. In studying the two histories, one can move from one to the other and perceive little or no difference in the stories. In the one instance, the myth built around the people's blood; in the other it focused on the people's color. The differences, however, are trivial. Both are classical instances of the power of myth once it captures the imagination of human beings. In these cases it diminished everyone. In another instance, however, another myth, used for the betterment of all, could conceivably uplift and renew a world.

## D. The Impact of the Myth-Story at the Personal Level

That the myth-story has ever held an appeal for the human imagination is granted by all. What is most interesting, however, is the change that the myth has undergone—a point that Claude Lévi-Strauss has made in his *Myth and Meaning*. Like a chameleon, the myth-story has been camouflaged; but even in its new form it continues to exert the appeal as of old. It is a matter of history that the influence of the myth-story began to wane in the Western world sometime during and after the late Renaissance. No doubt the intellectual revolution that we have previously described helps explain the decline of the myth-story, as the emphasis on logical, rational thinking became so pronounced. Then, with the Enlightenment and the strong rise of science, the force of the myth became almost negligible. However, this development in no way lessened the appeal of the story. That has continued to the present day.

It is Lévi-Strauss's contention that the role of the myth-story was taken over in the seventeenth and eighteenth centuries by the rise of the novel-story and in the nineteenth century by classical opera story, many of which, like Bellini's *Norma*, Verdi's *La Traviata* and *Il Trovatore*, Mozart's *Don Giovanni* and *Magic Flute*, Bizet's *Carmen*, and others build expressly around mythical themes or capture the imaginative dimensions of dark passion. That there is considerable truth in his views would seem to follow from the intense interest that such novels and operas continue to exert at the present time. The myth, to be sure, no longer commands our attention as such, but the opera, the novel, the play, the oratorio, the concert, the symphony certainly do. And all such instances build around a narrative, not a mere metaphor as did the more Baroque music. Musical themes now tell stories, create plots, lead to altercations, and depict resolutions every bit as exciting as any novel or any ancient myth. Indeed the story is as alive and appealing as ever (1979).

Another area in which the importance of the myth-story and the story is asserting itself is the domain of religion, where the rise of narrative theology is most pronounced. This attempt to see in the inspirational stories of religion a significant way in which to impart religious truths marks a trailblazing departure from the more traditional approaches. It is an effort based on the realization that the story approach is not an empty venture. It is one that speaks to the heart of the person with a profound appeal to the imagination, and, being so, it is one highly calculated to touch heart and lives in a manner that a mere didactic approach could not hope to equal. As John Shea puts it, speaking of Elie Wiesel,

His telling of the Isaac story is a case in point. Isaac, like Wiesel himself, is a survivor of a holocaust. God ordered his slaughter, then relented. Yet the name Isaac means laughter. The story of Isaac is a tale of the affirmation of life in the face of the despair and nihilism of holocaust. As Wiesel tells the story his own story is taken up and moved beyond madness and murder. (Shea, 1978, p. 58)

Subsequently Shea addresses himself to the Christian story or stories, all of which spring from a rich and powerful tradition that allows each to have an integrity of its own while at the same time being gathered up in mega-stories with their connecting patterns: hope and justice, trust and freedom, invitation and decision (p. 75). Casting religious understandings and/or truths in such a narrative form bequeathes to them a power that is by no means negligible, an appeal that cannot be overestimated, and a fascination that lingers in the memory and personal history long after the hearing is over.

Needless to say, the influence wielded by the story in the novel, the opera, the symphony as well as the theological narrative, is manifested primarily at the individual novel-reader or opera-goer or church-attender level. In these instances it is the person who is touched, inspired, transformed, or moved. The end result may be primarily aesthetic or practical, and in all instances it is highly personal. And this we expect. However, there is another sphere where the story becomes personal but also professional. Here we might not expect that it even belongs, but it does. It is to this that we would now turn.

### 1. StoryTelling in Psychotherapy

The history of psychotherapy is complex, and it has been told by many authors. The styles of therapy and the techniques developed within the respective styles are centered, as one would expect, around the theoretical stances and its metaphorizations. Freud, for example, building around his picture of human nature, sought in a very specialized technique to bring to consciousness the unconscious repressions that were exacting their toll on the client's living. Sullivan focused on the impact of the interpersonal experiences that were at the heart of the individual's personalizations. The same could be said of Jung, Rogers, and others. It is true of the gamut of theorists, in the vast majority of which the role of the therapist is a relatively passive one.

During the 1950s a variety of therapeutic stances and techniques began to appear on the scene. These were multiplied during the 1960s, and, as a result, many new therapeutic approaches were introduced in which the therapist's role moved from a relatively passive one to a distinctly active one. Such an innovation was the work of Milton Erickson, considered by some as the outstanding of modern therapists. Founding president of the American Society of Clinical Hypnosis, and founding editor of the *American Journal of Clinical•Hypnosis*, Erickson had an impact on the American scene that has grown since his death in 1979. Master of strategic therapy, in which the .therapist plays the critical and significant role in effecting changes in the lives of his clients, Erickson, who had become recognized as the world's leading medical hypnotist, developed a style and technique, an approach, that grew directly out of his hypnotic orientation. Indeed it has been said that his strategic therapy was a logical extension of hypnotic technique (Haley, 1973, p. 19).

Central to the therapeutic stance of Milton Erickson, and critical to the theme of our present study, is his extraordinary emphasis on the matter of storytelling. Not only was Erickson a masterful storyteller himself, but his understanding of the importance of storytelling for the therapist and the client was truly remarkable. In this respect he would appear to have been a cut all his own.

In all aspects of his work, be it hypnosis or therapy, Erickson had constant recourse to the telling of stories. To be sure, the choice to do so was not a happenstance or a mere personal preference. Ultimately it was a conviction Erickson shared with colleagues and followers that the real change is effected within a person by communicating in metaphor. It should be pointed out here that the form that the preoccupation with metaphor took with Erickson was always the narrative. His genius for metaphor was captured in and embodied in the narrative. All his students acknowledge this fact. As one has put it,

> Having paced the client's conscious mind with an initially direct allegory, Erickson often will then begin to vary the content of what he says further and further from the literal and recognizable situation with which he began. . . .
>
> Careful management of the story's content will occupy and distract the client's conscious mind and the fixed set of associations contained within it. Further tangents and new turns in the story

leave the listener suspended and continually anticipating some direction. This state of attention allows the storyteller to access more powerful and flexible processes that are functioning out of the client's awareness but evident to the therapist's sensory experience. (Haley, 1973, p. 27)

In brief, Erickson's anecdotal or storytelling method enabled him to deal indirectly at all stages of hypnosis or therapy with his client. It was this indirect approach that caught up his client in an engaging way and yet put the person at ease to such an extent that Erickson was enabled to move into very difficult issues and areas in the person's life without arousing needless fears and anxieties. In so doing he was able to tap the person's own resources and to foster the individual's own sense of autonomy.

Jeffrey Zeig, president of the Milton H. Erickson Foundation, in his *Teaching Seminar with Milton H. Erickson*, speaks to this aspect:

There are a number of other things to keep in mind regarding Erickson's teaching stories. Erickson was a very consistent individual. He lived and worked by telling stories. This was true if he was talking to his family, colleagues, students or patients. If one asked him for advice, Erickson usually replied with an anecdote. Therefore, in this book one gets a good impression of Erickson's therapeutic, as well as his educational, approach.

Additionally, Erickson was very involved in the telling of his teaching stories. One often got the impression that he was reliving the story as he told it. Erickson told his stories with a sense of drama; he orchestrated his stories in a lively manner. (1980, p. xxviii)

Proceeding to synopsize for the reader just how Erickson did employ the story, Zeig points out that he used it in regular therapy for purposes of making a diagnosis, of establishing rapport with a client, of carrying out a treatment with an individual. That treatment might involve a story so that something could be illustrated, a solution suggested, a measure of self-recognition promoted, an idea or seed of ideas implanted, or some other purpose. Similarly in hypnosis Erickson would use the story toward the same three ends: diagnosis, rapport, and treatment. In other words the possibilities Erickson saw in the story were almost beyond estimation. Using it, then, was a means of reaching the person as effectively and non-threateningly as possible. And it was his conviction that the story approach guaranteed that the experience would remain with the subject for a considerable length of time. Good stories are not quickly forgotten.

Many examples could be cited from the literature concerning Erickson's use of the metaphor, especially in its story form. Haley gives countless instances of such. So too does Zeig. One such instance in the *Teaching Seminar* is the inspirational story of Joe, a young man whom Erickson met when Erickson himself was only ten years old. After describing expertly the young man's struggle during the imprisonments, his meeting a local farmer's daughter whom he came to respect and love, the metamorphosis that the man underwent over the ensuing years and his extraordinary living of an ordinary life to the age of seventy, Erickson concludes his comments by remarking to the students, "Now all the psychotherapy he had was, 'You can, if you are a gentleman.' " (1980 p. 121).

This particular remark was made to Joe by the young woman the first time he ever asked her if he could take her to the Friday-night dance. It was not much, perhaps, but it stated enough to start him imagining himself as a gentleman, and it stayed with him for a lifetime.

It was Erickson's contention that the therapist's task required that he understand his client as well as possible and provide the right metaphors and stories around which the client could build. These, he contended, are what works the changes once the client has been genuinely touched. As Erickson puts it himself in one of the seminars:

> I don't think the therapist does anything except provide the opportunity to think about your problem in a favorable climate. And all the rules of Gestalt therapy, psychoanalysis and transactional analysis . . . many theorists write them down in books as if every person was like every other person. And so far I've found in fifty years, every person is a different individual. I always meet every person as an individual, emphasizing his or her own individual qualities. (1980, p. 219)

## 2. *The Story and the Integrating Process: Story-Living*

### WHEN I HAVE FEARS

When I have fears that I may cease to be
  Before my pen has gleaned my teeming brain,

Before high-piled books, in charact'ry
  Hold like rich garners the full-ripened grain;
When I behold, upon the night's starred face,
  Hugh cloudy symbols of a high romance,
And think that I may never live to trace
  Their shadows, with the magic hand of chance;
And when I feel, fair creature of an hour,
  That I shall never look upon thee more,
Never have relish in the faery power
  Of unreflecting love!—then on the shore
Of the wide world I stand alone, and think
Till love and fame to nothingness do sink.

John Keats

The fears expressed by Keats are the fears of everyone. The realization that all things will pass away, that many a talent will go unfully used, that many would-be accomplishments will never come to fruition, that the great capacities for love in life will scarcely be touched before one's life comes to its close—such realizations do give one reason to think, and to think alone, about the meaning of love and fame and life itself. Life will indeed see its end long before its end has truly ended, long before one's dreams are fully and finally brought to their happy close. Such is the human lot.

But Keats's words have also depicted the nature of the human venture. We live with our goals, we pursue our ideals, we follow after our dreams, we seek to implement our plans. Coming out of our past, we embrace the present with our minds and hearts turned toward the future. And, as Heidegger has said so well, we see our past coming to us out of the future. In short, our lives are unique combinations of the past, present, and future, and any effort we expend toward the integration of that life is a highly imaginative achievement. It is the imaginative projection that brings the future to us in the present, that makes the future a burning, moving force in the living of our present moment. Our motivations are our present's grasp on our future realizations. They are the future burning in the present's heart. Thus the thought that much of that future will be left unrealized when one's life is drawing to a close is a sobering one indeed—as Keats has well said. But at the same time the understanding that the present's imaginative projections are the secret of our future's accomplishments, however many or few, however great or small, makes the dreaming of the dreams and the pursuing of ideals all worthwhile.

Thus it is that we all turn to the story that is our lives with its past, present, and future dimensions. One may word his life many ways, and one does. We may metaphorize its phases or moments in unique and often spectacular styles, as we certainly do, so that we may make sense of the many discrepancies that threaten to bewilder us. And we may find ourselves bringing together whole areas of our lives in rich symbolic forms, as a consequence of which we move with subtle but real familiarity in great reaches of our lives made emotionally accessible to us because of the symbolism that they awaken, often so unexpectedly. Still it is necessary that we do more. Metaphorizations and symbolizations are inadequate for comprehending our whole life narrative. It is necessary that we paint in broader strokes, so to speak, to bring it all together for ourselves, to garner a picture of the entire spread of our lives—if we would seek to effect some kind of an intelligible unity in the whole. That is why it is necessary to imagine it more as a story with its past roots, its present opportunities, and its future possibilities, and with, to be sure, its share of meaningful symbols and vital metaphors. For the broad picture encompasses many aspects of life that metaphors and symbols of themselves do not account for or allow. In fact they themselves are ultimately intelligible only in the light of some kind of greater interest or life trajectory or personal dream that we are itching to live out or reenact. In its light the other details may take on deeper meaning, for that life span provides a larger context in which they can all be understood.

We are not suggesting that our life at any time can be laid out before us as a map, much less a blueprint. We are suggesting that we feel it at various stages taking great strides in certain, and often varying, directions, much as an ice-skater takes her strides far to the left and far to the right while still moving ahead down the ice. New ideas, new persons, new causes, new choices come into the picture, or perhaps new appreciations of old ideas, familiar persons, older causes, and former choices. In time, as in the writing of a novel, different plots and subplots appear, and we find ourselves working them out—some of our satisfaction, some to our disappointment or even chagrin. At this time, the entire situation may undergo more and significant changes, and we find ourselves at another place, school, country, situation with new learnings and appropriations called for by the situation. It is not that we are moving helplessly or chaotically; it is just that we are unable to command every scene. Fortunately it is not necessary that we do so. As our body assimilates various foods and makes them its own, so we assimilate varieties of experiences and make them ourselves. Like the body, we can in the assimilation process also undergo our own changes. This is the give and take of life. We are never in its total command, nor is it ever totally subjected to us. The story keeps unfolding all the while; and since it is our story, we have much to say about its unfolding.

When, on some special occasion, we assume a somewhat Olympian stance to see where our life might be heading, and how we are putting it all together, it is quite possible that some kind of picture begins to emerge: of our journey across life's stage. And we do have such moments: a period of meditation, a retreat, the writing of a novel in which we cull from our own life experiences, the thoughtful viewing of glorious sunsets being swallowed by the ocean and enveloped in vast darkness. Such pacifying experiences may come at any time. Robert Frost tells of one such experience for him:

### Stopping by the Woods on a Snowy Evening

Whose woods these are I think I know.
His house is in the village though;
He will not see me stopping here
To watch his woods fill up with snow.

My little horse must think it queer
To stop without a farmhouse near
Between the woods and frozen lake
The darkest evening of the year.

He gives his harness bells a shake
To ask if there is some mistake.
The only other sound's the sweep
Of easy wind and downy flake.

The woods are lovely, dark and deep,
But I have promises to keep,
And miles to go before I sleep.
And miles to go before I sleep.

                                   Robert Frost

It is the experience of promises to keep and miles to go before we sleep that makes us even more subtly aware that there are endless little projects, all meaningful in themselves and all giving meaning to lesser projects, even though they are themselves part of larger projects, that engages us for shorter and longer intervals in life's endeavors. Somehow, particularly as one gets older, the many details converge within limits and vectors begin to be discernible, and we get the feeling that the novelist must get as he works through plot after plot while making his story fit into a grander whole. To be sure, we see little of the magic about it, but much of the imaginative, far more than we once suspected.

We would bring this chapter to a close by listening to the testimonies of two authors who have sketched their own life journey. These excerpts provide us a flavor of what we have tried to capture: the subtle experience of direction in life that makes the journey a meaningful continuity, despite the experiences of bewilderment, lostness, and disappointment that allow the life journey to remain humanly disjointed.

The first is taken from a chapter by David J. O'Brien, "The Historian as Believer," found in Baum's work, *Journeys:*

> To those who always tell me that my hopes have no possibility of fulfillment, I can argue with Max Weber that without reaching out for the impossible, even the possible would not be achieved. In fact, the limits of the possible are always greater than they seem; definitions of human possibility always presume present inertia and pessimism. Throughout my life, people in and out of the Catholic community have constantly helped me to discover unknown parts of myself. I continue to believe that we in the Catholic community could do great work in the world if we could constantly offer one another a challenge and an invitation. The challenge—to change our lives to become more fully a people living for others—and the invitation—to be part of a community of people trying to do the same—both derive from continued faith in Jesus Christ, whose promises remain ever before us, calling us to be better than we thought we could be, together, all of us, with him. I, for one, have nowhere else to turn than to the tradition that inspired and empowered my parents and shaped and formed me. I cherish that tradition and retain a confidence in the final fidelity of God, because I have experienced in my own life and in the lives of those who have touched me the mysterious but wonderful benevolence of Providence. (1975, p. 85)

The second passage, also taken from *Journeys*, was written by a priest who looks back on his own life in this manner:

> There are three principal intellectual concerns that occupy me at the present: ethnicity and pluralism in American society, the Catholic experience in the United States, and the coming together of religion and social science. As I prepared this sketch, it occurred to me that these three themes have occupied me in one way or another for more than thirty years. But my pursuit of these themes has been very unself-conscious. Indeed, I became aware of the continuities only as I worked on this paper. It would be pompous for me to refer to these three interests as "life projects." Others may well lay out systematic plans for the next several decades of their lives (like Jaroslav Pelidan's projected history of Christian thought); I have never done that and probably never will. My own intellectual style, I think, is much more empirical, pragmatic, intuitive. I move from problem to problem as the spirit moves me, "playing it by ear" . . . If a subject or a book or an idea interests me, I pursue it without much thought whether it will fit into what I did last or what I may do next. If a project comes down the pike or NORC that seems intriguing, I get involved in it without much concern about whether it can be integrated into the other things I do. The three principal intellectual concerns that I have discovered only sitting down to think about the things I am doing can hardly be called "projects." At best, they are, to lift a word from biblical scholars, "trajectories." I have no notion where these trajectories are going, and in fact I would resist the temptation to plot them. I much prefer to continue as I have in the past to do things because I want to and not because of any obligation to some ponderous "life project." Maybe that's because I'm a Catholic and not a Protestant.

> Still, even before I began this paper, I did have the feeling that there is a convergence in my three lines of interest and thought. If there is such a convergence, however, it will take place in its own good time. I have no intention of trying to hasten the process by being self-conscious about it.

> So I usually laugh out loud when someone asks me what I will be doing in the next five years or even in the next year. The pertinent question might be, what I am going to be doing next week?

> Whether this be a good or bad way to think and live, I do not know. But as I watch the waves break against the wall at Grand Beach, I know it is the way I have lived and the way I propose to

continue. I guess it affronts some people, but that's their problem. (Greeley, 1975, p. 202)

Both of these passages impart to us the continuity-discontinuity that is the human experience of life. Often they are on a small scale, but often too they are on a large scale. We humans must and do deal with it all. If one had experienced great pain and little success at integrating it all into his or her life, the experience is indeed an ordeal. If, however, one has learned to metaphorize and remetaphorize, symbolize and resymbolize, the challenge is not only endurable; it can become a sweet yoke and a lightsome burden. The fact is, that every human being does somehow integrate the picture of his or her life, imaginizing it as this or that, filled with whatever. The important realization for all is the fact that it can always be re-imagined; not rewritten, but re-imagined. Whatever its details, the story of life can always be re-seen, newly understood, and newly appreciated. That was the great blessing that came to Ivan Ilych on his deathbed (Tolstoy, 1960). That was the great blessing that came to the thief dying on the cross alongside Christ.

It is a happy realization indeed if we are able to come to an appreciation of these truths while we are still actively engaged in the authoring of our life story, long before we have finished the final page. It makes the writing such a memorable experience.

# CHAPTER VII

# Unity and Temporality: Constituents in the Integrating Process

THROUGHOUT our study we have spoken often about the process of integrating our lives in some fashion or other. At the same time we focused on the plethora of details with which our Being-in-the-world involves us. The interpersonal and impersonal realities of the world are many and complex. These two aspects of the question—unity and plurality—now call for reflection in their own right: But there is another constituent in the process worthy of attention, about which we have said little thus far: temporality. It is proper to single it out for the unique role that it plays in the human achievement of integration.

The unity and plurality experience go together: our experience of the one in the many of life. Temporality, on the other hand, could be seen almost as the context in which that oneness is brought forth into the light. Such a description provides us with a hint of the manner in which the two could conceivably be related to each other. The experience of personal unity amid the plurality of life's give and take, and the experience of temporality are both intrinsic to all that we have been exploring to date.

## A. UNITY

The question of human oneness—unity—is a subject that has engaged thinkers over the centuries. It is to be found in the writings of Aristotle, Plato, Plotinus, Augustine, Descartes, Aquinas, and many others. Their focus was on the structure of human nature and the conceptualizations that attend it: the soul and the body, prime matter and substantial form, and many ways in which the two or more elements could be conceived as part of one united nature, if united they could be.

The focus that we are bringing to bear on the question—that of psychology—is something else. We are speaking to the experience of oneness that an individual person has while living out his life. And this topic is of considerable importance to the professional psychologist, the clinician, and the human being who must confront the world before him. This is the experience of integration of which we have made frequent mention. In this experience one feels himself as a self, a unity, at the center of life, so to speak. One feels himself as an integer, a whole person, much as one would imagine an integral number—such as one, two—feeling itself to be a whole. A human being who feels fractionated—only one-half or one-third,—is one who feels the self to be split, half operative, at loggerheads with self. Such a person feels helpless, inundated by life, tossed about like flotsam on water. He would appear to be going in many directions at once, with no assurance that he will ever successfully arrive anywhere—an unhappy experience indeed.

## 1. Monotheistic-Polytheistic Psychology

Psychologists, as we discussed in chapter four, are well aware of the experience of scatteredness that many people endure and do not take it lightly. There is debate on the matter, of course, and some there are who would attempt to extol it as a positive experience. Most psychologists, however, would deem it a dangerous and undesirable experience for a given human being. We cited at the time Hillman's defence of the phenomenon as a constructive event, upholding as he did the position of polytheistic psychology, as distinct from what he terms monotheistic psychology. In Hillman's view the latter in its emphasis on unity actually diminishes the person by ignoring the rich possibilities for human growth that he finds in the person's pathological condition. Indeed the presence of pathology in one's life is metaphorized in polytheistic psychology as a positive situation that admits of new and rich imagery. In his words,

> We are driven, therefore, to learn something from psychology, taking imaginal persons as seriously (if not as literalistically) as does someone with his delusions of hallucination. Then our idea of personifying would include its full "pathological" implications. This means nothing less than dethroning the dominant fantasy ruling our view of the world as ultimately a unity—that real meaning, real

beauty, and truth require a unified vision. It also means that we would abandon a notion of our personality as ultimately a unity of self. Instead of trying to cure pathological fragmentation wherever it appears, we would let the content of this fantasy cure consciousness of its obsession with unity. By absorbing the plural viewpoint of "splinter psyches" into our consciousness, there would be a new connection with multiplicity and we would no longer need to call it disconnected schizoid fragmentation. Consciousness, and our notion of consciousness, would reflect a world view that is diverse and unsettled. (1975, p. 41)

This view, an extreme one, would dismiss the effort at integration, unification, as itself a futile fantasy. It sees the various styles of consciousness as secondary personalities that affect the role of the so-called ego through symptomatic interferences or psychopathologies, just as supposedly the secondary personalities of our dreams affect the person's ego in direct confrontation or conflict. Thus, as we pointed out previously, this effort to see the person not as an integer or whole or unity but as a plurality of personifications, each of which presents a certain style of consciousness, appears diametrically opposed to the concept of integration of which we have been speaking. We have already noted, however, that the appearance is deceptive and that it remains but another effort to effect a special kind of integration, called by Hillman a "disintegrated integration." Not only does it admit a privileged position to the Number One personality which presumably seeks to effect unity by bringing all the lesser conscious states or forms under its aegis; it also grants that the strenuous effort to coalesce the coexisting splintered psyches, the psychic fragments, the little people into a loose federation is itself an attempt to realize but a different species of unity.

## 2. *Positive Disintegration*

A second theoretical position espoused by some psychologists that would presumably militate against the concept of integrated unity is that of positive disintegration, a position identified with the Polish psychiatrist, Kazimierz Dabrowski. It was his contention that the human person's development is actually furthered by the disintegrative experience, an experience that enlarges the personal horizons, enriches one's life and brings forth genuine creativity. In his words,

In contrast to integration, which means a process of unification of oneself, disintegration means the loosening of structures, the dispersion and breaking up of psychic forces. The term *disintegration* is used to refer to a broad range of processes, from emotional disharmony to the complete fragmentation of the personality structure, all of which are usually regarded as negative. The author, however, has a different point of view: he feels that disintegration is a generally positive developmental process. Its only negative aspect is marginal, a small part of the total phenomenon and hence relatively unimportant in the evolutionary development of personality. The disintegration process, through loosening and even fragmenting the internal psychic environment, through conflicts within the internal environment and with the external environment, is the ground for the birth and development of a higher psychic structure. Disintegration is the basis for developmental thrusts upward, the creation of a new evolutionary dynamics, and the movement of the personality to a higher level, all of which are manifestations of secondary integration. (1964, p. 5)

Distinguishing as he does between unilevel disintegration and multilevel disintegration, partial and global disintegration, permanent and temporary disintegration, and positive and negative disintegration, Dabrowski by no means identifies all disintegration as growth indications or possibilities. Indeed he is at pains to distinguish the harmful effects of a disintegrative process that would be negative. In the latter instance the disintegration would be adevelopmental, having no developmental effects, or would cause involution. If, on the other hand, the process would give indications of advancing the development of the person, its presence would certainly be termed beneficial. In that case, one could compare, so to speak, the disintegration process with the breakup of the shell that once protected the embryonic chick, but now must be demolished so that the peep might emerge. Thus the kind of disintegration is critical, and disintegration as such is not the issue.

The process of positive disintegration as conceived by Dabrowski, then, has to do ultimately with the development of a higher grade of integration. As he sees it, the positive disintegration process is sowing seed for a secondary integration, the entire process preparing the way for the formation of higher structures integrated at a more advanced level. Those seeds would be the feelings of dissatisfaction, discouragement, protest and lack of higher values and needs, the congeries of which ultimately generates a transformation toward a more refined, sophisticated synthesis. At no time does the theory of positive disintegration as outlined by Dabrowski deny the significance of the integrative process, the effort toward unity. Quite the contrary: it emphasizes the critical importance of the unity that the person must experience for genuine growth to transpire.

In brief the position of positive disintegration and that of polytheistic psychology, with its complex of a disintegrated integration described earlier, are themselves variations of theory, both aimed at furthering the growth of the human person through an integrative process. In the one instance (Hillman) the theory emphasizes the positive values that conceivably can be found in the apparent disarray and scatteredness, and would point up such values as growth potentials for the person in question. In the other instance (Dabrowski) the theory would suggest that a given disintegrative experience could conceivably be the shell-breaking process that allows the individual to emerge into life a stronger and better integrated person than ever. Thus both presentations would point to the possible positive potential that may lie within an apparently pathological experience, and urge us to exploit it for the benefit of the human being in whatever way we can. Neither theory—and this is our primary focus—extols the disintegrative process or pathology for its own sake. Each in its own way would turn it toward the greater integration and unification of the individual. Thus, while seeming to extol the disintegrative experience, they actually see it furthering the person's efforts at unity.

## 3. Self-Theory

*a. Some earlier versions.* It is in the realm of self-theory that psychology has witnessed the most serious efforts to bring its thought into line with its clinical experience and to advance formulations that attend to the individual's attempts, particularly conscious attempts, to integrate the complexities of his personal life experientially. Early in American psychology there was interest in the self, as can be seen in the work of William James (1890) and later in the introspectionists. This attention, however, slowed down considerably during the second, third, and fourth decades of the twentieth century, as the introspectionists proved none too successful in dealing with the essence of self and the behaviorists found it meaningless. Meanwhile Freud and the Freudians, while developing theory that called for a self-referent, were wont to focus on the powerful concept of the id and its function in human living, even though they gave recognition to the ego and related functions to some degree. Jung likewise emphasized the self in contrast to and in conjunction with the conscious functioning ego, while Adler looked upon his notion of the creative self as one of his principal contributions. For various reasons, moreover, the later Freud began to stress ego development and functions, while neo-Freudians made much of the notion of the self-picture and the ego ideal.

Thus the notion of self had a history prior to the 1940s and 1950s, but during and after these years personality theories of all kinds assigned value to the phenomenal and nonphenomenal self, particularly the self-concept with its emphasis on cognitive and motivational dimensions of human life. The work of Carl Rogers (1951) comes readily to mind, famous not only for its more phenomenological thrust (meaning by this his stress on the role of the conscious self-concept in the determination of human behavior) but also for Rogers's own eagerness to submit his clinical theory to the scrutiny of experimental testing in an effort to establish, if possible, significant nomological principles governing human behavior.

In the formal Freudian circles it was Hartmann who brought about the serious awakening in the area of self-study. Speaking in Montreal in 1949, he clarified theoretical narcissism (Levin, 1969). This he did by emphasizing the libidinal cathexis, not of the ego, but of the self, one's own person. Prior to his clarification, narcissism had found its place in the domain of the ego. Subsequent to Hartmann's formulation, however, Freudian structural theorists sought to establish greater harmony with clinical observation. The self now became the great resource center from which the ego would be seen to draw, or at least significant psychoanalytic thinkers began to see it in this manner. Of them Heinz Kohut was among the more prominent, but his treatment of the subject, in the spirit of Hartmann, has been conducted in relation to the question of narcissism. Others have taken issue with him in this matter. Roy Schafer, for one, while conceding the merits of Kohut's efforts to develop the self as a new dynamic and structural entity as well as a vital life theme, thus serving to bridge the gap between theory and practice, faults him for his ambiguity. In Schafer's words,

"Like identity, however, Kohut's 'narcissistic self' mixes two different types of discourse in that it represents an attempt to inject the person as agent into a natural science model" (1976, p. 116).

The observation that Schafer makes he would also apply to others in the psychoanalytic movement. With misgivings, he sees the language of self (and identity) seeking to become the dominant language in modern Freudian theory. Indeed he would suggest that these efforts would appear to be reformulating Freud's earlier statement that where id was there ego shall be into a new version: where ego was, there self or identity would be (p. 188). In so doing, he contends, the psychoanalytic movement is actually entering into whole new realm of discourse that will necessitate its abandoning the traditional natural science model of classical psychoanalytic theory (p. 192). In the meantime, of course, Schafer has continued his own efforts to develop through action language a psychoanalysis that would jettison its psychodynamic origins, if not its nomenclature and understandings.

Finally mention would be made of the prominent contribution of Erik H. Erikson. To be sure, his work has centered more on the topic of identity, but, as Schafer has indicated, Erikson's identity sounds at times much like the notion of self. Through his work our understanding of the unification process has been advanced. He spoke of Freud's conception of the task of the ego as:

> the domain of an inner "agency" safeguarding our coherent existence by screening and synthesizing, in any series of moments, all the impressions, emotions, memories, and impulses which try to enter our thought and demand our action, and which would tear us apart if unsorted and unmanaged by a slowly grown and reliably watchful screening system. (1968, p. 218)

Erikson himself prefers to speak of the I (which he would describe as all-conscious) in contrast to the ego (which he sees as unconscious, functioning for the psyche much as do the heart and brain for the body), as the very core of human self-awareness, the capacity which makes self-analysis possible. He spelled out the unique position held by the I, the self, the subject, the agent around whom the complexities of life revolve and to whom the task of integrating the totality is assigned. As Erikson sees it, this I and its identity functions are uniquely permeated by the mysteries of a languaged existence. He speaks in terms that smack of the mystical:

But "I" is nothing less than the verbal assurance according to which I feel that I am the center of awareness in a universe of experience in which I have a coherent identity, and that I am in possession of my wits and able to say what I see and think. No quantifiable aspect of this experience can do justice to its subjective halo, for it means nothing less than that I am alive, that I *am* life. The counterplayer of the "I" therefore can be, strictly speaking, only the deity who has lent this halo to a mortal and is Himself endowed with an eternal numinousness certified by all "I"'s who acknowledge this gift. That is why God, when Moses asked Him who should he say had called him, answered: "I AM THAT I AM." He then ordered Moses to tell the multitude: "I AM has sent me unto you." And, indeed, only a multitude held together by a common faith shares to that extent a common "I", wherefore "brothers and sisters in God" can appoint each other true "You"'s in mutual compassion and joint veneration. The Hindu greeting of looking into another's eyes—hand raised close to the face with palms joined—and saying "I recognize the God in you" expresses the heart of the matter. But then, so does a lover by his mere glance recognize the numinosity in the face of the beloved, while feeling, in turn, that his very life depends on being so recognized. (1968, p. 220)

*b. Existential-phenomenological thought.* The foregoing discussion on the self and self-theory has provided us a context for our discussion on existential-phenomenological thinking on the self. Such a discussion is needed; first, as Wylie (1961) and Schafer (1976) have indicated, the subjective and highly human, personalistic thrust that seems to inhabit self-theory appears relevant and related to phenomenological theorizing, and second, because the existential and phenomenological thinking has itself contributed significantly to the human understanding of the self. Our emphasis will center primarily around the Heideggerian explication of self, an understanding that Hall and Lindzey feel has the "greatest pertinence" for personality theorizing (1978, p. 312).

The phenomenological method employed by existential thinkers requires that one remain in close touch with the phenomenon under scrutiny and make every effort to elucidate its self manifestation as faithfully as possible: that the phenomenon be depicted as it shows itself from itself in the manner in which it shows itself from itself. Hence the major role played in existential thought by description, as well as contextualization. The former is necessary, so that the being in question may be made manifest; that latter is necessary so that its ground may enable the phenomenon to be the better figured. Finally there remains the role of interpretation, an elaborate and almost unending attempt slowly, painfully, and care-fully to further the understanding of that phenomenon through a part-whole, back-and-forth, progressive-regressive dialectic. Such a method was employed by Heidegger in his depiction of the human self in *Being and Time.*

Often the self is described as an isolated phenomenon, an individual set apart, one distanced from its world and the others with whom it must nonetheless be related. And it is understandable how such a notion of self could come about. It would appear to capture the human being alone, autonomous and seemingly at his best. Man the thinker, the cogitator has its appeal to the philosophically minded, and it is not without its appeal to the imaginative individualism of the populace. In such a view the self is indeed a polarized isolate that would transcend the limits of existence, pursuing in almost solipsistic reflection the world beyond the mundane and trivial in which most humans are engulfed. Heidegger, however, sees this description of the self as misleading and unfaithful to our human experience, for it simply does not depict the phenomenal self as that self is found existing in our lives.

There are two features about human existence that Heidegger would highlight: first, that it is always an existence that is caught up, involved in the world (Man is a Being-in-the-world, a *Da-sein,* as he describes man), and second, that that existence is characterized by a mine-ness (1927/1962, p. 150 ff). The first of these two observations, at first glance, appears banal; nothing could be more obvious. It has, however, certain philosophical and psychological implications that have usually been overlooked. It is not the fact that we are spatially and temporally localized in the world that is significant. What is significant is the fact that our every act finds us thrown into the world at every moment, during our every experience. We experience seeing the world, hearing the world, smelling the world, touching the world, feeling the world, tasting the world, loving the world, hating the world, mistrusting the world, enjoying the world. And when we would cogitate, think, we think about the world in one way or other. Our efforts at abstraction are abstractions from the world; our attempts to transcend seek to transcend the world. In essence, the world is built into our entire existence. Even when we would attempt to bracket some aspect of the world imaginatively in a given study, performing what Husserl called the epoche by setting aside some dimension of the experience and concentrating intently on the remaining focus, we experience the pull of the world on our consciousness. As Merleau-Ponty stated it, the effort to perform such a reduction of consciousness proves ultimately the impossibility of doing so completely. Be it the world of physics, aesthetics, mathematics, literature, art, poetry, philosophy, theology, or whatever, we cannot be without some such. To be human is to be worlded; we are never unworlded. And we find to our amazement that we are always already there. Everything begins from that fact. Our problem is not the stepping into the world, but the stepping out of it—if we can. But we cannot.

There is, then, the second characteristic that Heidegger cites: the fact that our existence is characterized by a mine-ness (1927/1962, p. 67, 152). His phenomenological description of the human experience makes this ineluctably clear. That which I see is seen by my seeing; that which I hear is heard by my hearing; that about which I think is thought about by my thinking. All my experiences, in short, have about them a reference back to me. And it is at this point that the issue of self arises. As Ricoeur has pointed out (1970, p. 45), the human being, thanks to its intentional consciousness, is scattered among the objects of its experience, is lost, so to speak, among the works that bear witness to one's efforts to exist and to desire. The human being is in a state of *diaspora* or scatteredness among its works, its achievements, its acts, its objects—all of which mirror the me or self that has brought them about or made them the object of its concern. It remains then for the me, to which they have their reference, to gather them up and return them, as it were, to the center of my existence, to reappropriate them to me, to the mine-ness that brought them to consciousness, to the self that is their referent, their home. This task is accomplished by an imaginative reflection upon the existence that I am, wherein I re-collect the mirrored self from these mirroring selves or objects (if you will, the mirroring selves of my scatteredness), and, through the imaginative re-collection, move toward making the concrete experience of me somewhat equal to the positing of me that took place in the existing that I am. Thus it is that Ricoeur states that the positing of self is not a given; it is a task, an accomplishment, a challenge.

We have before us, then, two vital considerations, both attested to by everyman's experience. In my existence I find that I am always *there* (*da*), in a world, a *Da-sein*. And in my existence I find that the thereness of which we speak is mine. I am both there and here, and the self is the hereness of that thereness. Indeed the thereness and the hereness are mutually implicatory. Thus our self is not an isolated ego polarized against the world, a subject withstanding an independent object. Our self is an existence to the structure of whose mine-ness belongs the world.

In the light of these considerations we can see how the process of integrating involves the person's world. The unification of which we speak is a unification of the personal self: the imaginative integration of the worlded me. Thus the putting of one's self together is a putting of one's world together. Integration, like existence, pertains to the Being-in-the-world that each human is. It is around the self that the unification or integration takes place. It is to the mineness-existence that one attributes feelings, emotional responses, thinking and thoughts, dreams, hopes, difficulties, relationships, and so on. It is to be the worlded self that one turns in situations of responsibility where decisions must be formulated; to the thered-here that one attributes the credit for achievement realized or blame for tasks left undone. The worlded-self is the center of my existence, whether one considers that worlded self to be intelligent or uninformed, attractive or unattractive, friendly or distant, confident or uncertain, poised or fearful. It is this self whom in memory I see sitting at a desk in first grade and whom in memory I also experience ascending the stairs years later at a commencement exercise to receive a doctoral degree. That the I has changed during the interim is beyond doubt, but equally doubtless is the fact that that much-changed self has retained an undeniable identity throughout the intervening years. I can return in imagination and memory to myself-experiencing of my mother's funeral thirty years ago with the same ease that I return to myself-experiencing of a conversation yesterday. And I can move imaginatively to an anticipated meeting next month with a person whom I have not seen for twenty-five years. Already we two selves have talked on the phone and planned the get-together. Our phone conversation took both our selves back to experiences which we both recalled so easily and vividly. Our conversation next month will do very much the same. Despite the changes that we have both undergone over the years, I have no doubt that our anticipated discussion will find us more and more experiencing the person we knew in each other a quarter of a century ago.

Milton Erickson tells a simple but magnificent story in his most recent book, posthumously published, *My Voice Will Go with You* (1982, p. 57). The story captures some of the thought we have just been examining: the self that perdures.

### LIGHT SNOW

In the village of Lowell, Wisconsin, it snowed for the first time that autumn on November 12, shortly before 4:00 P.M. And that kid in the third seat, in the third row of seats, right beside the window, wondered, How long will I remember this?

I was just wondering. . . .

I knew exactly. . . . I knew it was November 12, in the year 1912. It was a very light snow.

So wondrous and powerful is the experience of the self that Immanuel Kant, a philosophical genius who was much touched by the psychological thought of his day, saw the self-subject as the critical dimension even in the constituting of nature. In his so-called Copernican revolution in human thought, Kant pointed out the unique role played by the constituting subject in the study and mastery of nature. As he put it:

When Galileo caused balls, the weights of which he had himself previously determined, to roll down an inclined plane; when Torricelli made the air carry a weight which he had calculated before hand to be equal to that of a definite volume of water; or in more recent times, when Stahl changed metals into oxides, and oxides back into metal, by withdrawing something and then restoring it, a light broke upon all students of nature. They learned that reason has insight only into that which it produces after a plan of its own, and that it must not allow itself to be kept, as it were, in nature's leading-strings, but must itself show the way with principles of judgment based upon fixed laws, constraining nature to give answer to questions of reason's own determining. Accidental observations, made in obedience to no previously thought-out plan can never be made to yield a necessary law, which alone reason is concerned to discover. Reason, holding in one hand its principles, according to which alone concordant appearances can be admitted as equivalent to laws, and in the other hand the experiment which is has devised in conformity with these principles, must approach nature in order to be taught by it. It must not, however, do so in the character of a

pupil who listens to everything that the teacher chooses to say, but of
an appointed judge who compels the witnesses to answer questions
which he has himself formulated. Even physics, therefore, owes the
beneficent revolution in its point of view entirely to the happy
thought, that while reason must seek in nature, not fictitiously
ascribe to it, whatever as not being knowable through reason's own
resources has to be learnt, if learnt at all, only from nature, it must
adopt as its guide, in so seeking, that which it has itself put into
nature. It is thus after the study of nature has entered on the secure
path of a science, after having for so many centuries been nothing
but a process of merely random groping. (1929, p. 20)

In thus extolling the significance of the constituting self-subject
in the study of nature, Kant was emphasizing the truth that the
subject, the I, the self was ultimately the central factor in the entire
scientific and human enterprise. He likened this position to that of
Copernicus, whose formulations, contrary to the apparent common
experience, provided nonetheless the understanding mankind needed
in its attempt to grasp the movements of the heavens. Kant refers to
this in a footnote in his second edition:

> Similarly, the fundamental laws of the motions of the heavenly
> bodies gave established certainty to what Copernicus had at first
> assumed only as an hypothesis, and at the same time yielded proof of
> the invisible force (the Newtonian attraction) which holds the
> universe together. The latter would have remained for ever undis-
> covered if Copernicus had not dared, in a manner contradictory of
> the senses, but yet true, to seek the observed movements, not in the
> heavenly bodies, but in the spectator. (p. 25 note) 1929

[i. *The unifying self as historical and rooted*]

The Kantian emphasis on the primacy of the self-subject was
focused on the importance of the a priori conditions that the mind
brought into the rational and scientific investigations. They have
been termed the transcendental conditions, since they precede the
empirical study and its findings. Subsequent critiques of the Kantian exposition have led to a more profound appreciation that
human study and investigation, to say nothing of human living
experience, have about them a historicity of which Kant was
undoubtedly aware but which in fact he did not fully incorporate in
his analysis itself. Heidegger, however, not only allowed for the
constituting power of the subject or self, but also pointed to the
historical factors and development in a culture or epoch that wield

every bit as powerful a force in the human experience as the constituting quality of the self's rational and personal powers. In brief, if we are to understand the self's role in the development of science or in the unification of life, we must take cognizance not only of its unique constituting power but also of the historical development that the self-subject has undergone at both the cultural and personal levels.

The above considerations are germane for our study of the process of unification. They make us aware, first, of the constituting power of the human self, and, second, of the impact of cultural traditions and historical experience on the integrational achievement. More than that, they enable us to appreciate the impact of language as well as imagination in the realization of unification. My own hereness, my self, is brought to bear on my thereness, the world of my existence, but it does not do so out of nowhere. I step forward out of my personal history, just as that history steps forward out of the cultural milieu, which in turn steps forward out of its antecedents. Thus no individual is ahistorical and untouched by the past. On the contrary, everyone is both a benefactor and a transmittor of history to which he has somehow contributed.

To phrase it another way, we could say that it is possible, when the person goes about unifying one's life, that one does so in a manner already for the most part imagined for it by historical others. We seldom appreciate the fact that little of the mores, culture, and customs passed on to us in our everydayness has been thoroughly thought out by our ancestors. Most of it has simply been imagined by them. To assume that our predecessors thoroughly thought through all of life is preposterous, any more than we have done. Yet it remains a fact that every people transmits what it has to its descendants, who in turn seek to embody that highly imagined tradition, putting their lives together just as did their tribe, their teachers, their parents, their neighbors.

This is not to be misconstrued as an evil. Indeed there is much of the meritorious in it all, for it enables descendants to avail themselves of the accumulated wisdom of their forebears. The danger, if danger there be, lies rather in the fact that the descendants may come to imagine that there is no other way of imagining it. If this should come to pass, then we witness a person or a people slipping into inauthenticity and, in effect, imprisoning themselves. Conceivably this could lead to a dictatorship of the they as its worst.

At the other end of the spectrum is the person who has come, by whatever course, to a critical examination of his or her traditions. Such a person has appropriated those traditions, making them truly a part of the self and thus moving to a style of existence that is far more authentic, where the self is the instrument. This is a more fully human existence. It does not entail a repudiation of ancestral values and mores; rather, it entails a genuine examination and owning of them. It is an owning of the historicity without which we would not be. Thus our unification effort, such as it is, is by no means ahistorical. Whether it be of a people or an individual, the integration taps the genius of the self or selves and the giftedness of our ancestors, our heroes, personal or collective. In effect, then, this points up at once our indebtedness to others as well as our need to take up the ancestral bequeathment in our own unique way. To bring about my integration asks that my feet be planted on the earth of my ancestors and that my head be focused, as it were, on the ideals, dreams, and understandings I have come to treasure. Making that integration an authentic one would require that I critically appropriate both aspects of the project.

[ii. *The unifying self as imaginative*]

Several times we have spoken to the imaginizing of life that enters a culture's making and a person's development. We did not address ourselves to the singular role of imaginative thought in the promotion of human understanding. It should be addressed now, however, since the integration of life is a process that partakes of understanding, and that understanding is a unique blend of both rational and imaginative thought.

In his discussion of the meaning of our Being-in-the-world, Heidegger concentrates on three significant aspects of this question:

1. *Befindlichkeit*, Moodedness, Affectivity
2. *Rede*, or Discourse
3. *Verstehen*, or Understanding (1927/1962, p. 172ff)

In so doing he pursues the critical features of the affectivity that attends human existence in the world. That affectivity has about it much of the enigmatic, not admitting of the apodicticity and assuredness that mark our knowledge of the things that are at hand about us. To be sure, affectivity makes its own disclosures about life, just as does perception, but they are of a different genre. Moods, feelings, emotions tell us much, but they do so in a different way than do our sensation or our conceptualizations. As Heidegger points out, that affectivity is not to be identified with the rational in the human. Nor is it to be identified with the irrational. It is not to be identified with the logical, nor with the illogical. Rather it leans toward the analogical or imaginative. In brief, the affectivity of *Befindlichkeit* bears close affinity to the imaginative, the metaphorical, the analogical dimensions of human thinking (1927, p. 175).

A second existential or characteristic of human existence Heidegger cites is discourse. In saying this Heidegger is pointing up the fact that articulation is intrinsic to human existence, whatever form it may take, and that it inheres in the disclosure in which *Dasein* is ever engaged. By its very existence *Dasein* is constantly unveiling, disclosing of reality. Indeed reality is that which emerges in the human disclosure, in the clearing that people bring about. Thus language and hence discourse bring to light, reveal the events of life. And it enters their being what they are as entities. As George expressed it in the poem we quoted in the third chapter:

Where word breaks off, no thing may be.

Hence, language and discourse are forever bringing to light for ourselves (and thus for others, too) an awareness of what is, for, as Merleau-Ponty had put it, we speak so that we may become aware. But it does more: it serves to communicate to another the event of reality, such as it is. It is no exaggeration to say that people are ever engaged in some kind of articulation—an articulation that is not always vocal, never mindless, and always meaningful. That this articulation calls for understanding and explicit interpretation goes without saying. By their existence people are always speaking to those who have ears to hear and eyes to see. And the language used in their discourse—whether it be with or without words—is often logical but inevitably imaginative. By no means is it restricted to rational exchanges. More likely than not, the rational dimensions are eclipsed by the powerful attraction that the analogical and the imaginative hold out to the inquisitive as well as the meditative self. A silent gesture may speak more powerfully than a multitude of words.

Finally, in his enumeration of the existentials Heidegger cites *Verstehen*, or understanding itself. It is essential to existence that people be forever attributing, finding, scrutinizing, mulling meaning. Humans bring not only affectivity and articulation to their existence; they also bring the human preoccupation with meaning. But that quest for meaning is built on the quest for understanding.

It is in his treatment of understanding that Heidegger spells out in a special way the full impact of the self's imaginative presence. To say that the human is understanding something is to say that it is pressing toward a grasp of the entity's possibilities. Only when we know a being in terms of its possibilities can we be said to have some understanding of it. Conversely, if we were to lack a grasp of its possibilities, we would be said not to understand it. In common parlance we ask another what something is for, for what it is intended. Indeed even when speaking of *Dasein*, we do much the same. A person is many things, and the details are endless. But knowing one's achievements of the past alone would never give us the secret of another's uniqueness. For that we must come to see in another a being that deals forever in the light of and in the movement of the fact that it is ever possibilitizing. In humankind we have a being that brings onto the scene the possibility of possibilities—thus a being that can change the face of the earth. In humankind we have a being the very being of whose being is the possibility-to-be. And in gaining an understanding of that feature of the person we start to grasp the key to existence.

This distinction befits *Dasein* because of his remarkable kind of existence: he is forever projecting, imaginatively projecting, his existence. It is not of his nature to simply confront entities in a mumified manner, not to be in the world worldlessly. On the contrary, people are ever existing in an engaged, confronting, intrigued, fascinated manner. It is their nature to be not only in the world but to be ahead of themselves in that world, to be caught up in the destiny of things, to be engaged with beings as possibilities for their possibilitizing. Thus they experience a double movement. People experience themselves as thrown into existence (Heidegger refers to this aspect as *Geworfenheit*, a throwness, inasmuch as we are born into a whole world of history that predates us and with which we must deal whether or not), and also as a project, forever creating a horizon in which to deal with entities (Heidegger refers to this as *Entwurf*, the ongoing projecting ahead of ourselves). As long as he is, man is both thrown and projecting: ever in touch with the past from which and the future toward which. In his own words:

> Because of the kind of Being which is constituted by the existentiale of projection, Dasein constantly is "more" than it factually is, supposing that one might want to make an inventory of it as something-at-hand and list the contents of its Being, and supposing that one were able to do so. But Dasein is never more than it factically is, for to its facticity its potentiality-for-Being belongs essentially. Yet as Being-possible, moreover, Dasein is never anything less; that is to say, it is existentially that which, in its potentiality-for-Being, it is *not yet*. Only because the Being of the "there" receives its constitution through understanding and through the character of understanding as projection, only because it is what it becomes (or, alternatively, does not become) can it say to itself "Become what you are", and say this with understanding. (1927/ 1962, p. 185ff)

In his Kant book Heidegger speaks several times about the role of the imaginative projection in the task of understanding. For example:

> "The imagination forms in advance, and before all experience of the essent the aspect of the horizon of objectivity as such" (1929/1962, p. 138).

In short, whether one emphasizes the moodedness, the understanding, or the discourse dimension of *Dasein*'s Being-in-the-world, one is dealing with an aspect of human existence that is highly imaginative. This is apparent in the experience of affectivity that accompanies our existence. It is also apparent in the use of discourse and language—both highly imaginative. And it is most obvious of all in the experience of understanding that *Dasein* undergoes. The imaginative projection lies at the heart of the experience wherein possibilities enter our awareness. Hence it is that the understanding people develop about anything is a blending of both the imaginative and the rational dimensions of their thinking. Something of this is captured by Heidegger in the following passage:

> That traditional logic does not treat of pure imagination is indisputable. But if logic wishes to understand itself, the question as to

whether or not it need be concerned with the imagination must at least remain open. It is also undeniable that Kant always borrows from logic the point of departure for the problems which he formulates. And yet it is doubtful whether logic, merely because it has made pure thought, taken in a certain sense, its only theme, offers us a guarantee that it can delimit the complete essence of pure thought or even approach it. (1929/1962, p. 155)

[iii. *The unifying self as languaged-languaging*]

Having seen that the realization of unity involves the agency of a constituting self; that historicity is a critical element in the realization of such unity; and that the imaginative thought that accompanies the moodedness, discourse, and understanding that attend our existence in the world permeates the task of unification and integration, we shall now conclude this section on the unity experience by focusing briefly on the issue of language itself—a factor that makes it possible for a being to Be, for a self to constitute something for what it is, for history and tradition to make their mark, and for the imaginative thought of *Dasein* to realize effectively the unifications and higher integrations that it seeks in its metaphorizations, symbolizations, and story-making.

Without repeating thoughts that have been developed in previous pages, we would attend to the manner in which language furthers the unity experience. To effect an integration, it is critical to bring together similar or disparate dimensions in some form of higher synthesis. In some instances the unification may be realized easily and naturally, much as a picture might be framed into a more finished item. In other instances the unification would be more analogous to the coloration of water that takes place when new substances are placed together in a vial. In still other cases the end product may be a synthesis completely unanticipated and scarcely imaginable at the outset. Whatever the details, the choice of language is always central. Each perception of an entity or situation presents a perspective of the totality. As one moves to another perspective, one is in a position to view the totality differently. A clash of perspectives is always possible and in many instances probably inevitable. Multiperspectivity can indeed complicate the process and render unification an arduous task. In such instances, however, the naming of the object and description of the perspective are prerequisites. Until it is named and the perspective

described, no unification is possible. Once named, described, reflected upon, and restudied in terms of other properly described
perspectives, the process of unification remains well within the
limits of possibility. So too with the integration of one's life. To
initiate the process of unifying the perplexities of one's life, the
situation must somehow be languaged, and our movements toward
clarification and restructuring depend intrinsically upon one's
ability and success at imaginatively languaging and restructuring
by our words, metaphors, symbols, and stories the situation in
question.

It is commonly known that the psychoanalytic treatment at a
certain time in its history became known as the "talking cure."
That is to say, that it became known as an attempt to cure that was
allied with the use of language in the therapeutic hour. The reason
is apparent inasmuch as the therapeutic experience employed
language as the critical medium. It was the language of the therapist with his various interpretations that assumed primacy in the
process. However, it should not be overlooked that the interpretations advanced by the therapist were themselves intended to enable
the client to effect a more effective and satisfying integration. Thus,
in practice, the patient's languaging was the ultimate ingredient for
success, for it was the client's languaging (with or without the
therapist's influence) that effected his own integration.

The truth at which we are pointing—the significance of language
in effecting integration—is not new. It has a long history, which
Watzlawick has described this way:

> That language is a powerful determinant of moods, views, behavior
> and especially of decisions was, of course, known at least 1500 years
> before Frederick II. Suffice it to think of the high esteem in which
> already the pre-Socratic philosophers held rhetoric and its closely
> related discipline, sophistry. It is interesting to note that rhetoric, as
> a consistent doctrine, was in a very real sense the precursor of
> modern communications research in that it was related not to a
> specific subject area or topic, but was a discipline *in itself*—just as
> the study of the pragmatics of communication deals with communi-
> cation as a phenomenon *in its own right* rather than with the contents
> and meaning of messages in a specific context or subject area. . . .
> But of all the thinkers of that distant era it is Antiphon of Athens
> (480-411 B.C.) who appears to have come closest to the modern
> concept of therapeutic communication. . . . Antiphon would first

encourage the patient to talk about his suffering and would then help him by means of a rhetoric which utilized both style and content of the patient's utterances—a procedure which in a very modern sense amounted to a *reframing* of that which the sufferer considered "real" or "true," and thereby changed his pain-producing world image.

Plutarch writes of Antiphon: "While he was still engaged. in poetry he invented an art of liberation from pain, just as for those who are sick there is a treatment by physicians. In Corinth he was given a house beside the Agora and put up a sign to the effect that he was able to heal by words those who were sick." (1978, p. 6ff)

Thus the realization of a personal integration—a lived unity—is a complex matter, involving a self, history, imaginative thought, and language. Moreover, it is never realized in isolation from the world and its people—those among whom one is too, to use the phrase of Heidegger. One must always deal with the pluralism of life experiences and their mysteries in an imaginative way, as well as the realization that we are all very much a part of each other's lives. To effect a movement toward a oneness with self entails a movement toward oneness with our world and fellow humans.

*c. The self as othered:* Dasein *a decentered center.* With all his concern for the issue of authenticity in human living, Heidegger knew well that the style of humankind in its average everydayness was shot through with inauthenticity. Indeed authenticity, as he explained it, was but an existentiell modification of that inauthenticity that is lived everywhere by humankind at large. This was not intended as a putdown; he saw it simply as a statement of fact. We live very much a *Das Man* existence, a they-existence, and in our I-hood, so to speak, there is found a goodly portion of the not-I—the not-I that belongs to us, our I-hood. The human being is an *In-der-Welt-Sein,* an in-the-world-being. The human being is also a *Mit-Sein,* a with-being, meaning that its experiences are ever shared or peopled experiences, even though it may be alone at the time. The human being is also a *Mit-Dasein* being, a with-*Dasein* being, meaning that it bears a unique relation to Others who are *Daseins,* too, and that this dimension of its existence weighs heavily not only in its coming into being but also in its continued existence and development. It is not enough that *Dasein* be in a world, nor that it be ever open to sharing that world. It is necessary that *Dasein* be in the felt presence or the felt absence of others who are also *Daseins.* Whatever the degree of Otheredness, there must ever be that Otheredness that is part and parcel of *Dasein*'s I-hood.

With these critical comments we have introduced a subject that has received considerable attention from Lacanian psychoanalysis. We speak of the question of Lacan's theory of the decentered self. In some respects it smacks of the Heideggerian position; in other respects it does so only dubiously. The fact is, however, that much of Lacan's work is imbued with a Heideggerian viewpoint, so that the similarity of views on the question of the *subject* of *Dasein* becomes an intriguing one indeed (Wilden, 1968, p. 179).

Lacan's focus was on the rooting of the self at a pre-verbal, pre-Oedipal stage, known as the mirror stage. Since the infant does incorporate so many of the parental and societal values and imaginings from birth, if not even before birth, this concentration on the mirror stage and the mirror experience was seen by some, such as Louis Althusser, the Marxist, as a truly revolutionary concept that held out new hope for the possible resocialization of human beings (Kurzweil, 1980, p. 135ff). Altering the Oedipal situation with the resultant bourgeois family relationships could conceivably lead to a growth of socialism. Certainly unified conceptions of the ego and the self could, or at least so it appeared, be effectively overcome. Isolating the locus of self-emergence and intervening in the process was, to say the least, exciting and sobering. Such were some possible social implications of the mirror stage, if true. At the same time it promised to perfect Freud's own understanding of human development.

The mirror stage is alleged to occur somewhere between the sixth and the eighteenth month of the infant's life. Prior to this time the infant's body is seen to be fragmented and uncoordinated with no awareness of the perceptions it forms. Thus the anatomically incomplete development lies at the base of this remarkable experience. Somehow, somewhere the child during this period comes joyously to experience its own reflection in a mirror. In Lacan's view this becomes the child's initial awareness of itself as a biological organism, as a being bound up with the human species and on the threshold of what it would become. Thus it is at a critical stage in the process of its identification, and the experience is invested, as an anticipation of its future self, with all the complex emotions and intellections that go into one's future relations with the world within and the world around. Hence, this first impression will impact upon all of the child's future mental development, including his resolution of the Oedipal complex. It sets up an imaginary dual relationship, becoming the basis for its personal relationships with Others and for its primary narcissism and a source of aggressivity. As is apparent, the imaginative has entered uniquely into the picture, and we are witnessing the birth, so to speak, of an inchoate subject, a subject that will soon commence bespeaking its existence. When this comes to pass and language has really made its presence felt, we have entered into the reign of the symbolic. As one author has put it, "we may say that the jubilatory assumption of the mirror image by the infans represents a mould for the symbolic, a prefiguration of his roles" (Lemaire, 1970, p. 178). This taste for the power of the symbolic is experienced by the child who finds, in the absence of the desired mother, that the pain of her absence is mediated, so to speak, and assuaged by playing a game with inchoative verbal sounds. Thus it is that desire, not libido à la Freud, but desire becomes human, and the child is born into language.

It should be pointed out that the mirror-stage experience is not to be taken too literally. As William Richardson had indicated,

> To be sure, this "mirror" experience is no more than a "convenient symbol" of what takes place here. The essential is that there be some human form, some external image that the infant takes to be a "reflection" of itself. Presumably this human form could also be— and in the concrete is more likely to be—the mothering figure. In any case, the image is "other" than the subject, and identification with it constitutes a primordial alienation of the subject. The consequences of this, of course, are enormous. (1978-1979) p. 98

Be this as it may, the critical issue in this depiction of human development is the consequences (to use Richardson's word) that presumably take place—as the Lacanian theory would have it. In the words of Lacan,

> I have described elsewhere the sight in the mirror of the ego ideal, of that being that he first saw appearing in the form of the parent holding him up before the mirror. By clinging to the reference-point of him who looks at him in a mirror, the subject sees appearing, not his ego ideal, but his ideal ego, that point at which he desires to gratify himself in himself. This is the function, the mainspring, the effective instrument constituted by the ego ideal. Not so long ago, a

little girl said to me sweetly that it was about time somebody began to look after her so that she might seem lovable to herself. In saying this, she provided the innocent admission of the mainspring that comes into play in the first stage of the transference. The subject has a relation with his analyst the centre of which is at the level of the privileged signifier known as the ego ideal, in so far as from there he will feel himself both satisfactory and loved. (1973, p. 25)

The duality in the experience is that of the original subject (the experiencing infant) and the reflecting image in the mirror with which the infant imaginatively identifies. This image is the "I" or "ego" or the "other." To phrase it in another way: the originating subject is the O, so to speak, and the ego, the other image, is the 1, 2, 3, and so on that enter the original subject's making. Hence the jubilation and delight, as well as the primary narcissism. Hence, too, the alienation that lies presumably at the very origin of one's subjectivity. And this is only the first step in human alienation, for the mirror stage leads the infant down the path of alienation before the symbolism of language begins to restore the child's subjectivity. Nonetheless, a unity and stability of sorts are experienced, presumably, and the alienating identity seemingly provides the child with a strength and armor and beneficent rigidity that haunt it throughout its entire mental development, much in the manner of a lost Paradise. As one author puts it,

> The ego is the mirror image with its inverted structure, external to the subject and objectified. The entity of the body has been constituted, but it is external to the self and it is inverted. The subject merges with his own image and the same imaginary trapping by the double can be seen in his relationships with his fellows. It should be noted that the subject is ignorant of his own alienation and that this is how the chronic misrecognition of self and the causal chain determining human existence takes shape. (Lemaire, p. 178)

However brief, this exposition of the Lacanian mirror-stage experience, so critical in his understanding of the human person, should suffice to show the self's radical eccentricity to itself and the manner in which the Other, the mysterious ego ideal, could conceivably evolve through stages of alienation from a dyadic relationship with the mother through pluralized relationships with others of society in a world that is intrinsically and totally languaged and dominated by its historical languaged formulations. It is but a small step from the alienating Other who is part of the subject to the unconscious language that is part and parcel of the conscious self.

The preceding discussion certainly establishes the ground upon which a similarity can be claimed between the Lacanian and the Heideggerian understandings of the self. The absorption of the inauthentic *Dasein* in the world of the *Das Man*, the They, and the prevalence of inauthenticity in the life of human beings—both theses close to the heart of Heideggerian thought—and the intrinsic role played by the alienating Other as well as the unconscious language and the languaged unconscious in the life of the human being—theses close to the heart of Lacanian thought—sound very familiar, even similar, if not identical, with each other. Nor does this appear to be a mere happenstance. As Richardson has phrased it, "That Lacan needs a philosophical base presumably need not be argued here. That such a base is conveniently a Heideggerian one is suggested by Lacan himself" (1978, p. 107). Richardson then goes on to quote a passage from Lacan's *Ecrits* dealing with the question of Being and the subject. He then states,

> But this is certainly Heideggerian language, and Lacan acknowledges the influence explicitly. In fact, at one point in his career he personally translated into French and published an essay of Heidegger—the essay on *Logos* in Heraclitus (1956). In any case, we have reason to find in Heidegger some paradigm for Lacan's notion of an ex-centric subject. (p. 107)

That Richardson's thesis is not without merit is apparent, and he has certainly established it. It is a far cry from this position, however, to claiming an identity in thought, which Richardson, of course, does not. Another view is advanced by Anthony Wildon:

> Given these difficulties, the reader should therefore approach with some caution my opinion that, provided the very different orientation between Heidegger and Lacan is kept in mind, Lacan's early view of the unconscious as "the discourse of the Other," his notion of the neurotic as "appealing to the Other," and the ideological concept of the alienated *moi*, are in part a psychological development of a point of view which, while not exclusively Heideggerean, is particularly emphasized and developed in the Heidegger of *Sein und Zeit*. Later on, however, similar expressions will occur in contexts where the divergence between the philosophical epistemology of Hegel and Heidegger and the "linguistic" epistemology of Lacan is much more advanced. (1968, p. 182)

In the arena of this controversy we would advance several considerations before bringing this section to a close. Aside from the contention that Heidegger is working in the area of the onto-logical while Lacan focuses on the ontic, we would concentrate on the structure of the *sum* that is *Dasein*: his very existence. Heideg-ger's intent is to depict the basic human structure that underlies our existence, and his contention is that the human is found in a state of ontological comprehension of Being, always-ever-already in a state of ontological understanding of the There, be that There a world, a person, a thing. On the basis of this underlying unity of *Dasein* with the world it is possible for human experiences to transpire, and transpire they certainly do, in different ways and at different stages. It is all possible, however, simply because *Dasein* is already at one with the world, with the Other. Lacan, on the other hand, introduces the mirror stage long after *Dasein* has already been in the world and only when *Dasein* experiences the Other of the mirror and has its ontic experience of the mirror image. Lacan, in brief, has totally missed the significance of the intentionality that characterizes *Dasein*'s entire existence, and which constitutes *Da-sein* a There, a worlded being at every moment of its existence.

Second, the notion of the There, the Other as alien to *Dasein* is foreign to the thought of Heidegger. The Other, in virtue of *Dasein*'s intentionality, is a constituent in the very structure of *Dasein*. It is the There or the Here, and thus is not alienated. On the ontic level, that of founded knowledge, Heidegger would point out that in the ego cogito cogitatum, the cogitatum is that which primarily spec-ifies the cogitation of the ego. The cogitatum, then, is the fulfill-ment of the cogito, inviting it, plenishing it, bringing it into action. To specify this as alienating, rigidifying is simply gratuitous. That such experiences do occur in human living is obvious, but they occur amid the Oneness-with-the-world that *Dasein* is, the unity-with-the-Other that *Dasein* already is. Lacan's position has not only established an infinite chasm between *Dasein* and the world (the first point above), but it has also construed the ontological or basic structure of *Dasein* as intrinsically nihilating. The truth is, that the human being has had countless human experiences with the Other prior to the mirror stage and there is no reason to assume that they have not contributed powerfully to the non-alienating development of the human being, even at preconscious or conscious level, except for the fact that the Lacanian theory would have it so. Human developmental problems can be studied without such assumptions. Making them, however, is one way of guaranteeing that they will be verified.

Finally, we would speak to the issue of the imagination. The Lacanian position makes much of the imaginative, and rightly so. There is no reason, however, to restrict its significance to the mirror stage, or to demarcate it from the symbolic. Nor should it be distanced in any way from the issue of language. As we have seen in previous chapters, the imaginative cannot be divorced from the languaged, any more than language can be divorced from the infant's experience of life from the moment it is born. Every experience of the child has its languaged dimension as well as its imaginative dimension. Current research is much too primitive as yet to enable psychology to speak authoritatively on such difficult issues, but it certainly is advanced sufficiently to date to warrant skepticism about easy generalizations and theoretical prejudices. Lacanian psychoanalysis, it would appear, has more than its share of both.

## B. TEMPORALITY

To speak of temporality in connection with unity may appear a bit incongruent. In one respect unity may seem to be at variance with the subject of temporality. Unification seems to require a gathering of multiplicities from many quarters and the integration of those pluralities into a oneness of sorts. This underlying identity apparently defies time, for it perdures despite the transformations of life over the years. That, however, is only part of the story. The truth is that the unification itself does not happen in a moment, is not completed overnight, and in fact is an ever-ongoing process over a lifetime. The sameness felt at an earlier and later age may be very much part of each other, but the interval between the ages is a temporal event and the changes, such as they are, were events occurring in time. Thus temporality and unity do speak to each other.

### 1. Temporality and the Self

The concept of temporality used in the preceding discussion is not the notion toward which we have been moving. Time is indeed often viewed as a series of "now" moments successively experienced. They are the moments that are marked off between appointments and meetings. They are the succession that is meant when one speaks of birthdays and annual picnics. They are not, however, the concept of time that Heidegger used. In his *Being and Time* he is not speaking of clock time, even though he would not deny the importance of clock time under the appropriate circumstances. In his work Heidegger is referring to that temporality which is *the* characteristic of *Dasein*'s existence. It is not high noon, twilight, or midnight; it is a temporality that is far more basic in *Dasein*'s humanity, so basic that Heidegger identifies it with imaginative thought itself.

Things exist all around us. There was a time when they were not, and there will come the time when they will cease to be. Such is their finite endurance. They come into being, and they ultimately return to a nothingness. Such things can be said to endure for a while, but they are not said to be characterized in their existence by temporality. This is said only of the human person. Thus, in a given situation, when a self appears on the scene and commences his or her co-constitution of reality, there is present a being whose existence, marked by temporality, bestows upon the other entities a time significance. Prior to that things just endured. Now, however, they endure in time, because the temporalizing human is in their midst. We are saying, you see, that it is *Dasein* whose nature makes the clock time experience possible; and that this time experience, born of *Dasein*'s temporality, makes all the difference. When a being whose Being is marked by temporality appears, the entire scene changes.

The human being supplies a temporal horizon in which the many things in the world begin to have meaning and thus come to their being in time. It is as though all existence were viewed against the backdrop of the *Nicht*, the Nothingness that surrounds Being, and against that backdrop the Wonder of Wonders (that there is something rather than mere nothing) looms up before us. The human being is cognizant of the marvel of existence, as he is aware too of the finitude of the many existences about him, including his own. Each entity shines forth in its Being even though it is ever slipping away into its inevitable non-Being. Each person stands forth in its *Dasein* splendor even though it too moves toward its ultimate demise. And, more remarkably still, each person moves through his or her life keenly aware of that death that awaits him or her. As a Being-toward-death (a *Sein-zum-tode*, to use Heidegger's phrase) the human person proves to be a cut all its own, existing in the world with a sense of responsibility for that existence which he or she enjoys; a call to conscience. It is the person's own finitude, and the keen awareness of that finitude, that constitutes the horizon, the temporal horizon, that marks the person's existence. Thus, before the backdrop of Nothingness stands the existing human marvel of *Dasein* which, unlike the rest of entities, sketches out the temporal horizon that encompasses its existence and the existence of all other entities it beholds. In the light of that temporal horizon *Dasein* can mark time in clock fashion regarding the details of some involvements or engagements, but this is incidental. Far more significant is *Dasein*'s capacity, despite its finitude, to move almost infinitely in the direction of its past and its future. It can encompass almost infinity in its horizontal sketch or projection, and can extend its care in every direction. Nothing escapes *Dasein*'s horizon, *Dasein*'s care, *Dasein*'s concern and solicitude—at least in principle. With his imaginative thought and his language *Dasein* can move freely as he wishes, even to the threshold of eternity, as he does in his religious and theological reflections.

With this we start to garner some appreciation of the temporality that is *Dasein*'s, and the scope of its implications. Moving into the concept more deeply, we find that Heidegger would describe temporality in terms of three principal exstacies: the ex-stasis of the present, the ex-stasis of the past, and the ex-stasis of the future. In each instance the person moves out into the world and embraces in his temporality the present, the past, and the future. It is not as though each were separate from the others or that all three were added together to constitute a whole. Rather it is a description of the way a finite being projects a temporal horizon in which each dimension is present at all times, entering the respective experiences in its own unique way while benefiting at the same time from the presence of the other dimensions in its own peculiar modality. Thus, while the person is engaged in his present activity, the temporal dimensions of the past and future contribute significantly to that experience. So too does the past enter the present and the future, and the future play its role in the present and the has-been of the past. It is impossible, in short, to experience any temporal exstasis without being influenced by all at the same time. One is tempted to draw an analogy with a water bed, in which each section at every moment enters the experience of every other section, even though the concentration of pressure in a given moment may be limited to a certain portion of the bed.

Of the three temporal exstases that characterize human existence Heidegger points to the exstasis of the future as being most singular. It is in the future projections that he finds prime significance. It is in these that the person uncovers the plans and ideals that beckon, the hopes that sustain, the motivations that arouse, the dreams that uplift, the strength that will enable one to continue even if the present should end in failure. It provides the key to understanding. Thus, for example, the student attending a classroom lecture presumably shares it with many other students. But the experience of each will vary considerably if he or she is preparing to become a future chemist, nurse, philosopher, psychologist, minister, musician, or writer. Those plans, still years from fulfillment, are as meaningful to the experience as the lecture itself.

Thus in dealing with an object in the present, from whatever perspective, one brings to bear upon the experience in a prolonged presence—and we do extend our present imaginatively in a prolonged way, as, for example, a Thanksgiving Day dinner which is seen as a glorious meal, not many happy seconds—the wealth of his past, and the anticipations of his future. The experience becomes what it becomes in the light of all three temporal considerations. Each enters each, and in virtue of the temporal dimensions every experience is quite different than it would have been were there no consideration of temporality at all. As it is, the self's capacity to project these horizons into its every activity enables it to encompass in an extraordinary way unlimited reaches of the past and the future in the seemingly small moments of our present.

## 2. Temporality and Imaginative Thinking

In discussing the temporal exstases Heidegger speaks of them as primordial ground, and he identifies temporality with the imaginative thinking a person performs. This may be a bit perplexing, but it is an acute observation. As we have seen, imaginative thinking can stretch into past and future infinity and engage the old and the new of temporality. He refers to it as a spontaneous receptivity and a receptive spontaneity—a kind of thinking that admits of both activity and passivity, or, if you will, an active passivity and a passive activity (1929/1962, p. 202). In virtue of it people are enabled to transform at will that which they will in the interest of their recollections and anticipations. As he phrased it,

> Primordial time makes trancendental imagination, which in itself is essentially spontaneous receptivity and receptive spontaneity, possible. Only in this unity can pure sensibility as spontaneous receptivity and pure apperception as receptive spontaneity belong together and form the essential unity of pure sensible reason. (p. 202)

The imaginative effort, then, identifies with the temporal effort of *Dasein*, to use Heidegger's metaphor, as the root combines with the earth in which it is implanted. Each becomes the other and the human being, gifted so uniquely with the endowment of both, brings into his experience whole new dimensions, enabling the person to transform experiences with the world and reality in such a way that they, the world and reality are caught up into contexts that would simply never be without the presence of *Dasein*, and into possibilities that would be just unimaginable were *Dasein* not present.

Thus it is *Dasein* in his temporal and imaginative experience who can say what "is," what "is" was, and what "is" might well become. Only *Dasein* can say when "was" was, how it conceivably was, and how it entered the transformations of the present and the tentative schemes of the future. Were there no such being as *Dasein*, there would be no one to imagine and reimagine the past, to reconstruct it from findings, to surmise the possibilities that once were extant, and to trace the impact of former choices and decisions on the developments now before us—all of which, of course, are intrinsic to historical study, and all of which require the presence of that imaginative temporality found only in humans. By the same token there would be no one to imagine the future, to draw up its agenda, to study the possibilities that abound, and to make the elections that careful implementation presupposes. Says Heidegger, "Dasein's Being finds its meaning in temporality. But temporality is also the condition that makes historicality possible as a temporal kind of Being which Dasein itself possesses, regardless of whether or how Dasein is an entity 'in time' " (1927/1962, p. 41).

The whole matter of temporality hinges on the individual's imaginative capacity. It is not the past event, any more that it is the future event, that matters in the person's life. It is the way in which the past has been imaginatively picked up, transported, and sustained in the seemingly enduring present that is the critical issue. The events of the past are countless, and most of them will scarcely be remembered in their details. How they have been imaginatively incorporated into the person's scheme of things is something else, and this can prove devastating or inspirational. It similar ways the future remains to be unfolded, obviously, but it becomes a powerful factor in human life long before the unfolding ever transpires. It is the manner in which it is imaginatively depicted and brought close to the present that gives experienced, phenomenological and personal time its significance, long before it can be recorded in clock time. As such it could be frighteningly paralyzing or incredibly uplifting. The spontaneous receptivity and the receptive spontaneity make all the difference in the person's life. Seen as a ghastly ordeal, the future bears heavily and quickly upon us; seen as a life's dream come true, it cannot happen soon enough for any of us.

Thus it is that history is so intrinsically related to temporality and to our imaginative thought. The events themselves, to say nothing of their recounting or understanding, are permeated with time, thought, and the imaginative. History itself is possible only for that being which exhibits historicality: the capacity to imagine the past in terms of its own anticipated future and to study the present and future in imaginative ways that allow us to discern in the present and future living influences that owe their origin to past historical decisions. If, as Heidegger insists, we look into the future only to see the past coming toward us, by the same token we can say that we look into the past only to find the future already ingeniously spelled out. To be sure, there is much of the imaginative in both stances.

There is another aspect of the matter that we would briefly address. We speak of the many stages of life, the fleetingness of time, and the inevitability of change. All are ways to state the fact that there is no standing still. This is the lot of human finitude. Not only does our life run its course and our days their numbering, but the experiences of life we do have never see the full blossom of their possibility. Our experiences are limited, and so too are our comprehensions of those experiences. In essence, we never know the whole of our life, and even that which we do know is not known wholly. Our existence is very finite indeed. Only in the experience of imaginative temporality does one begin to approximate the experience of one's whole wholeness. We have the capacity to rise above ourselves imaginatively, as it were, and to glimpse our life sojourn by moving imaginatively throughout the spread of the temporality that is ours. We can take the imaginative stance and gaze at our existence *sub specie aeternitatis* (from the viewpoint of eternity), to employ an ancient and beautiful phrase. We can see it in the spread of creation or, if you will, in the unfolding of Providence. We can see ourselves as humans destined with the care and protection of other creatures who are incapable of such a marvelous comprehension of their own existence, and in so doing gratefully appropriate our unique humanity. This possibility is ours, thanks to the singular endowment of *Dasein*'s temporality and imaginative thought.

Pondering such realizations about *Dasein*'s existence and its existentialia, Heidegger was led to metaphorize *Dasein* as the Shepherd of Being. One can imagine the sheep gravitating to their shepherd, milling around him, looking to him for protection, relying on him for whatever direction or guidance they might need. And one can imagine the shepherd watching carefully and responsibly over his flock, attending those needs and providing the protection required. To depict the human experience in the world in such metaphorical language is to see that existence as something that must be owned and responsibly discharged. It makes the human presence in the world a meaningful enterprise. In fact such an appropriation becomes itself a salvific experience for us, for it enables us to be truly grateful for the gift and gifts of our finitude.

### 3. Temporality and Integration

It remains for us, in the light of these reflections, to take up the question of temporality vis-à-vis personal integration. Having some appreciation of the meaning of temporality/imagination, we should be in a position to ponder its significance for personal unity. The question is important, for the issue of integration is ongoing and the realization of unification has about it an element of impermanence. There is a past, present, and future about the human, and there is the same in the integration process. Temporality indeed is an ever-present dialectic between my past and my future.

In one of his stories Milton Erickson speaks about his father. The story he tells is entitled "*Oats*":

I spent one summer grubbing up brush on ten acres of land. My father plowed it that fall and replanted it, replowed it in the spring, and planted it into oats. And the oats grew very well and we hoped to get an excellent crop. Late that summer, on a Thursday evening, we went over to see how that crop was getting alone, when we could harvest it. My father examined the individual oat stalks and said, "Boys, this is not going to be a bumper crop of thirty-three bushels per acre. It will be at least a hundred bushels per acre. And they will be ready to harvest next Monday." And we were walking along happily thinking about a thousand bushels of oats and what it meant to us financially. It started to sprinkle. It rained all night Thursday, all day Friday, all night Friday, all day Saturday, all night Saturday, all day Sunday, and in the early morning on Monday the rain ceased. When we were finally able to wade through the water to that back field, the field was totally flat; there weren't any upright oats.

My father said, "I hope enough of the oats are ripe enough so that they will sprout. In that way we will have some green feed for the cattle this fall—and next year is another year."

And that's really being oriented to the future, and very, very necessary in farming. (1982, p. 235)

In some ways this story has already made our point by highlighting the importance of temporality, and particularly future thinking. We have already seen how the individual self, in dealing with any object, brings into the present the wealth of the past and the anticipations of the future. In considering integration in the light of temporality, we are moving toward the heart of the matter, for it weighs heavily in the quality of the experience. Erickson's father taught his sons a valuable lesson about life: the handling of serious adversity with which one is presented. He provided them a wisdom that grew out of his own rich experiences of the past. And he enlightened them to see that the strength to handle it all lay in a reformulation of the future. His son never forgot it and shared it years later with his own clinical patients.

In all the experiences of our lives we deal with the ever-present present, whether we spend ourselves in our work, in our reminiscing on the past, or in our planning for the future. Should we devote ourselves to an event of the past, we do so from our present perspective while mindful of its repercussions for the future. In such an instant the effort is expended again in the present, while the focus is on the events of the past, but the principal implications, perhaps still uncertain but inevitable, lie in the future. This is true whether we are exploring archeological excavations in the Middle-East or thinking through a client's childhood experiences with his parents. By the same token our creative plans for the future must cope with the circumstances of the current situation and tap the resources that the past has bequeathed. There is no dispensing with any of the temporalities, but integration requires that we pay special attention to the temporality of the future. The human being is unique in that it lives ever ahead-of-itself. No matter how engrossed in the past or present, it is never oblivious or mindless of the future; and the future horizon ever colors its experience. In living ahead of itself the person has a unique quality of being able to transform the history of his past and to inspirationally change the history of the present. Thus we are led to see that our personal unification owes a special deference to the temporal exstasis of the future. It is true, of course, that beings other than humans have shared his past with him, as they share his present now. No being, however, shares his future with him at the present moment except other *Daseins*. It is their personal and communal genius to make future developments possible in the present by their gift of possibilitizing. When they do so, that future is in the experienced present. *Dasein* can enter it long before it ever comes to pass. The human can do this—and this dealing with the future temporality in the present temporality makes a genuine personal integration possible. Our ability to live an anticipated future in the temporality of the present gives us a unique position, power, and responsibility among all the creatures of the earth. It also bids us take our own integration seriously that we might more humanly carry out our responsibilities to our selves, our fellow persons, and to the rest of creation.

What we have done in our discussion, then, is simply this: we have backed into the issue of self that we pursued in the early section of this chapter. And properly so, for the temporalizing self is undergoing the integration, and its temporalizations, particularly that of the future, are, to repeat, and the heart of its integrating experience. Without its past and present there is no *Dasein*. Without its future even the gifted *Dasein* evaporates. Kierkegaard pointed out long ago that the self is at every instant becoming, and it is only that which it is to become. The self, then, is *what we are becoming*. This is intelligible in light of the fact that the future is uniquely present *in the present* by way of our anticipation. The anticipation is the present's hold on the future, and thanks to the imaginative anticipation, we are what we are becoming even before we become it. Thus too the imaginative metaphorizations, symbolizations or storying that we create regarding our being-in-the-world permeate our anticipations and begin to effect transformations and new integrations of our existence immediately. To be sure, the feat is highly relative and at first tentative and indiscernable, having more than its share of the mystique and the mysterious. But for all that it is nonetheless real and experience-able. In principle a single experience can change a person's life; in practice it usually takes a while. But the right metaphorization at the right time can renew the face of the earth for a person, even though he or she stand in the midst of debris.

This is what the future temporalization can do for one's present. It can also bring alive one's past. In fact the past does come alive by virtue of the part that it plays in our future. Everyone's past has its share of riches: achievements, learnings, skills, knowledge, wisdom, stories, powerful experiences. For the most part they lie dormant, waiting to be awakened by some energizing commitment to a cause. It is as though they were buried, and buried they are—but not dead. When a new sun appears in the East in our lives, a new day dawns and new life starts to stir. The listless and the lethargic stretch their muscles, while the sleeping awake. Discourse happens; things get done; and the discounted or the underestimated stun us all by making their mark. Even the person himself is awed by his own ability to tap his past, bringing it all to the fore in the present, now that the anticipations of the future are lighting up his life.

The self is not what I was. The self is not solely what I am. The self is what I am moving into, am becoming, with my living anticipations of the future.

## SONG OF A MAN WHO HAS COME THROUGH

Not I, not I, but the wind that blows through me!
A fine wind is blowing the new direction of Time.
If only I let it bear me, carry me, if only it carry me!
If only I am sensitive, subtle, oh, delicate, a winged gift!

If only, most lovely of all, I yield myself and am borrowed
By the fine, fine wind that takes its course through the chaos of
  the world
Like a fine, an exquisite chisel, a wedge-blade inserted;
If only I am keen and hard like the sheer tip of a wedge
Driven by invisible blows,
The rock will split, we shall come at the wonder, we shall find the
  Hesperides.

Oh, for the wonder that bubbles into my soul,
I would be a good fountain, a good well-head,
Would blur no whisper, spoil no expression.
What is the knocking?
What is the knocking at the door in the night?
It is somebody wants to do us harm.

No, no, it is the three strange angels.
Admit them, admit them.

         D. H. Lawrence

# CHAPTER VIII

# *Some Concluding Reflections for the Time Being*

THE study which we have engaged throughout this work is, ultimately, the integration of the human personality as it is achieved by the individual person in the course of life. Since this achievement is one that entails the full panoply of imaginative resources that a person may possess, as well as the multiple forms that language may take, we dealt with those matters as we proceeded. From the outset, however, we sought to make clear the fact that our study, even though concerned with the imaginative thought in diverse forms, was centered on the person's living out life in the real world. Thus we focused on the perceptual field rather than the purely imaginary. It is there that people live and integrate themselves. Our emphasis on the importance, if not the primacy, of imaginative thinking was intended to point up its significance on the life of perceptual and cognitional experience. Many, it is true, have elected to focus on the imaginative as the power to deal with the unreal, the fanciful, the absent. We pointed out early, however, that this was only one aspect of that imaginative thought of which human beings are capable. Far more important for the task of integrating our lives is the impact that imaginative thought has on the world of the real that emerges in the horizon of our thought. This has been overlooked. The imaginative thinking we do impacts on the real world far more than is ever suspected and contributes to our judgments and decisions far more than we are accustomed to acknowledge. This is not to suggest that the person is totally unaware and thus totally helpless in endeavors in the presence of imaginative thought. The fact is that most people are keenly conscious of their imaginative thought but simply do not appreciate its full significance.

A careful study of the conversation of many a person or group will indicate to a surprising degree the extent to which the conversation is carried out in terms of imaginative thinking and language. While critical points are being made, metaphors abound on all sides; analogies are constantly employed; similes are forever suggested; symbolic aspects of life are brought to the fore; stories, jokes, fables are constantly interjected; dreams are shared; fantasies are depicted and embellished; poetry is recited; pithy quotes are rendered. In short the conversation is replete with countless imaginative diversions, colorations, illustrations, creations that continuously flesh out whatever logical skeleton may be present. Such is the human endeavor: one whose meritorious achievements are not only bedecked and bejeweled with the beautiful, the poetic, and the imaginative, as Holderlin has well stated, but one whose meritorious achievements are themselves the offspring of the imaginative thought that one has brought to bear on the hard realities of life. Imaginizing the real, having it shot through with genuine imaginative thought, is a potent dimension of the full life, the integrated existence.

It was this realization about life that gave rise to the reflections of chapters three to six. Language obviously is at the heart of the enterprise, but it is the metaphor specifically that is at the origin of semantic breakthroughs. The symbol and the myth-story are the metaphors embellished, full-blown, stretched big, and written large. They bring into the human picture dimensions that the mere metaphor can only hint at, but they are in the end but magnificent developments of the understandings that are seen to originate in the metaphorical grasps of life. Thus, to say that imaginative thought permeates and vibrates throughout life is to say that that thinking which is the human claim to fame (humankind being the ζῶον λόγον ἔχον that it is) is vibrant because it is characterized by the vitality, the fluidity, the nonrigidity that characterize human living itself. It is not enough that it be logical and rational; it must also be imaginative. Life is languaged; otherwise it is not human. But the language has *vita*, vitality, life only insofar as it genuinely prompts and promotes the life that it would depict and describe. Otherwise it is dead. And that life is undergoing constant change and becoming. Hence the language that would permeate and effect life, as well as describe and communicate it, must allow for that selfsame change and becoming. This is precisely what imaginative thinking and languaging do.

In the light of all this, then, we paused in the seventh chapter to reflect on the significance of temporality. Personal integration, to be sure, entails imaginative thought, language, and metaphorical syntheses, but it also entails temporality. This is due not only to the fact that the human person is constantly engaged in temporalizing every experience in terms of its past, present, and future dimensions, but also to the fact that the human person during his lifetime cultivates an ongoing identity that remains at once a unique, conscious, persistent individuation throughout a lifetime as well as a never-ending process of significant change and development— every stage of which can rightfully claim that identity while being claimed by it in return. Thus the fullness of a personal identity, such as it is, is never experienced until death itself intervenes, while each moment allows the person at a given stage of development to claim ownership over all of one's life. Temporality, in brief, is an intriguing phenomenon that introduces one to some of the most subtle aspects of the mystery that is the human person.

It remains now to advance a few final considerations, reflections that seem relevant to the study that we have undertaken in these pages. In all, we would focus on three:

A. Human existence: a dialectic between logical and imaginative thought
B. The presence of significant metaphorizers at the societal level
C. The unique role of religion in the human integrational process

## A. Human Existence: An Ongoing Dialectic Between Logical and Imaginative Thought

The discussion that we have entertained at various times in our study about the eminence accorded logic in the course of Western thought has enabled us to see and understand the reluctance to accord to imaginative thought a similar prestige. As has been stated, this entire question constitutes a major discussion in its own right. Important for us is the fact that meaning, respectable meaning, was identified with the logical thinking of humankind, while human imaginative thought was identified with the animistic, the irrational, the illogical, the instinctual, the represssible, and ultimately the dangerous. It has taken philosophy many centuries to come to an appreciation of the nature of language, its relatedness to thinking, and the inevitability of the metaphorical flavor that permeates both language and thought. One of the few great philosophers to recognize this was the eighteenth-century Italian, Giambattista Vico. Even so great a thinker as Plato, whose recourse to myth and analogy are well known, had great misgivings about the significance and truth value of the poets. Questioning their contribution, since it dealt with an image of an image and not with the ideal reality itself, he failed to see that his own efforts to depict life's truths were characterized by the same metaphorical qualities that the poets manifested. Likewise the medieval genius, Thomas Aquinas, whose love for the logical thought of Aristotle is evident on every page, was wont to question Plato himself for the simple reason that his thought was indeed so metaphorical. This is illustrated by his famous passage in his commentary on the *De Anima* of Aristotle, I, 8:

> *Plato habuit malum modum docendi. Omnia enim figurate dicit, et per symbola docet: intendens aliud per verba, quam sonent ipsa verba; sicut quod dixit animum esse circulum. Et ideo ne aliquis propter ipsa verba incidat in errorem, Aristoteles disputat contra eum quantum ad id quod verba eius sonant.* (Plato employed a bad method of teaching. For he spoke constantly in figures or metaphors, and taught by the use of symbols: intending in his words something other than what the words themselves signified, as when he spoke of the soul as a circle. And thus, lest someone because of these words fall into error, Aristotle disputed with him in regard to what his words actually meant.)

As we have seen in the course of our study, the appreciation of metaphorical, symbolic, and mythical thought has mushroomed particularly since the turn of the century—in many circles. In some ways it could be said that the pendulum seems to be swinging completely to the other side, and logical thought finds itself very much on the defensive at the present time. The United States courts, for example, witnessed in June 1982 the Hinkley trial with its decision to exonerate the defendant by virtue of the fact that he was deemed insane at the time of shooting the president of the country. During the course of the trial, the government argued for the sanity of the defendant and hence his responsible guilt. Now, however, by virtue of the verdict rendered and Hinkley's confinement to a mental institution, the same government is arguing equally for his insanity, lest his established sanity lead to a precipitous public release. This is but a passing but significant instance of the turn of events in human thought and life, now that rational and logical thought no longer go unchallenged. Indeed in the current debate between logic and rhetoric, debate that is pursued in the courtroom as well as in the realm of national and international politics, logic is as apt to suffer defeat as it was once to score victories.

Pascal saw it quite differently, and Wallace Stevens speaks to Pascal's dismissal of imaginative thought whose good is so often evil and whose evil is so often good.

> Pascal called the imagination the mistress of the world. But as he seems never to have spoken well of it, it is certain that he did not use this phrase to speak well of it. He called it the deceptive element in man, the mistress of error and duplicity and yet not always that, since there would be an infallible measure of truth if there were an infallible measure of untruth. But being most often false, it gives no sign of its quality and indicates in the same way both the true and the false. A little farther on in the *Pensees* he speaks of magistrates, their red robes, their ermines in which they swathe themselves, like furry cats, the palaces in which they sit in judgment, the fleurs-de-lies and the whole necessary, august apparatus. He says, and he enjoys his own malice in saying it, that if medical men did not have their cassocks and the mules they wore and if doctors did not have their square hats and robes four times too large, they would never have been able to dupe the world, which is incapable of resisting so genuine a display. (1942/1951, p. 133).

Having spoken of the preeminence once enjoyed by reason and logic and which is now under seige, Stevens continues:

> What, then, is it to live in the mind with the imagination, yet not too near to the fountains of its rhetoric, so that one does not have a consciousness only of grandeurs, of incessant departures from the idiom and of inherent altitudes? Only the reason stands between it and the reality for which the two are engaged in a struggle. We have no particular interest in this struggle because we know that it will continue to go on and that there will never be an outcome. We lose sight of it until Pascal, or someone else, reminds us of it. We say that it is merely a routine and the more we think about it the less able we are to see that it has any heroic aspects or that the spirit is at stake or that it may involve the loss of the world. Is there in fact any struggle

at all and is the idea of one merely a bit of academic junk? Do not the
two carry on together in the mind like two brothers or two sisters or
even like young Darby and young Joan? Darby says, "Is it often true
that what is most rational appears to be most imaginative, as in the
case of Picasso." Joan replies, "It is often true, also, that what is
most imaginative appears to be most rational, as in the case of Joyce.
Life is hard and dear and it is the hardness that makes it dear."
(p. 143)

The question raised by Stevens is appropriate: Is there in fact
any struggle at all? We can answer this by appealing to history and
seeing that the struggle has indeed gone on. And we might also add
that we might have expected that, with the historical triumph of
logical and rational thought, it would only be a question of time
until we would witness the swing of the pendulum and the upsurge,
if not the triumph, of imaginative thought. This is precisely the
situation that is developing today. Increasingly, we are being faced
with the paradox of the coexistence of unparalleled scientific,
rational thought and achievement and a growing, unbridled, emo-
tionalized, highly imaginized enthusiasm that feels no need to
provide rational justification for its iconoclasm. The latter, which
bids fair to become a return to barbarism, does indeed offer its
share of riches, but it can no more, of and by itself, do justice to the
human condition than did the previous triumph of logical-scientific
thought.

Personal integration at the individual level and societal integration at the mass level call for the recognition of the legitimacy and
the necessity of both logical and imaginative thought at all levels in
an ongoing dialectic. When in its early days Greek thought described the human being as an ζωον λογον ἐχον living being
endowed with the power of logos, it understood that logos to be the
power of wording, thinking, reasoning, imagining, meaning. It is
this fullness of the concept of λογος that must be restored in all its
dimensions. Fortunately, such is now becoming possible, particularly since we have come during this century to the deeper appreciation of languaging, wording, and imaginative thinking, three
aspects of the question that previously were either taken for granted
or irreverently dismissed. Giving all dimensions of λογος their due
would be a significant step in the right direction.

The rational resources of the human being are imperative.
Human life is beset with endless complexities compounded by the

fact that human perception is perspectival. Realities that emerge within our respective perceptual horizons undergo constant change, not only because of the realities themselves but also because of the changing perceptions. And yet they must be dealt with and intelligently so. We can no more hope to cope successfully with the complexities of life without the resource of rational thought than we could have hoped to bring into existence the wonders of human achievement without that same logical reasoning, scientific, legal, or whatever. The fruit of human genius surrounds us on all sides, and the methods of rational investigation have proved their worth time and time again. If human beings are to continue living on this earth in a manner "full of merit," they will need as never before the benefits of our best rational thinking.

By the same token, it has become ineluctably clear that rational thought of and by itself will not suffice for the human condition. It has failed and will continue to fail without the benefits of imaginative thinking permeating its realm. We need not turn to Freud to learn that there is much in the human person that is not encompassed by the terms rational and logical. Everyday experience provides testimony to the power and significance of human feelings, emotions, human irrationalism and violence and the like, even amid the most logical and rational of settings. To attribute this aspect of human living to unconscious forces that escape human control, as Freud did, is to acknowledge that the human person is more than mere rationalism. Unfortunately, however, such an explanation becomes quickly self-defeating, for in denying the person the power of self-determination over such nonrational dimensions of his own person, we are throwing out the baby with the bath, robbing the human of that which is his claim to humanity. Phenomenological study has demonstrated the significance of consciousness, responsibility, choice, and self-determination in the human scheme of things, while at the same time acknowledging the presence of nonrational resources within the person. To term such resources unconscious and inimical is to throw dubious light on the matter. Since the person does experience consciousness and a sense of responsibility and limited freedom, to deny such is to fly in the face of human experience and to reduce the human to the subhuman, explaining away the experience in terms of instincts and biochemical forces. On the other hand, to see the nonrational resources of a person as configurations that come into existence and under human experiential control when the person indulges in imaginative thinking of countless kinds is to provide the individual person with an understanding of self, an appreciation of the findings of biofeedback studies, a sense of autonomy and self-responsibility while still corrobating one's conscious experiences of life.

Human experience, in short, indicates clearly that we are constantly engaging in thinking that is at once rational and imaginative or, if you will, logical and analogical. It is not a question, then, of upholding the virtues of logical thought against those of imaginative thought, or conversely of upholding the virtues of imaginative thought against those of logical thought. Nor is it a question of upholding the virtues of both, as though they operated in parallel lines within the human endeavors. None of these explanations is satisfactory, since they either set them at loggerheads with each other, or keep them at a comfortable distance from each other. The fact of the matter is that in every human endeavor we find both the logical and imaginative dimensions of thought operative. At no time is thought purely and simply rational or purely and simply imaginative. At all times our thinking partakes of both features. All of which is another way of saying that human thought is ever engaged in a dialectic between both kinds of thinking, whether those efforts be expended in the realm of philosophy, science, law, literature, theology, politics, or interpersonal exchange.

It is this give-and-take of thought that leads us to term it a dialectic rather than a dialogue. In the latter we would expect the rationality to accost the imagination and vice versa. It simply does not work that way, as every human knows full well. What happens is quite different. We start out with our careful thinking, and in the midst of it embark on an imaginative excursion, a brainstorming session, that in turn leads us to question, if not rethink, our whole rational explanation. On the other hand we begin to indulge in an imaginative endeavor and soon come to see that it will simply not do, since it is so completely at odds with what we realize is rationally established, plausible, or doable. Whereupon we adjust our imaginative scheme and bring it more into line with the data that we have accumulated. Each kind of thinking is bequeathing to the other that which it knows, so that the end product profits from the contribution of both. In so doing, our enterprise moves ahead in whatever realm we are occupied, and hopefully it moves toward some achievement. If such be the case, the human person is tapping all his thinking potential at the time and widening the possibilities into which he is moving. Failing to recognize this fact is to truncate the effort. Rational thought without imaginative input is lifeless and sterile; imaginative thought without rationality is delusional and ultimately impotent.

All this being the case, we cannot but insist that life calls for every person to be ever human, that is to say, ever mindful of the full remarkable thinking power that is at his or her command. And personal integration, to be more specific, demands that a person put his life together by tapping the contributions that can be had from both kinds of thought. Anything short of this is an invitation to failure and a pledge of futility.

Such would seem to be one realization that flows from our study.

## B. The Presence of Significant Metaphorizers at the Societal Level

If, as Ricoeur has stated and we have shown in describing the metaphor as the midwife of unification, the metaphor is at the origin of all semantic fields, it takes but little thought to perceive the critical importance of those people in society who are so positioned that they are able to influence the formation of metaphors on a grand scale. To a certain degree we should say this of everyone inasmuch as we can all influence our own circles. That having been granted, however, it would appear that there are still persons in our midst of whom it can be said in a very special way. And it is of these that we would now speak—for two reasons.

First of all, people in their efforts to cope with life's vicissitudes often find themselves with little recourse for help outside very limited circles. An extended family may provide help, but such is not always available—and too often only when it is too late. Such persons are often helpless, or at least imagine themselves as helpless—and thus they are. If, then, they imagine that there is no other way to imagine their lives, the future becomes bleak indeed. Simplistic or even desperate strategies are frequently employed. One is reminded here of the hillwife of whom Frost wrote in his work:

## THE OFT-REPEATED DREAM

She had no saying dark enough
    For the dark pine that kept
Forever trying the window-latch
    Of the room where they slept.

The tired but ineffectual hands
    That with every futile pass
Made the great tree seem as a little bird
    Before the mystery of glass.

It never had been inside the room
    And only one of the two
Was afraid in an oft-repeated dream
    Of what the tree might do.

It was too lonely for her there,
    And too wild,
And since there were but two of them,
    And no child,

And work was little in the house,
    She was free,
And followed where he furrowed field,
    Or felled tree.

She rested on a log and tossed
    The fresh chips,
With a song only to herself
    On her lips.

And once she went to break a bough
    Of black alder.
She strayed so far she scarcely heard
    When he called her—

And didn't answer—didn't speak—
    Or return.
She stood, and then she ran and hid
    In the fern.

He never found her, though he looked
    Everywhere,
And he asked at her mother's house
    Was she there.

Sudden and swift and light as that
 The ties gave,
And he learned of finalities
 Besides the grave.

     Robert Frost

Many, of course, do not take the path of the hillwife, but instead endure their lives in whatever way they can. Such people, along with everyone for that matter, turn to society's metaphorizers to enable them to reimagine their problems or struggles more effectively or satisfyingly.

Second, while such moments are being experienced at many levels of life, the metaphorizers themselves do not always appreciate the significance of their own efforts. Because feedback or words of appreciation are not spoken out, particularly on a personal level, such persons can easily begin, on their own part, to imagine their efforts as fruitless, if not futile. The truth of the matter is, it is easy for them to forget who they are and the powerful influence that they actually do wield in human lives, on the human scene.

Uppermost among such people, and perhaps we should even say first among such, are the clergy in the pulpit. Even though they may often question, as do teachers, the effect of their efforts, the fact remains that they are in a position to work wonders for their people. For the most part they enter the pulpit, not with a captive audience as cynics would phrase it, but with a congregation that for the most part could just as easily be elsewhere. It is improper to take the congregation lightly or to entertain the thought that they would be just as well pleased if one did not preach that day. Entering his sermon with such imaginings in his own mind, the preacher renders himself ineffective. What is important for him or her to understand is the fact that every person in front of him is dealing with life and engaged in a process of integrating his or her life. A few thoughts, a worthy message, a serious preparation, carefully chosen words, an honest reflection, an apt metaphor, a symbol or two, a meaningful story—all these are in order. Any one of these, if handled well, can touch another's heart, proving inspirational or providing uplift. And even if such does not appear to happen, that is really inconsequential. What is important is the fact that the preacher has shared a message, thoughtfully prepared and imaginatively presented, that has had its impact. The full effect will not—indeed cannot—be forthcoming immediately. If the person has been imaginatively touched, mission has been accomplished. And the preacher has done properly by his people, for they have come to derive much from him, not only because of his well-conceived and delivered message, but also because of the tremendous symbolism that characterizes his office and performance. Few in society can rival the metaphorical significance of a people's spiritual leaders, and that congregation and community are truly blessed if their clergy have come to appreciate just how powerful their role is in the life of their people, and particularly how meaningful their words are when spoken amid the solemnity and sacredness of the pulpit scene.

Much of the same could be said of the teacher, although in this instance we are dealing with a situation quite different from the pulpit and, for that matter, from the home from which the student (child or adult) comes. The imaginative appeal of the teacher is legend. Unlike the clergyman whose sermon impacts in a dramatic but periodic manner, the teacher finds herself or himself in a more quasi-parental position (even in these days of student consumerism). There takes place in the classroom, particularly at the elementary and high school level but by no means exclusively there, a give-and-take quite analogous to the interchange in the home. The teacher's position is unique, however. There is about his role an aura much like that surrounding the preacher and the parent. Unlike the preacher, however, the teacher has frequent personal contact, or at least the opportunity to effect it, that the pulpit does not easily provide. Unlike the parent, the teacher is able to speak out to the student and gain a hearing that would be emotionally denied to the parents. There is about the teacher an emotional distance and professionalism that command a hearing, based principally on the assumed informed competence. No parent can claim that as a rule, even when the parent also has the requisite competence, since the emotional relationship between student and parent is so powerful, the contact so constant and close, and an inevitable authoritarianism present in the picture of the home. Teachers, on the other hand, spared the intricacies of the home's emotional labyrinth, may speak forth, touch the heart, introduce delicate but relevant considerations, fire the imagination, open up new worlds and perspectives, share their own reflections, recommend readings, read meaningful poems—all of which are designed to effect marvels in the casual and studied exchanges, during which the teacher also has the opportunity to model life for the impressed and suggestible student.

Unfortunately it is a fact that many teachers do not see their role in this way. But it still remains that students of all ages are integrating their lives, as is the teacher, and are seeking proper metaphors for their living. Knowing this and appreciating their unique psychic impact upon students, teachers can introduce into the student's life and thinking many rich observations, examples, stories that enable the student to remetaphorize their homes, their problems, their relationships—and all this with relatively little emotional opposition. The task, of course, makes its demands on the teacher; but the teacher who has come to appreciate the importance of these metaphorizations can through imaginative appeals work wonders for many in the classroom, even for the seemingly unreachable students who apparently are just sitting there listlessly. They too are caught in moods, and the imaginative content of these moods can be challenged by a caring and ingenious teacher.

The third member of this significant triumvirate is the parents. Preachers can work their wonders; teachers can give life entirely new dimensions; but it is the parents whose impact is so foundational. In this instance, however, it is not by preaching or even by teaching that the parent imparts metaphorizations to children. It is by modeling. We would not want to suggest that a parent's words are insignificant. We would want to point out that the powerful emotional impact parents have on children is realized through the modeling. Again we would say, as we have previously, that a child will take up the modeling and give it a unique coloring of his or her own. But this is as it should be. Modeling should appeal to the imaginative genius of the child or subordinate, who in turn embellishes it in a child's own way. By no means does this imply that the modeling is irrelevant. Quite the contrary: the modeling embodies the actual parental metaphorizations, and it takes little effort on the child's part to read the text that a parent embodies. Say what he might to a child, it is the manner in which the parent handles situations that speaks to the youngster and teaches him or her the art of handling life. Along with the preacher and teacher, the parent constitutes a powerful pedagogical triumvirate. Together they show by word (the preacher), by provocative challenges (the teacher) and by significant example (parents), how one puts life together. One need not be speaking his metaphors all the time. His living of them will say all that should be said.

There is a second category of metaphorizers that we should mention whose impact on life is simply unmeasurable. They enter into the inner person, they stir up feelings, they enlarge our vistas, they carry us aloft, they challenge our views and stereotypes of the world and of life. Unlike preachers, teachers and parents, these metaphorizers deliberately appeal to the imaginative in the human— making capital of it—and they would give us no choice but to rethink or reimagine the quotidiana of life. In this category we would find the playwright, the novelist, the poet, the artist, the composer, the musician, the writer, the sensitive actor. People such as these have seen something in life that they are convinced must be languaged, be it in words, musical sounds, stone, steel, paint, sand, wood, or just mime. They are aware, as few others about them, that the human longing for the beautiful is every bit as powerful as the yearning for the good and the true. Indeed they would identify all three, and speak out that conviction in their work.

In this category we would do well to include the architect, the gifted architect, who has come to appreciate the human need to dwell fittingly on this earth if we are going to dwell humanly. Such persons spark the imagination of the dweller and would make of his dwelling, his churches, his office buildings, his roads, his bridges subtle testimonies to the transcendental significance of the human's aspirations.

This extraordinary group of people is touching our lives every day. Their creative masterpieces, and even nonmasterpieces, allow the rest of us the opportunity to distance ourselves from life's stressors and to gain fresh and freeing perspectives on life itself. Their creations speak to us as does modeling to a child, and the inspiration they impart is every bit as real as the impact of the parent, teacher, and preacher. It is different, but every bit as real. In addition, there is about their work so often a goodly measure of ambiguity that can be misleading. But we must allow for that, for they are speaking in an extraordinary language that the rest of us are trying to learn. One might be tempted to underestimate their work because of that ambiguity, but really we should treat it as we would treat striking rhetoric. The truth may very well be that in the ambiguity lies the imaginative appeal and the potential for new and more astounding metaphorizations for the rest of humanity.

In his work, *Music and Imagination*, Aaron Copeland writes about meaning and ambiguity in his creative world:

> The precise meaning of music is a question that should never have been asked, and in any event will never elicit a precise answer. It is the literary mind that is disturbed by this imprecision. No true music-lover is troubled by the symbolic character of musical speech; on the contrary, it is this very imprecision that intrigues and activates the imagination. Whatever the semanticists of music may uncover, composers will blithely continue to articulate "subtle complexes of feeling that language cannot even name, let alone set forth." (1952, p. 22)

In a subsequent section of his work Copeland takes up the question of the artist's communication, more particularly the musician's communication:

> What, after all, do I put down when I put down notes? I put down a reflection of emotional states: feelings, perceptions, imaginings, intuitions. An emotional state, as I use the term, is compounded of everything we are: our background, our environment, our convictions. Art particularizes and makes actual these fluent emotional states. Because it particularizes and because it makes actual, it gives meaning to *la condition humaine*. If it gives meaning it necessarily has purpose. I would even add that it has moral purpose. (p. 117 ff)

These comments of Copeland sound quite akin to those that we have made regarding preachers, teachers, and parents. The reality of the dialogue cannot be denied; the power of the communication is evident. The purpose of the revelation from composer to listener would, to Copeland, even appear to be moral; meaning thereby, no doubt, that it would be the composer's hope that his musical disclosure would touch an audience's way of living life. Art in all its forms *speaks* to human life, and its justification does indeed lie in the life about us. Man lives full of merit, but yet poetically, imaginatively. The playwright, poets, composers, and artists realize this better than anyone, and they address their talents to that aspect of existence which has to do with the unabashedly imaginative dimensions of life. It is humankind's blessing that they do, for there is not a source of metaphorizations comparable to the creations that they have bequeathed in their unique artistic way.

A final category or classification, if you will, that we would suggest is that of the seemingly prosaic amalgam of civic leaders and communication experts: those who make the news and those who share it with others. It would be a serious mistake to underestimate the power of metaphorization that lies within their respective areas. Ever since President Franklin D. Roosevelt's use of the phrase "New Deal" the nation has been particularly conscious of the impact such slogans or battle cries have on the populace at large. The history of the last two decades is replete with similar phrases: the New Frontier, the Great Society, Black is Beautiful, and many other catch phrases. Such words fire the public imagination for a program or a cause, galvanize public energy toward some enterprise, create momentum toward a goal. Even today, some twenty years later, the word Camelot has about it a ring that stirs memories, awakens forgotten dreams, and initiates a weak hope that maybe all is not lost and that something can be recaptured nationally and set afire. Such phrases are not empty and their power not negligible. Civic leaders on all sides have recourse to the magic of the right phrase, and all the while the phrase constitutes an attempt to metaphorize a human movement. In the same spirit chambers of commerce throughout the country formulate highly imaginative phrases to appeal to tourists: Sky Country, Vacation Wonderland, Land of Lakes. On all sides and at all levels of leadership we witness this phenomenon. It is no mere happenstance. It is a public acknowledgment of the power of the metaphor on the public mind, and the need for metaphorizing movements in striking, imaginative ways.

That civic leaders can use their position to fire the thinking of their people in many areas of life is a historical truism. The leader can capture his position in a powerful slogan and then use that slogan with its inevitable ambiguity toward the realization of other purposes as well. It is not easy for a people to set aside a significant phrase or dream that has been formulated for it by its leaders, so great is the latter's symbolic impact. The people want to believe their leader and to live by the metaphors he or she provides.

By the same token the communicators of news are masterful in their own unique metaphorizations of events, tragedies, episodes, conversations, public addresses, programs, and the like. Their ability to capture the news in pithy, imaginative phrases allows the public mind to rest with their analyses. Their words become the public view overnight and their imagining of it the public understanding. A classical instance of this was the image projected by

Walter Cronkite. In the public mind the full and true story was that which he presented. It was inconceivable that he would engage in any duplicity, that he would allow falsity to go out under his name, that he would not be thorough in his investigation or analysis. And the public rested with his characterizations. Needless to say, this phenomenon is seen at work in newspapers and periodicals everywhere. A brilliant cartoon can provide a metaphorization of the most complex issue and enhance the public understanding of the matter at a glance.

Thus it is within the power of newsmakers and news commentators/communicators to metaphorize life situations for the masses of people and in so doing to play significant roles in the life of a nation. A people can be put at rest by the right metaphor phrased by the right person, or it can be noticeably upset by the wrong metaphor phrased by the right person. People are living imaginatively all the time, and it is the responsibility of our public metaphorizers to respect the seriousness of their position and the trust that the populace at large places in them. In all avenues of life, there is nothing so effective as the right metaphor said by the right person at the right time. It will live long after he or she has died.

## C. THE UNIQUE ROLE OF RELIGION IN THE HUMAN INTEGRATIONAL PROCESS

We shall bring our reflections for the time being to a close by a focus on the question of religion and the integrational process. It will be remembered that in the first chapter we spoke of the growing appreciation for imaginative thinking that was being manifested in religious circles. Then in our previous section we mentioned the significant role of the preacher in the pulpit as a societal metaphorizer. We now wish to conclude with a consideration of the unique part that religion plays in the effort of many people to integrate their lives. Some, of course, would question its value, but the vast majority of humankind sees it differently. We would speak to its worth.

Freud's work, *The Future of an Illusion*, has been judged by some as one of the most serious attempts in the twentieth century by a partisan of science to face up to the disenchantment of the world. As two contemporary authors phrase it,

> The underlying issue in the work is not so much the future of religion or even of civilization, but the question of how to give principle to one's life when nature is no longer a home, when human beings have no more sanctuaries or sacred territories to which to withdraw for communion with the source of their being. Freud found his own sanctuary within the recesses of his ego, but regardless of his protests to the contrary, his solution is an invitation to despair. By failing to acknowledge the limits of science he had to affirm a transcendental rationalism which undermined the very contributions which he had made to self-understanding. (Weinstein & Weinstein, 1981, p. 463)

This evaluation of Freud's position on the significance of religion in human living may appear harsh, but the truth is that it expresses accurately the view that he ultimately developed on the matter. It was not that Freud felt that religion had made no contribution to humankind, or that he saw no merit in the religious aspect of human living. It was just that he felt it had more than outlived its usefulness and could well be replaced—to the benefit of humankind. Marx, as we know, had seen religion as an opiate for the people. Freud saw in it an illusion that, however meritorious in the past, had little or no contribution to make the human future. He termed it a grand human illusion, so called because he saw at the heart of the religious experience a grand wish fulfillment, and wish fulfillment in Freud's view was the critical motivating force in any illusion. Religion, then, being the great illusion for the human race in its primitive years, its practice was nothing less than an obsessive-compulsive neurosis, not unlike the obsessional neuroses of children (1927/1961, v. XXI, p. 43).

In the debate that he conducts with an imaginary opponent in his *Future of an Illusion*, Freud states clearly that he is casting his chips with the realm of science. Despairing of the illusion and realizing the human need for life answers, Freud opts for science, the clear, rational thought that will have none of the obfuscation of the imaginary wish fulfillment that religion embraces. He spells it out in a forthright way in the final pages of the work:

> Education freed from the burden of religious doctrines will not, it may be, effect much change in men's psychological nature. Our god Logos, is perhaps not a very almighty one, and he may only be able to fulfill a small part of what his predecessors have promised. If we have to acknowledge this we shall accept it with resignation. We shall not on that account lose our interest in the world and in life, for

we have one sure support which you lack. We believe that it is possible for scientific work to gain some knowledge about the reality of the world, by means of which we can increase our power and in accordance with which we can arrange our life. If this belief is an illusion, then we are in the same position as you. But science has given us evidence by its numerous and important successes that it is no illusion. . . .

No, our science is no illusion. But an illusion it would be to suppose that what science cannot give us we can get elsewhere. (1927, p. 55)

In the second chapter of his *Civilization and Its Discontents*, written some three years later, Freud refers back to this same topic:

In my *Future of an illusion* (1927) I was concerned much less with the deepest sources of the religious feeling than with what the common man understands by his religion—with the system of doctrines and promises which on the one hand explains to him the riddles of this world with enviable completeness, and, on the other, assures him that a careful Providence will watch over his life and will compensate him in a future existence for any frustrations he suffers here. The common man cannot imagine this Providence otherwise than in the figure of an enormously exalted father. Only such a being can understand the needs of the children of men and be softened by their prayers and placated by the signs of their remorse. The whole thing is so patently infantile. (1930, 1961, v. XXI, p.74)

Such a faith and trust in science, seen from the perspective of the last quarter of the twentieth century rather than the first, certainly strikes one as naive and simplistic. It would appear that science in Freud's view held out solid and sound guarantee for human peace, confidence, and reassurance, while religion ultimately held out nothing but illusion. Near the end of his life Freud, now forced into exile, undoubtedly had misgivings of sorts about the inevitability of human progress and growth under the aegis of pure science. Today, some fifty years later, we have even greater misgivings than he. The current world concern, manifested in many mass protests over nuclear proliferation and annihilation, has many—not the least of whom are scientists themselves—wondering whether science, after a century of unbridled freedom and almost unlimited financial support, can of and by itself offer humankind anything of permanent value. It may well be that the human race can no longer survive without the benefits of its science, but it may also be that the race has even less chance of survival with it. Certainly there are few today who do not welcome every sincere gesture that religion can make to help humankind from the horrible threats to humanity that modern science has now made patently possible and real.

In a recent article one scientist phrased it this way: "In my recent book I have made the case that only religion is a strong enough human force to guide technology" (Roy, 1981B p. 224). The reference that Roy makes here is to his own book, *Experimenting with Truth: The Fusion of Religion with Technology, Needed for Humanity's Survival*. The author captures his theme in these words:

> My experience in the world of science policy at the microscopic level of choosing between alternative routes for the disposal of radioactive wastes as well as the level of greatest complexity in dealing with the use of SbT* in the development of nations has driven me to an unexpected conclusion. "Science" policy, I am convinced, must be done in a framework of, or under the hegemony of, a specific "religious" world view. Since so many national policies are infused with science-policy components, this means that SbT and religion must become extremely interactive to help mankind govern itself. (1981A, p. 2)

In brief, while it is certainly possible that Freud and others saw in religion only an illusion that will eventually but inevitably fail humankind, it can be said just as convincingly that the same judgment can be, and today is being, made against science. It too could prove to be an illusion that offered the human race so much at a certain stage of its development, but which is now starting to fail the human race. The truth undoubtedly lies somewhere in between these two extreme positions for both science and religion. Certainly few contemporary psychologists would be willing to endorse Freud's apodictic position and repudiate the worth of religion. By far the majority, I suspect, would be wont to view the issue more in the spirit of Erik Erikson:

> If I name religion as the institution which throughout man's history has striven to verify basic trust, I disavow any intention to call religion as such childish or religious behavior as such regressive, although it is obvious that large-scale infantilization is not foreign to the practise and the intent of organized religion. . . . Religion, it

*SbT: Science–based–Technology

seems, is the oldest and has been the most lasting institution to serve the ritual restoration of a sense of trust in the form of faith while offering a tangible formula for a sense of evil against which it promises to arm and defend man. (1968, p. 106)

Our own study has introduced for our consideration many aspects of human life and living. Throughout this work we have sought to focus on the manner in which persons seek to move into life and bring together for themselves its complexities. It is in the nature of the human to ponder the meaning of it all: to wonder, to marvel, to guess, to imagine, to move into the great beyond of all that surrounds us, to reach out to touch the intangible, to speak the ineffable, to embrace the mysteriosum of life. Every human being can affirm the experience of Keats, cited before, captured in his beautiful sonnet:

When I have fears that I may cease to be
  Before my pen has glean'd my teeming brain,
Before high piled books, in charactry,
  Hold like rich garners the full-ripen'd grain;
When I behold, upon the night's starr'd face,
  Hugh cloudy symbols of a high romance,
And think that I may never live to trace
  Their shadows, with the magic hand of chance;
And when I feel, fair creature of an hour!
  That I shall never look upon thee more,
Never have relish in the faery power
  Of unreflecting love;—then on the shore
Of the wide world I stand alone, and think
Till Love and Fame to nothingness do sink.

John Keats, "When I have fears"

These are thoughts of every thinking person, and they call for responses that can not always, maybe seldom, be made with logical, rational thinking. They call also for considerable imaginative thinking that enables one to formulate answers that bring about profound understanding and emotionally satisfying reflections. It is at such times that we seek to put in language that which we have come to understand, notions that we have found quite strengthening, hopes that we experience as meaningful, sound, and uplifting. And it is at such moments as these that we find ourselves having recourse to metaphors that enable us to span the chasms of life and to symbols that reverberate throughout our person, reaching into our past, our culture, our family, our history in a way that we can'affirm with quiet strength. At moments such as these the recourse to religion is natural for humankind. It calls for the effort for us to transcend mundanities, to escape the limits of our own finitude and to seek the company of the Lord. It is as natural for humankind to move upwards toward God, the spiritual largess of the Lord, as it is for the swimmer to hurry to the top of the water where he can breath in the welcomed influx of oxygen. One is as necessary here as the other, and the wonders of the world about us are no more capable of quieting our expansive needs for the Transcendent than is the inundating water able to quiet the mounting spasms of the lungs.

It is an axiom of psychology and of religion that the human person finds self when one loses self, when one genuinely moves toward the world, toward creation, toward people, toward others. This is no less true for the person when he or she moves toward God. This entire dimension of life must be accounted for, must be reckoned with, must be assimilated into life in some kind of a synthesis. Even to dismiss it as superstitious is to encompass it in an intelligible whole. How satisfying such a synthesis might prove to be for a person is another question. But it is one way of dealing with the issue of religion, obviously. The vast majority of humankind has never rested secure with such a grand and grandiose dismissal. They prefer to look for meaning on a grand scale in life just as they do for meaning on a small scale. It is the nature of the human to look for meaning at all levels. To be sure, we are prepared to find those who will find great joy in studying the world of the subhuman—animals, fish, plants, minerals, rocks—and who dismiss the world of the human, of people, as almost meaningless. So too some would find the world of the human unbelievably fascinating and the world of God boring. We must be prepared for that, too. The vast majority of people, however, whatever their interest in the world of the subhuman, find their fellow humans a source of love, strength, and inspiration and seek to foster relationships with them. So too do the vast majority, whatever their appreciation of the purely human, find the relationships of which religion speaks equally meaningful and strengthening, and seek to foster relations in that domain as well. The proof one offers is not that of argumentation; it is the proof that originates in the experience.

Thus the person whose life story in all its fullness and temporality leads him or her to seek intercourse with God, and to live the life as a vast meaningful love exchange with God and the whole of creation, has indeed significant possibilities at his or her command. Every relationship contributes possibilities to our lives, and the spiritual relationships offer beautiful possibilities for those who cultivate them. Indeed history has shown that genuine religious living with its metaphors, symbols, and inspirational stories can effect wonders in the lives of people, and, in the lives of some individuals, enable them to acquire the stature of saints. Among them we find some of humankind's most heroic people and the most inspirational of persons. But even those who fall short of this stature still find their efforts fruitful and their accomplishments noteworthy. Indeed in the religious understanding of things, the least impressive of persons merits to be taken seriously, the most hypocritical of humans remains entitled to the benefit of the doubt, the most heinous of individuals could end up finding salvation at the last hour. In short, no human being is ever beyond redemption. Such are the understandings of people and of life that are the heritage of religion, and such understandings are invaluable for one who is intent on putting life and world together in a meaningful way.

There is no realization in life more devastating to a human being than the fact that he is totally alone in life, in this world. By the same token there is no realization quite as important to all of us as the realization that we are not alone and never really ever alone. Such an understanding lies at the heart of a genuine integration of life. Thanks to religion in life, a person is brought to an appreciation of this and many other truths about life. No other field of study is comparable. It holds out hope to all, excluding none. And calling all the while for imaginative thinking, it would bid the person to look far, to see far, to think far into life. And it would urge the person to imagine even in the darkest of moments, the light of hope that makes integral living possible.

## "Early Illusions"

Early illusions are beautiful,
Early illusions are wounding
But what does it matter! We are above vanity,
We embrace the highest knowledge,
    saved by our happy blindness.

We, who are not afraid of taking a false step—
fools, from the common point of view—
still keep enchantment in our faces
through all the disillusioned crowd.

We are driven towards the distance
    by a glimmering of something,
away from the daily grind, the calculations of everyday
    living,
from pale skeptics and pink schemers,
transforming the world with our reflections.

But the inevitability of disappointments
makes us see too clearly. . . . On all sides
everything suddenly takes shape,
all unknown to us till now.

The world appears before us, unhazed; unmisted,
no longer radiant with something priceless,
but with all this truthfulness unmasked
as deceit. But what is gone—
    was no deception.

You see, it is not the knowledge of the serpent,
it is not the doubtful honor of experience,
but the ability to be enchanted by the world
that reveals to us the world as it really is.

Suppose someone with illusions in his eyes
flashes past, pursuing some distant gleam,
then it doesn't seem to us that he is blind—
it seems to us that we ourselves are blind.

Yevtushenko (1967)

# REFERENCES

Altieri, C. (1971). Jean Paul Sartre: The engaged imagination. *The quest for imagination*. Cleveland: Press of Case Western Reserve University.

Barbour, I. (1974). *Myths, models and paradigms*. New York: Harper & Row.

Barfield, O. (1964). *Poetic diction: A study in meaning*. New York: McGraw Hill, Co.

Baum, G. (Ed.). (1975). *Journeys*. New York: Paulist Press.

Berger, P. (1967). *The social construction of reality*. New York: Doubleday and Company.

Bidney, D. (1969). Vico's new science of myth. In G. Tagliacozza & H.V. White (Eds.), *Giambattista Vico: An international symposium*. Baltimore: John Hopkins Press.

Black, M. (1962). *Models, myths and metaphors*. Ithaca: Cornell University Press.

————. (1979). Afterthoughts on metaphor. In S. Sacks (Ed.), *On metaphor*. Chicago: University of Chicago Press.

Booth, W. (1978). Metaphor as rhetoric. In S. Sacks (Ed.), *On metaphor*. Chicago: University of Chicago Press.

deBono, E. (1971). *Lateral thinking for management*. New York: American Management Association.

Bolgar, R. (1972). Rhetoric. *British Encyclopedia*, Vol. 19. Chicago: W. Benton. (Originally published 1768)

Casey, E. (1974). Toward a phenomenology of imagination. *Journal of the British society for phenomenology*, 5 (1)

————. (1974, Spring). *Toward an archetypal imagination*. New York: Spring publications.

————. (1976). *Imagining: A phenomenological study*. Bloomington: Indiana University Press.

Cassirer, C. (1944). *Essay on man*. New Haven: Yale University Press.

Copeland, A. (1952). *Music and imagination*. New York: New American Library.

Crossan, J. (1975). *The dark interval: Towards a theology of story*. Niles: Argus Communications.

Dabrowski, K. (1964). *Positive disintegration*. Boston: Little, Brown and Company.

Davidson, D. (1978). What metaphors mean. In S. Sacks (Ed.), *On metaphors*. Chicago: University of Chicago Press.

Derrida, J. (1974–75). White mythology. *New literary history*, Vol. 6.

Descartes, R. (1972). Meditations. *Philosophical works of Descartes*. (E.S.

Haldane and G.R.T. Ross, Trans.). London: Cambridge University Press.

Dorfles, G. (1969). Contemporary aesthetics. In G. Tagliacozza & H. V. White (Eds.), *Giambattista Vico: An international symposium*. Baltimore: John Hopkins Press.

Edie, J. (1976). *Speaking and meaning*. Bloomington: Indiana University Press.

Eliade, M. (1961). *Images and symbols: Studies in religious symbolism*. New York: Sheed and Ward. (Original work published 1952)

Eliot, T. (1932). *Selected essays*. New York: Harcourt, Brace and World, Inc.

Erickson, E. (1968). *Identity: Youth and crisis*. New York: W.W. Norton and Company.

Franklin, J. (1972). Negro, American. *British Encyclopedia*, Vol. 16. Chicago: W. Benton. (Original published 1768)

Freud, S. (1961). The interpretation of dreams, Vol. IV. In J. Strachey (Ed.), *The standard edition*. London: The Hogarth Press. (Original work published 1900)

_____. (1961). New introductory lectures, Vol. XXII. In J. Strachey (Ed.), *The standard edition*. London: The Hogarth Press. (Original work published 1932)

_____. (1961). The future of an illusion, Vol. XXI. In J. Strachey (Ed.), *The standard edition*. London: The Hogarth Press. (Original work published 1927)

_____. (1961). Civilization and its discontents, Vol. XXI. In J. Strachey (Ed.), *The standard edition*. London: The Hogarth Press. (Original work published 1930)

Giorgi, A. (1970). *Psychology as a human science*. New York: Harper & Row.

Gordon, D. (1978). *Therapeutic metaphors*. Cupertino: Meta Publications.

Greeley, A. (1975). Nothing but a loud-mouthed Irish priest. *Journeys*. New York: Paulist Press.

Gurwitsch, A. (1964). *Field of consciousness*. Pittsburgh: Duquesne University Press.

Haley, J. (1973). *Uncommon therapy*. New York: W. W. Norton and Company.

Hall, C., Lindzey G. (1978). *Theories of personality*. (Third ed.). New York: John Wiley and Sons.

Hardison, O. (1971). Preface. In O. B. Hardison (Ed.), *The quest for imagination*. Cleveland: Case Western Reserve University Press.

Hatfield, H. (1960). The myth of Nazism. In H. Murray (Ed.), *Myth and myth-making*. Boston: Beacon Press.

Heidegger, M. (1927/1962). *Being and time*. (J. Macquarrie and E. Robinson, trans.). New York: Harper & Row. (Original work published 1927)

_____. (1929/1962). *Kant and the problem of metaphysics*. (J.S. Churchill, trans.). Bloomington: Indiana University Press. (Original work published 1929)

_____. (1959/1971). *On way to language.* (P. Hertz, trans.). New York: Harper and Row.

_____. (1971). *Poetry, language and thought.* (A. Hofstadter, Jr.) New York: Harper and Row.

_____. (1947/1977). *Letter on humanism in Martin Heidegger: Basic writings.* (D. Krell, trans.). New York: Harper and Row.

_____. (1935/1977). The origin of the work of art. In *Martin Heidegger: Basic writings.* (D. Krell, trans.). New York: Harper and Row.

Hesse, M. (1967). Models and analogy in science. *The encyclopedia of philosophy.* New York: Macmillan Company.

Hillman, J. (1975). *Revisioning psychology.* New York: Harper and Row.

Hofstadter, A. (1967). Imagination—organ of actuality. *Review of Existential psychology and psychiatry, 7* (1).

Husserl, E. (1954/1970). *The crisis of European sciences and transcendental phenomenology.* (D. Carr, trans.). Evanston: Northwestern University Press.

_____. (1970). *Cartesian meditations.* (D. Cairns, trans.). The Hague: Martinus Nijhoff.

_____. (1969). *Ideas* (Third ed.). London: Macmillan Limited.

Jacobi, J. (1962). *The psychology of C. G. Jung.* New Haven: Yale University Press.

Jung, C. (1956/1965). *Two essays on analytical psychology.* New York: World Publishing Company.

_____. (1964/1969). *Man and his symbols.* New York: Dell Publishing Company.

Kaeline, E. (1971). An existential aesthetic. *The quest for imagination.*

Kant, I. (1929). *Critique of pure reason.* (N. Smith, trans.). New York: Saint Martin's Press.

Kepler, J. (1958). Harmonice mundi. In M. Polanyi, *Personal knowledge.* Chicago: Chicago University Press.

Kerrane, I. (1971). Nineteenth century backgrounds of modern aesthetic criteria. In O. B. Harbison (Ed.), *The quest for imagination.* Cleveland: Case Western Reserve University Press.

Kirk, G. (1973). *Myth: Its meaning and functions in ancient and other cultures.* Berkeley: University of California Press.

Kohut, H. (1977). *The restoration of the self.* New York: International Universities Press Incorporated.

Krell, D. (1935/1977). The origin of the work of art. In *Martin Heidegger: Basic writings.* New York: Harper and Row.

Kuhn, T. (1970). *The structure of scientific revolutions.* Chicago: University of Chicago Press.

Kurzweil, E. (1980). *The age of structuralism.* New York: Columbia University Press.

Lacan, J. (1968). *The language of the self.* New York: Dell Publishing Company. (Trans. and commenting by Anthony Wilden)

_____. (1973/1978). *The four fundamental concepts of psycho-analysis.* (A. Sheridan, trans.). New York: W. W. Norton and Company Incorporated.

Laing, R. (1967). *The politics of experience.* New York: Ballantine Books.

Langer, S. (1951). *Philosophy in a new key.* New York: New American Library. (Original work published 1942)

Lemaire, A. (1970). *Jacques Lacan.* (D. Macey, trans.). London: Routledge and Kegan Paul.

Levin, C. (1969). The self: A contribution to its race in theory and technique. *International Journal of Psycho-Analysis, 50,* 41–51.

Levy-Strauss, C. (1979). *Myth and meaning.* New York: Schocken Books.

Lonergan, B. (1957). *Insight.* New York: Longmans, Green and Company.

McKenzie, J. (1963). *Myths and realities.* Milwaukee: Bruce Publishing Company.

MacQuarrie, J. (1967). *God-talk: An examination of the language and logic of theology.* New York: Harper and Row.

Merleau-Ponty, M. (1962). *Phenomenology of perception.* New York: Humanities Press.

————. (1968). *The visible and the invisible.* (A. Linguis, trans.). Evanston: Northwestern University Press.

Marlan, S. (1981). *Depth consciousness.* In R. Valle and R. von Eckartsberg (Eds.), *Metaphors of consciousness.* New York: Plenum Press.

Murray, E. (1975). The phenomenon of metaphor. In A. Giorgi, C. Fischer, E. Murray (Eds.), *Phenomenological psychology,* Vol. II. Pittsburgh: Duquesne University Press.

————. (1974, Spring). Language and the integration of personality. *Journal of Phenomenological Psychology, 4* (2).

O'Brien, D. (1975). The historian as believer. In G. Baum (Ed.), *Journeys.* New York: Paulist Press.

Polanyi, M. (1958). *Personal knowledge.* Chicago: Chicago University Press.

Richards, I. (1936). *The philosophy of rhetoric.* Oxford: Oxford University Press.

Richardson, W. (1978/1979). "The Mirror Inside: The Problem of the Self." In *Review of Existential Psychology and Psychiatry,* Vol. XVI, Nos. 1, 2, 3, p. 95–112.

Ricoeur, P. (1970). *Freud and philosophy: An essay on interpretation.* (D. Savage, trans.). New Haven: Yale University Press.

————. (1976). *Interpretation theory.* Forth Worth: Texas Christian University Press.

————. (1976). *Symbolism of evil.* (E. Buchanan, trans.). Boston: Beacon Press.

————. (1975). *The rule of metaphor.* Toronto: University of Toronto Press.

————. (1973, Summer). Creativity of language. *Philosophy today, 17* (2/4), 97–112.

Rosen, S. (Ed.). (1982). *My voice will go with you: The teaching tales of Milton H. Erickson.* New York: W. W. Norton and Company.

Rosenberg, A. (1930). *Der Mythus des 20 Jahrhunderts.* Munchen.*

Roy, R. (1981B, May/June). Government's shaping of the future and the church's blind eye. *New Catholic World, 224,* 1341.

————— . (1981A). *Experimenting with truth: The fusion of religion with technology, needed for humanity survival*. Oxford: Pergamon Press.

Santayana, G. (1900). *Interpretation of poetry and religion*. New York:

Sartre, J. (1965). *What is literature?* (B. Frechtman, trans.). New York: Harper and Row. (Original work published 1949)

*Cf. *A. Rosenberg Selected Writings* (R. Pois, Ed.). London: Jonathan Cape.

Shakespeare, W. (      ). A midsummer's night dream. Act V. Scene 1. Richard II. Act IV. Scene I. Sonnet XXIX.

Shea, J. (1978). *Stories of God*. Chicago: Thomas More Press.

Stevens, W. (1951). *The necessary angel*. New York: Random House/ Vintage Books. (Original work published 1942)

Sullivan, H. (1958). Conceptions of modern psychiatry. In (Ed.), *Collected works of Harry Stack Sullivan*, Vol. I. New York: W. W. Norton and Company. (Original work published 1940)

Tagliacozza, G. and White, H. V. (1969). Vico's new science of myth. In G. Tagliacozza and H. V. White (Eds.), *Giambattista Vico: An international symposium*. Baltimore: John Hopkins Press.

Tolstoy, L. (1960). *The death of Ivan Ilych*. New York: New American Library/Signet Classic.

Tracy, D. (1981). *The analogical imagination*. New York: Crossroad.

Turbayne, C. (1962). *The myth of metaphor*. Columbia: University of South Carolina Press.

Vico, G. (1970). *The new science*. Ithaca: Cornell University Press.

von Eckartsberg, R. (1981). Maps of the mind. In R. Valle and R. von Eckartsberg (Eds.), *The metaphors of consciousness*. New York: Plenum Press.

Watzlawick, P. (1978). *The language of change*. New York: Basic Books, Inc.

Washington, G. (1972). A biography in his own words. *Newsweek, 2.*

White, J. (1973). *The legal imagination*. Boston: Little, Brown and Company.

Wheelwright, P. (1968). *Metaphor and reality*. Bloomington: Indiana University Press.

Weinstein, D. and Weinstein, M. (1981). Freud's encounter with religion: A study in bad faith. *Thought*, Vol. LVI.

White, H. V. and Tagliacozza, G. (1969). Vico's new science of myth. In G. Tagliacozza and H. V. White (Eds.), *Giambattista Vico: An international symposium*. Baltimore: John Hopkins Press.

Wilden, A. (1968). Translator and commentor of J. Lacan. *The Language of the Self*. New York: Dell Publishing Company.

Wylie, R. (1961). *The self concept*. Lincoln: University of Nebraska Press.

Yoos, G. (1971). A phenomenological look at metaphor. *Philosophy and phenomenological research, 32.*

Zeig, J. (Ed. and Com.). (1980). *A teaching seminar with Milton H. Erickson*. New York: Brunner/Mazel.

*Indexes*

# Author Index

# Subject Index

Aesthetics:
   and imaginative thinking, 12 passim
   and metaphors, 98
*Animal symbolicum,* 123
Archetypal, 129, 131
Authenticity, 66

Becoming self:
   and Kierkegaard, 230
*Befindlichkdit,* 210, 211
Being-in-the-world, 39 passim

Client:
   role in therapy, 88
*Climb Down, O Lordly Mind,* 118
Consciousness:
   as autochthonous, 46
   fringes of, 53, 55
   Gurwitsch on, 47
   and imaginative thinking, 56 passim
   indeterminacies in field of, 49
   James' view of, 53
   Rubin and, 48
   theme-thematic field-margin of,
     47, 53
Culture:
   and imagination, 68

Dasein, 4, 5, 39, 40, 59, 60, 63, 67, 73,
   84, 204, 212, 216, 221, 228
*Das Man* existence, 66, 69
Decenteredness, 216
Demythization:
   and demytholigization, 167

Depression:
   as imagination, 65
Disclosure:
   of Dasein, 59
Discourse:
   Ricoeur on, 77, 211

*Early Illusions,* 255
*Einbildungskraft,* 62
*Endymion,* 14, 138
Existence:
   *in diaspora,* 205 passim
   and mineness, 205
   as worlded, 204
Existential-phenomenological thought,
   91, 203

Finitude:
   of the human, 224, 226 passim
Freedom:
   and imagination, 21
   and Sartre, 21

*Gelassenheit,* 36
Good life:
   according to Freud, 89
   according to St. Paul, 89

History:
   and perception, 42
Horizontal projections:
   Heidegger on, 60, 63
   Hofstadter on, 63
   human possibility and, 67